YALE
HISTORICAL PUBLICATIONS

MISCELLANY

XII

THE SEVENTH VOLUME
PUBLISHED UNDER THE DIRECTION OF
THE DEPARTMENT OF HISTORY ON THE
KINGSLEY TRUST ASSOCIATION PUBLICATION FUND
ESTABLISHED BY
THE SCROLL AND KEY SOCIETY
OF YALE COLLEGE

THE ATTITUDE OF MARTIN BUCER
TOWARD THE BIGAMY OF
PHILIP OF HESSE

By

HASTINGS EELLS, Ph.D.

NEW HAVEN: YALE UNIVERSITY PRESS
LONDON: HUMPHREY MILFORD
OXFORD UNIVERSITY PRESS
MDCCCCXXIV

PREFACE

"If I should tell how many evil speeches of all kinds I have heard about this affair, that would make a long and tiresome story."[1] So Melanchthon expressed himself in his last recorded statement on the bigamy of Philip of Hesse. And yet if he had recounted fully all he knew, there would have been less investigation of this famous episode by the historians of subsequent centuries. In this study of the subject the attempt has been made to examine more fully than ever before the attitude of Martin Bucer toward the bigamy, and, wherever possible, to clear away any misunderstandings with regard to it.

Since, like many other men of his time, Bucer of Strasbourg has been overshadowed by the Hero of Wittenberg, he occupies a much smaller place in the pages of history. His exile from Strasbourg and later influences there tending to overthrow his work contributed to this result, as did also the fact that the sources for a history of his life have been difficult to obtain. As a consequence, even authorities upon European history know little about him, and the best histories of the Reformation ignore his work and give wrong impressions about his character.

This lack of acquaintance with Bucer and the influence which he exerted upon his time is particularly exemplified in the history of the bigamy of Philip of Hesse. For nearly four centuries various men have written about the matter, but Lenz was the first to give any serious consideration to the rôle played by Bucer. Most of the writers were interested in Luther's relation to the scandal and in the attempt which was made to defame or exonerate

[1] *Archiv für Reformationsgeschichte*, I, 371.

him. Yet it was Bucer, not Luther, whom the landgrave first consulted, to whom he expressed the inmost secrets of his soul, to whom he turned constantly for advice and aid, and by whom he was most restrained from making his disastrous treaty with the emperor. Luther's relation to the bigamy is important because he was a great reformer; Bucer's relation is important because he exerted a greater influence than any other theologian upon the course of events.

I wish to express my deep appreciation to those who have aided me in the preparation of this work. Miss A. S. Pratt, reference librarian at Yale University, has rendered untiring and efficient service in securing rare books. Dr. Rockwell has given me invaluable aid by his many suggestions and by generous loans from his library. Great assistance has been rendered me in preparing the manuscript for publication by Professor Charles M. Andrews. Lastly, I am deeply indebted to the late Professor Williston Walker for his sympathetic encouragement and constant supervision.

HASTINGS EELLS.

Princeton, N. J.

CONTENTS

CHAPTER I

THE EARLY LIFE OF BUCER

Born on November 11, 1491, in Selestat, a town of
Lower Alsace less than thirty miles south of Strasbourg,[1]
Martin Bucer, the son and grandson of cobblers,[2] was
reared in a home totally devoid of wealth and worldly
grandeur.[3] The groundless rumor, circulated by his enemies in later years, that his parents were Jews, was a
malicious slander[4] against his parents, who compensated
for their poverty by a reputation for great piety,[5] and
having high ambitions for their son, they sent him to the
famous Latin School at Selestat.[6] This school, established
about 1424, had gained for itself in less than twenty
years an enviable reputation under the leadership of
Dringenberg, who was followed many years later by
Jerome Gebweiler,[7] a pedagogue privileged to number
Bucer among his two hundred and fifty pupils.[8]

So great was the fascination which his books exerted

---

[1] T. M. Lindsay, "Martin Bucer and the Reformation," *Quarterly Review*, Jan., 1914, vol. 220, pp. 116-133, see p. 117.

[2] J. Gény, "Die Reichstadt Schlettstadt und ihr Anteil an den social-
politischen und religiösen Bewegungen der Jahre 1490-1536," *Erlauterungen
und Erganzungen zu Janssens Geschichte des deutschen Volkes*, I, Heft 5
and 6, p. 59, n. 4.

[3] M. Bucer, *Verantwortung M. Butzers*, etc. (1523), p. aiij. For the full
title see Mentz, "Bibliographische Zusammenstellung der gedruckten Schriften Butzers," no. 3, *Zur 400 jährigen Geburtsfeier Martin Butzers*. M.
Bucer, *Der CXX Psalm*, etc. (1546; *cf.* Mentz, no. 70).

[4] *Der CXX Psalm*, p. G; J. Ficker and O. Winckelmann, *Handschrift-
proben des sechzehnten jahrhunderts nach Strassburger Originalen*, I, 47.

[5] *Der CXX Psalm*, p. G.   [6] *Verantwortung*, p. aiij.

[7] Gény, p. 54, ff.   [8] *Ibid.*, pp. 1, 13, 55.

upon Martin, and so intense was his desire to gain an education, that he preferred to enter the Dominican monastery when only fifteen years old rather than give up his studies.[9] His father had gone to Strasbourg November 23, 1501,[10] leaving him in the care of his grandfather, who, finding his slender means insufficient to provide an education for his grandson, persuaded the lad to join the Dominicans rather than the secular clergy, whose iniquitous lives he had long since learned to abhor.[11] Having assured the boy that he would find in the monastery ample opportunity for instruction, the Black Friars continually reminded him during the first year of his novitiate that no Dominican could be damned, but that anyone who forsook the order would have bad luck all the remainder of his life and die an unnatural death. So doubt made Bucer a monk.[12]

When the books on the Latin language which he had brought into the cloister with him were taken away and in their place he was given the desiccated and outworn scholastics, Bucer soon discovered that the monastic life was little suited to his needs or tastes. To complete his studies he was sent to Mainz and afterwards to Heidelberg,[13] where he received the degrees of Bachelor of Theology and Master of Students,[14] but his dissatisfaction with the cloister increased daily. Having incurred the bitter enmity of his order, and especially of Hoogstraten, the inquisitor at Cologne, by instructing the younger

9 *Verantwortung*, p. aiij, ff.

10 Gény, p. 59, n. 4. Bucer's father was a citizen of Strasbourg, and it was on this account that Bucer paid no fees when he received the ''Burgerrecht'' on Sept. 22, 1524 (A. Baum, *Magistrat und Reformation in Strassburg bis 1529*, p. 205).

11 *Verantwortung*, p. aiij.

12 *Ibid.*

13 G. Toepke, *Die Matrikel der Universität Heidelberg*, p. 509.

14 *Verantwortung*, p. aiij, ff.; M. Bucer, *Was in Namen . . . zu Bonn* (1543), pt. II, Ai (Mentz, no. 53).

brethren in Latin and Greek,[15] he was subjected to a cruel persecution which not only failed to make him relinquish his humanistic studies, but rather aroused him to greater perseverance and gained for him many friends among the partisans of the new learning.[16] His refusal to join in the immoralities common to cloister-life at that time was another cause for friction between Bucer and his monastic companions,[17] and it was not strange that irritated by these conditions he longed for freedom from the vows which he had taken at such an immature age. Not the least of the causes instilling this desire within his impetuous young spirit was a meeting with Luther in April, 1518, when the latter came to Heidelberg. Enthused with admiration for the way in which Luther defended himself at the disputation on April 26, and magnetically attracted by his evangelical interpretation of the Scriptures,[18] the young monk corresponded with him,[19] and found a way to read some of his works, preferring above others the commentary on Galatians.[20]

In September, 1540, Bucer definitely decided to seek freedom from his monastic vows,[21] and on November 11 left his cell never to return.[22] At first he took refuge with Maternus Hatten at Speier,[23] through whose influence he gained an order from the pope to the bishop of Speier, to free him from his vows in case investigation showed that he had taken them before reaching years of discre-

---

[15] *Verantwortung*, p. aiij.　　　[16] *Ibid.*

[17] *Ibid.*

[18] *Dr. Martin Luthers Werke* (Weimar edition), IX, 161-169.

[19] E. L. Enders, *Dr. Martin Luther's Briefwechsel*, II, 298. *Cf.* Krafft, *Briefe und Documente aus der Zeit der Reformation in 16 Jahrhunderts*, p. 16.

[20] J. W. Baum, *Capito und Butzer*, pp. 105-108; Enders, II, 299.

[21] Baum, p. 114.

[22] G. Anrich, *Martin Bucer*, p. 9.

[23] Bucer to Capito, Feb. 7, 1521, Thesaurus Baumianus (referred to as TB.), I, 33.

tion.[24] The bishop being absent, the decision was placed in the hands of the suffragan, Antony, who granted Bucer's request on April 29, 1521, giving him permission to leave the monastery and enter the ranks of the secular clergy.[25]

Meanwhile Bucer exchanged the hospitality of Maternus Hatten for that of Franz von Sickingen, the warlike knight of Ebernburg.[26] Here he found a congenial companion in Ulrich von Hutten, and was a member of the party sent by Sickingen in the vain attempt to persuade Luther to meet his adversaries within the sheltering walls of the knight's castle instead of at Worms.[27] Sickingen he admired in spite of his warlike nature, and praised his zeal in the evangelical cause.[28]

During May, 1521, Bucer accepted a position as court-chaplain to Count Frederick of the Palatinate,[29] but perceiving ere long that he "had nothing in common in the gospel" with this prince,[30] he returned about a year later to the patronage of Sickingen as pastor of Landstuhl.[31] Here it was that he married a nun named Elisabeth Silbereisen, thus being one of the first to take this step in support of clerical marriage.[32] In addition to preaching, he served his lord on a number of embassies,[33] but the defeat of the latter and the siege of his castle by several

[24] *Verantwortung*, p. b.; Baum, pp. 119-121.

[25] *Verantwortung*, p. b.; Anrich, p. 11.

[26] Thesaurus Baumianus, I, 151; *Verantwortung*, p. e.; H. Ulmann, *Franz von Sickingen*, p. 183.

[27] Ulmann, pp. 181, 183; Bucer to —, Thesaurus Baumianus, I, 154.

[28] *Corpus Reformatorum* (referred to as *CR.*), XCV, *Huldreich Zwinglis Sämtliche Werke*, VIII, 83. Later the reformer showed his gratitude by constant intercession with the landgrave on behalf of Sickingen's sons (Lenz, *Briefwechsel Landgraf Philipp des Grossmüthigen von Hessen mit Bucer*, I, viii).

[29] *CR.*, XCIV, 455.   [30] *Ibid.*, XCV, 81.

[31] *Verantwortung*, p. e.   [32] Baum, p. 137.

[33] Bucer to Sapidus, July 7, 1522, Thesaurus Baumianus, I, 244-245.

princes, among whom was the landgrave, Philip of Hesse,[34] made it necessary for Bucer to seek another place of abode.[35] With Sickingen's permission he resigned his office, and turned his face toward Wittenberg, contemplating a year of study under Luther and Melanchthon. On the way thither he passed through Wissembourg, where his whole career was changed when Heinrich Motherer persuaded him to stay for a half-year and help him in preaching the gospel.[36] Adopting an expository style of preaching and taking for his text the First Epistle of Peter and the Gospel of Matthew, he emphasized the ability and right of the individual to interpret Scripture; the free grace of God in salvation; and the inefficacy of good-works. Though he maintained a scholarly attitude and exhibited no inclination toward extravagances such as were later introduced by various sects,[37] the inevitable opposition of the clergy was aroused by his vigorous attacks on their iniquities, while the support that would ordinarily have been rendered him by other classes was weakened by the imminence of Sickingen's defeat.[38] When charges were entered against him, he disregarded a summons to appear before the Vicar of Speier and was excommunicated.[39] Not waiting for the publication of the sentence, he and Motherer had already left the city with the consent and by the advice of the council, whose sympathy with the reformers rendered them no less impotent to protect them.[40] To avoid any public disturbance, the preachers and their wives slipped

[34] *Der CXX Psalm*, p. Gi.
[35] *Verantwortung*, p. eij.
[36] *Ibid.*
[37] M. Bucer, *M. Butzers . . . Summary seiner Predig* (Mentz, no. 2); *CR.,* XCV, 81.
[38] Bucer to Lange, Jan. 19 (1523), Thesaurus Baumianus, II, 1.
[39] *Verantwortung*, p. diij.
[40] *CR.*, XCV. 81.

through the gates one night in May, and fled to Strasbourg.[41]

The Reformation was well under way in Strasbourg
when Bucer arrived.[42] Politically organized into an intri-
cate series of councils which gave the middle class citizens
greater power than the nobles, the town enjoyed by imperial right a freedom from outside control which favored
a struggle for independence from papal authority.[43] Long
years before Bucer's arrival the city had gained renown
as a centre for humanism, and here German mysticism
and sectarianism found a favorable field for development.
The most potent influence preparing the way for the
Reformation was the reforming zeal of that master of
eloquence, Geiler of Kaisersberg, whose attacks upon the
sins of the clergy made many a dent in their armor of
clerical sanctity.[44] His mantle fell upon the shoulders of
an equally popular and intrepid preacher, Matthew Zell,
who was chosen People's Priest on April 26, 1519; and
proclaimed not only the dire need of moral reform, as
had Geiler, but also many of Luther's revolutionary
teachings.[45] Others of the clergy followed his example,
and by the time Bucer arrived evangelicalism had already
laid the foundations of its future dominance over the city.

Bucer did not leave all his troubles behind at Wissembourg, for as he rode through the gates of Strasbourg
while the sun was casting its early morning rays over the
beautiful plains of Upper Alsace, he was still an excommunicated, married priest, almost without money, and
only the wildest imagination could have predicted that he
would oust from his power the bishop of Strasbourg to

[41] *Ibid.*

[42] G. Anrich, *Die Strassburger Reformation*, p. 4, ff. (This work will
always be cited with both author and title to distinguish it from the biography of Bucer by the same writer.)

[43] On the political organization of Strasbourg see Baum, p. 170.

[44] Lindsay, p. 119.   [45] Baum, p. 196.

whose diocese he came an ecclesiastical outlaw. He confessed to the vicar that he was married, and offered to let himself be stoned to death in true Mosaic style if his life and teaching were proved to be heretical, but the vicar forbade him to preach and said that the decision as to his orthodoxy must be relegated to the bishop.[46] A similar confession to the city-council, whose authority he acknowledged,[47] was more successful, for they refused to deliver him into the bishop's power, though they did not accord him the privilege of preaching in German as he had desired. Forced to content himself with lecturing on Timothy in Latin to a small audience, he wrote to Zwingli requesting a position in Zurich,[48] but fortunately for Strasbourg, the council appointed him a salaried lecturer,[49] and in March, 1524, he was chosen priest of the gardeners' chapel of St. Aurelia.[50]

There is not sufficient space here to relate the details of Bucer's subsequent life in Strasbourg until his exile in 1549. In a few years his abilities won for him the place of acknowledged leader of the church there,[51] though he was greatly assisted by others, chiefly Capito, Hedio, and Zell.

For convenience and clarity it will be best to consider separately his activities as a preacher, an educator, an author, and a polemicist. Bucer was not merely the reformer of Strasbourg, he was the greatest religious diplomat of his time, exerting a determining influence from Wittenberg to Geneva, and from London to Rome. Though never a popular preacher, for, as Luther said,

[46] *CR.*, XCV, 82.
[47] *Verantwortung*, pp. d, ff., dij, diij, e, ciij, ff.; *cf.* Bucer to the Council of Strasbourg, Thesaurus Baumianus, II, 45.
[48] *CR.*, XCV, 82.
[49] Lindsay, p. 120.
[50] E. Doumergue, *Calvin, les hommes et les choses de son temps*, II, 336.
[51] *Cf.* G. Anrich, *Die Strassburger Reformation*, p. 9.

his sermons were too involved and scholarly to appeal to the masses,[52] he displayed a forcefulness and persuasiveness which soon created a wide demand for his services, and after 1530 he was constantly away from home, answering calls like a knight-errant to assist in the Reformation of Augsburg, Ulm, Bonn, Hesse, and other parts of Germany. Only the plague of 1541 prevented him from returning to Geneva with Calvin, and it was not for lack of invitations to other places that he sought refuge in England in 1549. Evangelical leaders in Italy, France, the Low Countries, and England were among his correspondents, and refugees from persecution in foreign lands, especially France, were continually entertained in his own home.

Perhaps Bucer's most important work, in its results upon the local Reformation in Strasbourg, was his effort to improve the system of education. Undaunted by the numerous obstacles he encountered, he applied himself so vigorously to the task that when Gereon Sailer of Augsburg visited the city in 1539, he testified, "If his [Bucer's] whole life long he were to do no other good thing other than to establish the school at Strasbourg, yet he has done a magnificent, Godly, work, for I have never seen such a school in my whole life."[53] By his energetic efforts he persuaded several cities of Upper Germany to provide financial support for the students they sent to Strasbourg, and added prominence and dignity to its faculty by the appointment of such masters of education as John Sturm, John Calvin, Fagius, and others.

At the same time that Bucer was active in preaching, lecturing, contending with papists and sectarians, and traveling extensively in the interests of the Reformation, he was writing and publishing an enormous number of

52 E. Kroker, *Luthers Tischreden in der Mathesischen Sammlung*, p. 139.
53 Lenz, I, 347.

books. During his first eight years at Strasbourg, before he began his long journeys, he completed those commentaries on the Psalms[54] and the Gospels,[55] which are his most extensive works and most imposing in their size and erudition. In all he published about eighty books, some of them only pamphlets, others thorough and extended treatments of special subjects. Though many of them were controversial, Bucer seldom descended to the use of vituperative language so common in his age. He had two styles, one clear, precise, interesting, and convincing; the other, prolix, dull, involved, and scholastic. The latter is found in his commentaries, while the former is exemplified in the *Verantwortung* of 1523. The commentary on the Psalms was published anonymously that its circulation might be increased in France and other areas under strict papal censorship.[56] To erudite commentaries on Romans and Ephesians he added numerous books on the Supper Controversy, of which the most important are, the *Vergleichung D. Luthers, unnd seins gegentheils,* the warning to the Münsterites, and the confutation of the Bishop of Avranches. Though the last two did not deal with this doctrine extensively, they contained cunningly-worded conciliatory statements with which Bucer sought to bridge the gap between Lutherans and Zwinglians. His keen insight into conditions in Germany is shown in the books about the Nürnberg Colloquy, church-goods, and the Diet of Ratisbon, 1541, while the volume which he wrote and presented to King Edward VI of England under the title *De Regno Christi,* was his nearest approach to a systematic theology. Bigamy was seldom mentioned and never discussed in any of his writings except the *Scripta duo Adversia D. Barth.*

[54] Mentz, no. 23.   [55] *Ibid.,* no. 24.

[56] T. Schiess, *Briefwechsel der Brüder Ambrosius und Thomas Blaurer 1509-1568.* I, 198

Latomi[57] and the *Argumenta Buceri,* published more than three hundred years after his death. In none of his publications did he ever refer directly to the bigamy of Landgrave Philip.[58]

Although Bucer is noted for his efforts to gain religious peace in a time of religious strife, he was continually obliged to engage in controversies, both to defend his own views, and also to expose what he considered to be dangerous errors. Within a year after his arrival in Strasbourg, he joined Capito in a controversy with a Roman Catholic adversary named Conrad Treger,[59] and in addition he rendered valuable assistance at the Disputation of Bern in December, 1527.[60] Yet his most serious conflicts were with the Anabaptists, and those emissaries of discord who stirred up strife on the doctrine of the Lord's Supper. The Anabaptist leaven first began to ferment in Strasbourg in the late summer of 1524,[61] and two years afterwards this disturbing element found a vigorous leader in John Denk,[62] whom Bucer called the pope of the Anabaptists, complaining that his fanaticism had caused the expulsion of all evangelical preachers from Worms.[63] Another Anabaptist leader of no small ability was Pilgram Marbeck, against whose "stubborn heresy" Bucer warned his friends.[64] In December, 1531, Bucer disputed with him in the presence of the council of Strasbourg, and was officially declared the victor, but Marbeck refused to accept the verdict, though compelled to withdraw from the

---

[57] Published in 1544 after the bigamy of the landgrave.

[58] The full titles of these various books can be found in Mentz. His connection with the authorship of the *Dialogus Neobuli* will be discussed later.

[59] M. Bucer, *Ein kurtzer . . . bericht von Disputation . . . Treger (cf.* Mentz, no. 7); *CR.,* XCV, 241.

[60] M. Bucer, *Enarratio in Evangelion Johannis* (Mentz, no. 19).

[61] *CR.,* XCV, 440.

[62] Herminjard, *Correspondance des Réformateurs dans les pays de langue française,* I, 467.

[63] *CR.,* XCV, 184.   [64] Schiess, II, 790-791.

field.[65] The greatest leader of the Anabaptists at Strasbourg was Melchior Hoffmann, who, having proclaimed
Rome as Babylon and Strasbourg as the New Jersualem of
Anabaptism,[66] came to the city while Bucer was in the
midst of his final conflict with Marbeck.[67] The toleration
which Hoffmann enjoyed for a long time was finally terminated on June 11, 1533, by a disputation in which Bucer
tried to convince him of his errors.[68] In consequence of the
disputation Hoffmann was condemned and imprisoned,[69]
and, in order to combat his heresy more effectually, Bucer
published a book in July, which combined an account of the
disputation with a confutation of Hoffmann's errors.[70] The
condemnation of Hoffmann was praised by Melanchthon,[71]
for the tolerance shown him had brought such a bad reputation upon the city, that Bucer found it necessary to
defend the policy of the council, claiming that it was better
to allow such heretics an open defense, in order that the
refutation of their errors might also be public and more
effectual.[72] When it is remembered that the sects caused
a crisis in Strasbourg during these years and nearly
created a catastrophe similar to that in Münster, Bucer's
treatment of them appears remarkably tolerant. Though
willing to sanction all their teaching that agreed with his
own interpretation of the Bible, he objected to their sepa-
ratism and defined heresy as ''A passion of the flesh
through which one thinks he has something better in doc-

[65] Schiess, I, 300, 314-318.
[66] M. Bucer, *Handlungen in dem offentlichen gesprech . . . gegen . . .
Hoffmann* (1533), preface (Mentz, no. 30).
[67] Schiess, I, 308. Bucer to G. Schenk, Jan. 2, 1532, Thesaurus Baumianus,
V, 4.
[68] *Handlungen in dem . . . Hoffmann*, preface.
[69] Bucer to Christoph of Augsburg, Sept. 8, 1533, Thesaurus Baumianus,
VI, 153-155.
[70] Schiess, I, 404; see above, p. 10, n. 58.
[71] *CR.*, II, 676.
[72] Thesaurus Baumianus, VI, 153-155, 143.

trine and life than the common, divinely-ordained usage
of the universal church, conducts himself accordingly, and
on that account secedes from the church and betakes himself to some particularistic society or sect.''[73]

When the Anabaptists established their notorious kingdom in Münster, Bucer wrote a polemic against them,
hoping thereby to prevent the spread of their doctrines
in the Low Countries.[74] This book deals only with doctrinal questions, contains an extensive argument in favor
of child-baptism, and says nothing about bigamy or the
other errors in conduct at Münster. At the end there is
a brief statement of Bucer's doctrine on the Supper,
which he advanced as a preliminary platform upon which
all parties could unite.[75]

Caspar Schwenckfeld and his followers were the most
dangerous opponents encountered by Bucer in the maintenance of his leadership over the church of Strasbourg.
Several of the most influential members of the church were
subject to Schwenckfeld's influence, and for a time Bucer
was in danger of losing the support of his colleagues, Zell
and Capito.[76] But by 1535 he had established his suprem-
acy, and though he encountered opposition from other
sources, he had little to fear from the sectarians.

Bucer is best known today for his efforts to make peace
between Lutherans and Zwinglians in their strife over the
doctrine of the Lord's Supper. His activities to this end
have been greatly misunderstood because of prejudice, and
the failure to consider that his attitude was not stationary
but continually developing. Soon after the controversy
originated Bucer became a strong Zwinglian. His own account of his conversion to the teachings of Zurich is worth
quoting, because it shows how he approached matters of

[73] Schiess, II, 792.
[74] M. Bucer, *Bericht auss der heyligen geschrift*, etc. (Mentz, no. 33).
[75] Bucer to Bullinger, Jan. 17, 1536, Thesaurus Baumianus, IX, 15-16.
[76] Schiess, I, 441-442.

this sort. He wrote to a friend, "Moved by Luther's authority and not by the power of the Word, I made it a rule never to venture upon any speculations on this subject. . . . When the writings of Carlstadt appeared, I was forced to make an investigation . . . I wrote on a piece of paper the position of the evangelists and Paul, in Greek and Latin, next to each other. . . . What appears evident to me is, that as in baptism plain water, so also in the supper, plain bread, was used. They are in each case symbols, and you may add to the bread what you will, yet it will always be a token, and indeed a useless token if you are not inspired and led by faith in Him who has died for you."[77] In later years he considerably modified this symbolic view of the Supper, confessing in his *Shorter Catechism*, "I believe and do not doubt that our Lord Jesus gives me, through the holy sacrament, his true body and true blood . . . and he himself is truly dispensed through the holy sacrament, not physically or in the flesh, for he is no longer in this world, but yet truly and for a true and blessed food and sustenance to eternal life, as he has promised us."[78]

The part played by Bucer in the Marburg Colloquy of 1529 is important, because it was here that he first clasped hands with Philip of Hesse in the struggle for sacramental peace. It is probable that the landgrave was not personally acquainted with him before this meeting, because he invited him indirectly, writing to Jacob Sturm to send two Strasbourg ministers, one of whom should be Martin Bucer.[79] As far as is known, the first letter which Bucer ever wrote to the man who later exercised such an important influence on his life, is concerned with the route

[77] Bucer to Martinus, Thesaurus Baumianus, II, 213.
[78] M. Bucer, *Der Kürtzer Catechismus* (1544, Mentz, no. 58).
[79] *Politische Correspondenz der Stadt Strassburg im Zeitalter der Reformation* (referred to as *PCS.*), edited by Virck, Winckelmann, and Bernays, I, 382; Lenz, I, 16.

of the Swiss reformers from Strasbourg to Marburg. At first it was planned to have the party come through Wasslenheim, where they were to be met by a Hessian guard,[80] but when subsequent reflection caused Philip to decide that the route through Herrenstein would be shorter and safer,[81] this road was taken by the little group of reformers soon after Hedio had been appointed by the council on September 14 to be Bucer's colleague.[82] The cordial reception tendered Bucer by the landgrave, who granted him a private interview on the evening of the fourth day,[83] was in striking contrast to the greeting he received from his old hero Luther, who pointed his finger at him and said, "You are a scoundrel."[84]

When the colloquy had vented its strength in vain against the adamant wall of the irreconcilable beliefs of Luther and Zwingli, Jacob Sturm requested that Bucer be allowed to give a brief statement of the doctrine taught at Strasbourg, because during the discussion Luther had charged the city with certain doctrinal errors.[85] Bucer then gave a summary of Strasbourg theology, but when he asked for Luther's sanction the latter replied, "I do not wish to be your preceptor: you have the Scriptures and my confession."[86] To a further request that he recognize the Strasbourgers as brothers, Luther merely replied that he committed them to the judgment of God,[87] and a private interview with Bucer failed to make his attitude more favorable.[88] So the colloquy ended, but before Bucer left Marburg he had an encouraging conference with Brenz and Osiander.[89]

---

[80] Lenz, I, 3, 4, 6.   [81] *Ibid.*, p. 7.

[82] A. Erichson, "Strassburger Beiträge zur Geschichte des Marburger Religionsgespräch. I. Hedio's Itinerarium," *Zeitschrift für Kirchengeschichte*, IV, Heft III, 414-436, see p. 416.

[83] *Ibid.*, p. 417.   [84] *Ibid.*, p. 418.

[85] *Ibid.*, p. 435.   [86] *Ibid.*

[87] *Ibid.*, p. 435.   [88] *Ibid.*, p. 419.

[89] *Ibid.*, p. 435. On Oct. 13 he arrived at Strasbourg (Schiess, I, 197).

The Marburg Colloquy changed radically the direction
of the channel of Bucer's life. Here he first learned to
know and admire Philip of Hesse,[90] with whom he established bonds of relationship that drew them continually
closer together in the following years, and inevitably involved Bucer in the bigamy-affair when the landgrave
needed assistance. In many ways they had opposite
characteristics, but they were mutually attracted by the
common desire to unify the protestants politically and
religiously. Though in previous years Bucer had lamented
the sacrament-strife, it was not until after the Marburg
Colloquy that he ceased to be a partisan and began seriously to desire and to strive for concord.[91] Not only did
he learn to know the landgrave, but he also extended the
circle of his acquaintances to include many Hessian theologians. Here he won back the friendship of Francis
Lambert, who had been an enemy,[92] and here he impressed
Pistorius so forcibly that the latter wrote to him for further information about the disputed doctrine.[93] Unfortunately his relations with Luther and Melanchthon were
not so cordial. He thought that Luther was stubborn and
unreasonable, and declared that Melanchthon was largely
responsible for this attitude.[94]

During the decade that followed the Marburg Colloquy,
Bucer was indefatigable in his exertions for theological
peace. At the Diet of Augsburg he began official negotiations with the Wittenbergers,[95] and though his advances
were coldly received he continued his efforts undaunted.
Convinced that fundamentally Luther and Zwingli were
in accord on the essentials of the doctrine, and that the
conflict was rooted in the difficulties of expression,[96] he

[90] Schiess, I, 197.   [91] Cf. Schiess, I, 202-205.
[92] Herminjard, II, 236-244.
[93] Pistorius to Bucer, Nov. 1, 1529, Thesaurus Baumianus, III, 173.
[94] Schiess, I, 197-198.
[95] CR., II, 221-222, and other places.   [96] Schiess, II, 811.

persistently sought a formula to which both sides would subscribe. The untimely death of Zwingli hampered his efforts, but finally in 1536 he gained that partial agreement known as the Wittenberg Concord, and with this he let the matter rest.[97] When the strife threatened to break out again a few years later, he thought the wisest policy was simply to suppress all discussion of the subject,[98] and it is probable that one reason why he chose England as a place of exile was his longing to be free from this and other controversies.[99]

What has already been said of Bucer's early life before he became connected with the bigamy of Landgrave Philip, will have given some idea of his personal character. Distinguished predominantly by unflinching perseverance, he owed all that he ever gained in the way of position or influence not to fortune or favor, but to his own determined efforts to make the most of his opportunities. Only by indomitable persistence did he obtain his education, for when he was denied the classics that he desired, he made good use of the scholastics, so that his knowledge of this field and of the patristics was hardly excelled by any of the reformers. His unconquerable determination and energy, by which alone he overcame the difficulties he encountered continually, enabled him to counteract a frail constitution and onerous susceptibility to illness which increased with age.[100] After holding three pastorates and being more or less of a failure in all of them, he found himself a penniless refugee in Strasbourg; yet before ten years had passed he had won for himself

---

[97] *Politische Correspondenz* . . . *Strassburg*, II, 675-699; "Historia de Concordia," *Scripta Anglicana* (referred to as *SA.*), pp. 648-699.

[98] Lenz, II, 342, ff.

[99] *Scripta Anglicana*, pp. 546-550; cf. *CR.*, VII, 733.

[100] Cf. Schiess, I, 436, 764, 800; Thesaurus Baumianus, XX, 177, 192, and other places.

a place as acknowledged leader of the church there.[101] All his life he was a hard worker, simultaneously fulfilling the functions of a religious organizer, an author, and a professor, while also undertaking long journeys. For example, in the year 1540, which was a central year in the history of the bigamy, he spent more than five months of the year attending conferences at Smalkald, Hagenau, and Worms, published five books, and carried on an enormous correspondence—of which more than one hundred letters written by himself still exist—in addition to his regular duties as leader of the church at Strasbourg. Yet this year was not an exceptionally busy one.

Not only was Bucer a perseveringly hard worker, he also possessed certain personal gifts fitting him to be a leader of other men. By a dominant forcefulness he carried through what he undertook, and won over other men to his point of view. Well aware of this persuasive ability to which he owed what measure of success he gained in his efforts for concord, he always preferred an interview to a letter as a means of argument, while his opponents admitted it by seeking to avoid such an interview.[102] When a difficulty arose, Bucer invariably contrived some expedient for overcoming it, and although many of his schemes were of doubtful value, his ingenuity and versatility must be recognized. More than most men of his time he was broad-minded and able to distinguish between important principles and unimportant details. It was this trait rather than weakness which led him to make concessions on the wording of the doctrine of the Supper, for he

[101] His official title was ''Professoris der H. Schrifft und dess Kirchen-Convents Praesidenten zu Strassburg'' (Mentz, no. 41a).

[102] *Cf.* Bucer to Bullinger, Feb. 15 (1535), Thesaurus Baumianus, VIII, 61. Bucer was anything but a coward and often risked his life upon his journeys (*Politische Correspondenz . . . Strassburg*, I, 284, 446). One writer has styled him the ''klugste Politiker unter den Reformatoren'' (E. v. Borries, *Geschichte der Stadt Strassburg*, p. 127).

deemed peace and concord of more importance than formalistic expressions of faith, and when the essential idea was acknowledged, he was content. While a great leader himself, he showed little jealousy of others and was active in assisting men of ability. John Calvin and John Sleidan[103] were among his protégés, and while he disagreed with Luther, he acknowledged his services and abilities.[104] The years which have brightened the fame of Martin Luther, and almost obliterated the memory of Martin Bucer, must not be allowed to conceal the fact that in his own day his influence as an organizer was in some respects only slightly second to that of Luther and Melanchthon, while in others it was much greater. All through the valleys of the Upper Rhine and Danube Bucer was called upon for assistance, and in many cities the articles by which the Reformation was guided owed their origin to him.

Bucer's personal appearance, because of his noble manner and dignity, made a favorable impression in spite of his shortness of stature.[105] A small mouth, a Grecian nose, a high, prominent forehead, and short curly hair, gave him an imposing, if not a handsome appearance. In later years deep wrinkles formed upon his spiritual and expressive features.

Financially, Bucer was never in prosperous circumstances. His father, being poor, was unable to help him, and even the most skillful planning could not stretch the small salary that he received from Strasbourg to cover his

[103] M. Lenz, *Kleine Historische Schriften*, pp. 104-105. (This book will be cited with both author and title to distinguish it from the more important work by Lenz already quoted.)

[104] Lenz, II, 225-231.

[105] Baum, p. 346; *cf.* F. W. Hassencamp, *Hessische Kirchengeschichte* (1864), II, 345; A. Jung, *Geschichte der Reformation der Kirche in Strassburg*, p. 108, n. 57; J. B. Rady, *Die Reformatoren in ihrer Beziehung zur Doppelehe des Landgrafen Philipp*, p. 13.

regular expenses and the additional costs of his extended travels. The year 1533 seems to have been an especially difficult one, but Bucer's wife was thrifty[106] and with her savings he was able to keep out of debt.[107] It is significant that at this time Margaret Blaurer wished to help Frau Bucer with money,[108] and that the city of Augsburg sent her twenty gulden after Bucer had been there in 1534,[109] for Bucer was too proud to accept personally such gifts in return for his services though he stood in great need of them. Another indication of his poverty is the frequency with which he apologizes for not being able to give fine presents.[110] At the time of his connection with the bigamy his salary was barely eighty gulden a year, besides a moderate sized house in which to live.[111] This was not a munificent salary, yet in spite of his poverty he was always hospitable. At one time he mentions his house as full of guests even during one of his wife's confinements,[112] and at another he speaks of entertaining two Italians, four Frenchmen, and two Germans, while two of his children were sick.[113]

Such was the man who was the confidant and adviser of Philip of Hesse. How he became connected with the bigamy and what influence he exerted upon the course of events, is the subject of the following chapters.

[106] Schiess, II, 807.
[107] *Ibid.*, p. 797.
[108] *Ibid.*, I, 401, 404.
[109] *Ibid.*, II, 813.
[110] *Ibid.*, pp. 800, 812.
[111] *Der CXX Psalm,* p. Giii.
[112] Schiess, II, 808.
[113] *Ibid.*, p. 813.

CHAPTER II

BUCER'S TEACHING ON DIVORCE

An investigation of Bucer's opinions on divorce is a fundamental preliminary to a comprehension of his attitude toward bigamy, for the same basic principles are evident in his teaching on both problems. In his commentary on Matthew, originating out of the sermons he preached at Wissembourg in 1522-1523, and first published in complete form along with briefer commentaries on Mark and Luke in 1527,[1] Bucer outlined his position on the subject.[2] In 1530 a commentary on all four gospels was issued,[3] and, though he often discussed the subject later, his teaching on the doctrine of divorce, as stated in his exegetical works, was definitely fixed in final form by that year.[4]

The commentary on Matthew treats of divorce in three separate places: under Matthew V: 31-32, VIII: 4, and XIX: 1-10. There Bucer expresses the following ideas. Divorce in itself is wrong and an unnatural departure from God's first institution of marriage. If the injunc-

[1] Mentz, no. 13, p. 109.

[2] Anrich, p. 14.

[3] Mentz, no. 24, p. 115. The edition of 1553 was used in preparing this chapter: *In sacra quatuor Euangelia, Enarrationes perpetuae*, etc. (Mentz, no. 24b).

[4] When Bucer wrote his commentary on Romans (published in 1537, *cf.* Mentz, no. 40), he said of Romans VII:2, ''Nam mulier quae sub viro est,'' that this text had nothing to do with the question of marriage and divorce, and since it was an example taken from the Mosiac law, which permitted divorce and re-marriage, ''nihil ex praesenti loco colligendum esse contra diuvortium,'' (M. Bucer, *Metaphrasis et enarratio in epist. D. Pauli apostoli ad Romanos*, etc., p. 344).

tions, "these two shall be one flesh," and "for this cause shall a man leave father and mother," etc., are observed properly, there would be no necessity or desire for divorce, for any man who bestows the highest kind of love upon his wife will never desire separation from her. Yet a wish for separation, due in some cases to a precipitate marriage, in others to a lack of endeavor by both parties to cultivate a spirit of mutual esteem, will arise in spite of all precautions and necessitate a resort to divorce.[5]

The causes for divorce find their scriptural justification in the divine command, "these two shall be one flesh." If under any circumstances it becomes impossible to fulfil this purpose of marriage, or it is not fulfilled in actual practice, then there is a just ground for divorce. Nor is such a plea in any way contradictory to Christ's interpretation of the law of divorce (Matthew XIX) for Christ condemned the spirit of those who used this law, not the law which compelled them to restore what they had despised.

In cases where marriage is thus practically incomplete, certain cardinal principles make divorce a necessary and proper procedure. The first of these is the service of the state, or organized civic community, in which the individuals live. For example, the welfare of the state requires that a leprous husband should be separated from his wife, his children and others. "Surely no one is born, and should live for himself, but for the state."[6] Secondly, the welfare of the individual, especially in the spiritual sense, must be safeguarded. When a husband, through hardness of heart, torments his wife so as to make her

[5] In a marriage sermon, preached probably in 1543, Bucer took Ephesians V as his text and repeated the same ideas about the nature of marriage, already given in his commentary on Ephesians. He did not mention polygamy (cf. the edition and criticism by H. v. Schubert, "Zwei Predigten Martin Bucers," Beiträge zur Reformationsgeschichte, pp. 208-228).

[6] In sacra quatuor Euangelia, Enarrationes perpetuae, p. 80.

life unbearable, it is necessary today, as in ancient times, for the magistrate to liberate her. Conversely, when a wife refuses to live in subjection to her husband, it is best to dissolve the marriage. Divorce is a remedy instituted by God, which the magistrate should utilize for the benefit of those who, because of the hardness of heart of one or both, cannot live suitably and peaceably. This remedy may still be used today, because Christ would not condemn anything which the Father has taught. For the welfare of the husband an unfaithful wife may be divorced, because she is *ipso facto* not a wife, and has failed to meet the requirement of being one flesh with him. Since it is an essential characteristic of a wife that she fulfil the duties of a wife, a failure on her part in this respect justifies her husband in repudiating her, for Christ's words, ''Whoever shall put away his wife,'' apply only to one who genuinely merits the name of wife.

The doctrine of unbreakable marriage is a wicked device of Satan, not only pernicious to the salvation of the individual, but also based upon the false assumption that the vows taken in marriage are perpetually binding, since it fails to recognize that a promise is sacred to a Christian only in so far as it is not against God. Yet the other extreme of easy divorce is fully as evil and injurious, for it is this which Christ attacks in his answer to the Pharisees.

Among the specific causes for divorce may be mentioned leprosy. The proper regard for the health of his wife and children which demands that a leper be segregated from them, also requires that he be granted a divorce, while the obligations of his wife to her children and the state, which forbid her to follow him into a segregated life, justify her in seeking a separation from him. In case they do not have any children, then the love of each partner for the other should prompt them to live together. God him-

self divorces the leper by his command in Deuteronomy
XIII: 45. But this mandate cannot be applied to other
diseases, because there is not the same revelation of divine will concerning other diseases that there is about this
one. "Tum in raribus casibus necesse est Spiritum magis-
trum audire."[7]

Adultery is a legitimate ground for divorce. This is
not disputed, and equally universal should be the acceptance of the rule that adultery is a capital offense, punishable with death as in Old Testament times, for the effi-
ciency of this method for protecting the sanctity of
marriage has been recognized by the law of Leviticus XX:
10 and the Julian codex. Nor did Christ abolish this
punishment by what he said to the woman taken in adultery, "Neither do I condemn you, go and sin no more,"
for by that he only denied that it was his office to punish
external sins with the sword, since his kingdom was not
of this world. "Surely, good faith in marriage and its
lasting strength, could not better be guarded than by making adultery a capital offense."[8]

Hardness of heart is also an adequate ground for divorce just as much as it was under the law of Moses, for
the spirit of hardness of heart is equivalent to adultery.
By such a spirit the husband separates himself from his
wife, since he is no longer "bone of her bone and flesh of
her flesh," and the magistrate recognizing the hate of the
husband does not separate whom God has joined together,
but he saves from more serious peril a soul already re-
pudiated and separated. No one should be forced to live
under the name and regulations of matrimony, when such
conditions as hardness of heart make a true observance
of marriage, as a close union, impossible. In general, when
one partner is unfit for the duties of marriage, either

[7] *In sacra quatuor Euangelia, Enarrationes perpetuae*, p. 80.
[8] *In sacra quatuor Euangelia, Enarrationes perpetuae*, p. 148.

physically or spiritually, the other partner should be allowed a divorce.

Re-marriage after divorce is permissible. The two-fold scriptural basis for this is the admonition, "It is not good for man to be alone," and Paul's counsel that every man should have his own wife to avoid fornication. From these principles may be drawn four arguments why a divorced person should be allowed to marry again.

First, so that he may serve the state better. By marriage the citizenship is increased and also the honesty and discipline of the citizens. If it is true that families are instituted for the good of the state, then it is right to allow a woman divorced from a leper, for example, to marry again, in order that she may render full service to the state. As leprosy is not always an incurable disease, the law of love should impel the healthy partner to delay second marriage, but a leprous husband has no claim upon a healthy wife, for she must first seek the safety and service of the state.

Secondly, divorce is a complete, not a fictitious separation, and the person divorced is no longer bound in any way by the vows previously taken. This is evident from Christ's answer to the Pharisees in Matthew XIX, in which he was concerned as to the kind of divorce about which he was asked. He was asked about the kind of divorce which left a person free to marry again, such as the Romans performed with the words, "Res tuas tibi habeto, res tuas tibi agito." He was not speaking about the kind of divorce which left the partners still bound not to marry other persons. In the specific case of adultery, he allowed a divorce after which marriage might take place again, thus permitting re-marriage after any kind of legitimate divorce. Such a permission is not inconsistent with Paul's statement in Romans VII: 2, and I Corinthians VII: 39, "The wife is bound to the husband, while he is living," for Paul, who would in no case contradict the words of Christ, here refers to the special case of a wife who is capable of being bound to her husband but has left him, and so infringed upon the general law of marriage. When Christ says that whoever takes a wife that has been put away commits adultery, he refers only to that taking of her which is by fraud or deception of the first husband. Paul allows second marriage to a woman who has been put away by a believing husband, in no wise conceding that he who takes her commits adultery.

Thirdly, re-marriage should be allowed to avoid adultery. This is the strongest and most fundamental reason, just as it is above all important that everyone should live chastely. "Since the Lord created man male and female, he wished neither the man nor the woman to live apart, but he said, 'it is not good for man to be alone' (from which Paul states that each man ought to have his own wife, and each woman her own husband, in order to avoid fornication, I Corinthians VII: 2). No one is able to do more than is granted him by God, and in order that he should not sin, each man should have his own wife and each woman her own husband. If, therefore, there is anyone, man or woman, who has no partner and desires one, he should be allowed to take one.'"[9]

There is no doubt that celibacy is more harmful to the state than matrimony, and Christ himself bears witness that it is not given to all men to live celibate. In fact, the welfare of the state demands that even evil men should have wives, rather than be compelled to maintain a celibacy which forces them to commit crime. Likewise, a wife should be either tolerated by her husband or allowed to marry another. "For nothing may be done anywhere so that anyone is forced to sin, or is deprived of the means of a pure life if he desires it. Wherefore, to whomever it is

[9] *In sacra quatuor Euangelia, Enarrationes perpetuae*, p. 147.

not given to live purely outside of marriage, marriage
ought to be provided, whether he fell from it by his own
sin or by another's. Therefore, certainly, nothing at all
is to be denied to a Christian if it promotes honor and
piety."[10] A Christian who is fighting for God should have
all things which God has pronounced good and among
them marriage. Even the adulterer, if he has not been
punished by death for his crime, should not be kept from
a marriage without which he cannot live purely. Celibacy
is a gift which all do not have, and to deny marriage to a
person without this gift, whether divorced or not, is
equivalent to forcing him into a life of immorality. "Thus
to anyone who has a righteous cause, second marriage is
granted."[11]

The magistrate, to whose power all external things are
subject, should regulate and control divorce and second
marriage. His authority comes directly from God and is
in no way limited by the command, "Let not man separate," since it is not he but God who separates. The
magistrate only carries the law into effect. Christ denied
the right, not of the magistrate, but of the individual husband to put away his wife. In fact, the Christian magistrate is a successor of Moses. He should know how to
govern external affairs so that he may do all to the glory
of God and the advantage of the public welfare, and not
disgrace that which Moses permitted to the people of
God. "Our God is the same, and our state they should
govern just as divinely as Moses did that one."[12]

The authority of the magistrate has a worthy example
in the conduct of the Christian emperors of Rome, who did
not consider that matrimony and divorce were outside of
their jurisdiction, but passed laws to regulate these

---

10 *In sacra quatuor Euangelia, Enarrationes perpetuae,* p. 150.
11 *Ibid.,* p. 147.
12 *In sacra quatuor Euangelia, Enarrationes perpetuae,* p. 148.

things. Above all, the magistrate is under a divine guidance, revealing to him the limits of his jurisdiction, the extent of his power, and the laws he should enact. One of the most important of the magistrate's duties is to protect the weak and afflicted. For example, he should provide for the leper a maintenance sufficient to free the healthy partner from the burden of his care, and for unfortunate matrons, relief from the affliction of hard-hearted husbands. When either partner desires a divorce, the magistrate, after investigating the circumstances and deciding whether the causes are sufficient and just, should grant the divorce in accordance with the divine mandates and his own discretion, if he thinks it will be to the advantage of the state and the individuals concerned. Then, if anyone desires re-marriage, he should determine whether or not it should be granted him. If some seek marriage to avoid living in fornication (I Corinthians VII: 2), the wise ruler will act so sagaciously that no one will be caused to sin. He should permit re-marriage to the healthy partner of a leper, when it is piously sought, in everything acting as God's agent, aiming to regulate marriage relations so that all may live peaceably and with a good conscience, and seeking as his ultimate goal the prevention of immorality or impure living.

This, in brief, was the position on divorce to which Bucer had come by 1530. Needless to say, it was a very radical position. But most important of all, it contained within itself certain methods in the interpretation of Scripture, certain ideas of the nature and purpose of marriage, certain conceptions of the structure of human nature and society, which completely accorded with the attitude which he assumed ten years later on the more difficult problem of bigamy.[13]

Even a superficial examination of Bucer's teaching on

[13] See below, p. 63, ff.

divorce will reveal two fundamental doctrines which lay at the basis of his later attitude toward bigamy. First, divorce is a remedy employed to curb the natural inclination of men toward immorality and unfaithfulness,[14] in order that the perfect standard of righteous living may be maintained. This doctrine is founded on the idea that marriage has a two-fold purpose: first to avoid fornication[15] since celibacy is a gift bestowed upon a favored few,[16] who find it an indispensable aid to the preservation of continency outside of marriage;[17] and, secondly, to benefit the state by increasing its population and elevating its morality.[18] Inherently undesirable as divorce is admitted to be, it may often be a useful expedient to improve conditions that are far worse, because they endanger the salvation of the individual. Marriage is not a sacrament with an indelible character, but an institution designed to promote the morality of the individual, so that the desire to promote the integrity of the matrimonial bond should never be permitted to defeat this purpose.[19] For example, a leper must be segregated to protect the health of society. The integrity of the institution of marriage requires that a leper's wife remain bound to him, but the morality of the individual voices the higher demand that she be allowed to divorce him and re-marry in order to avoid fornication, unless she has the gift of continence. Because this latter demand takes precedence over the other, it should be granted when the two conflict.

The second doctrine is that Christ did not abrogate the

---

[14] See above, p. 22.   [15] See above, pp. 24-25.

[16] See above, pp. 25-26.

[17] This idea may have been borrowed somewhat from Bucer's own experience, for in his *Verantwortung* he wrote, ''Now we have learned to our sorrow, that the cloister-life is in many numerous ways a hindrance to a Christian life, and so we have married and find that it helps us in a godly life'' (*Verantwortung*, p. d, ff.).

[18] See above, p. 24, ff.

[19] See above, pp. 23-26; *cf.* Schiess, I, 269.

Old Testament law of divorce, but ruled that divorce for
hardness of heart is still permissible.[20] The law of divorce
was not condemned by Christ, but rather the spirit leading people to use it;[21] nor would he condemn anything
which the Father has taught.[22] The magistrate should not
disgrace that which Moses permitted to the people of God,
for "our God is the same, and our state they should
govern just as divinely as Moses did that one."[23]

The best proof that Bucer's opinion on bigamy developed naturally from his teaching on divorce, and was
founded on the same methods of exegesis, is that he argued from the permissibility of divorce to prove that
bigamy also might be permitted under the new dispensation, in order to cure the evil of fornication.[24]

During the last year of his life Bucer wrote *De Regno
Christi*,[25] one of his most extensive works. In this book,
presented to Edward VI as a New Year's gift, he made
his final and most complete statement on divorce, which
differs in no essential particular from the attitude which
he had taken in 1530, except that the arguments which
he used to justify bigamy are here emphasized and repeated. For example, he said that the laws of Moses are
to be highly valued. "How much more is it our duty to
observe diligently what the Lord hath commanded and
taught by the examples of his people concerning mar-

[20] See above, p. 23.

[21] See above, p. 21.

[22] See above, p. 22. *Cf.*, "quod enim deus admisit semel praesertim lege
publica totius gentis . . . id enim, si causa sit, et modo admittere credendus
est" (Schiess, I, 269).

[23] See above, p. 26.

[24] *Argumenta Buceri pro et contra. Original-manuscript Bucers, die
Gründe für und gegen die Doppelehe des Landgrafen Philipp des Grossmüthigen de anno 1539*, published by L., Cassel, 1878 (Mentz, p. 163), pp.
25-27. *Cf.* below, p. 84, ff.

[25] Harvey, p. 79; Mentz, no. 81, p. 152. This work is printed in the *Scripta
Anglicana*, p. 1-170.

riage, whereof we have the use no less than they.[26] . . .
What the Lord permitted to his first-born people, that,
certainly, he would not forbid to his own among the
Gentiles. . . . For being God he is not changed as man.'[27]
Arguing that Christ would not refuse to give these same
remedies of divorce and second marriage to the weak,[28]
he claimed that some persons are so predestinated to
marriage that they cannot be continent without it, and in
this case everyone is left to his own judgment and conscience.[29] In conclusion Bucer declared that his purpose
was to prevent and remove causes for immorality outside
of marriage by exalting the status of matrimony.[30]

This doctrine of divorce he was called upon to apply,
when the case of Henry VIII was submitted to his consideration. Returning to Strasbourg[31] from Ulm, about
the middle of July, 1531, he found that during his absence
Simon Grynaeus of Basel had visited the city on an extraordinary errand.[32] After talking with Jacob Sturm and
others, Grynaeus had departed, leaving at Strasbourg a
pamphlet and the instructions given him for his mission,[33]
yet as soon as he heard of Bucer's return he wrote to him,
further explaining the nature and importance of the question he had come to discuss, and asking for an answer.[34]

In brief, the following problem confronted Bucer. Grynaeus had just returned from England, where he had been
entrusted by the king with the difficult mission of securing
an opinion from certain theologians on the validity of the

[26] *Scripta Anglicana*, p. 87.

[27] *Ibid.*, p. 100.   [28] *Ibid.*, p. 101.

[29] *Ibid.*, p. 129.   [30] *Ibid.*, p. 133.

[31] Bucer had been conducting an evangelical campaign at Ulm and Biberach in company with Oecolampadius. He returned to Strasbourg by way of
Ulm during July (*Huldrici Zwingli Opera. Completa editio prima curantibus
Melchior Schulero et Io. Schultessio*, VIII, 624. This work will be referred
to as *Zwingli Opera*. Cf. Schiess, I, 253, 255, II, 789-790).

[32] Grynaeus to Bucer, Thesaurus Baumianus, III, 368-369.

[33] *Ibid.*   [34] *Ibid.*

king's marriage.[35] Catharine, the aunt of the emperor, had married Arthur, the elder brother of Henry VIII. She had no children by Arthur, and after his death Henry had married her, having received a papal dispensation for this purpose. But now, as some said, his conscience troubled him; others, that he loathed the queen and desired a certain girl. He had consulted various continental universities, all of whom had answered that the pope did not possess the power to grant the dispensation, and the marriage should be annulled as incest.[36] Henry claimed that his marriage was contrary to the law of Leviticus XVIII: 16, "thou shalt not uncover the nakedness of thy brother's wife, it is thy brother's nakedness." But it was a question whether this applied after the brother's death, and it was on this dispute that a judgment was requested from Bucer and his colleagues.[37] For more than seven years, so Grynaeus claimed, the king's conscience had been troubled by the thought that by marrying his brother's wife and continuing matrimonial relations with her, he had done a thing forbidden by divine and natural law.[38] Now he was convinced that it was wrong to live in marital relations with her, and since he had no male heir, there were most ominous prospects of a war over the inheritance of the crown.[39] Already factions had arisen within the kingdom asserting rival claims to the throne, and in foreign lands there were not a few aspirants to be found who might make trouble in case of a disputed succession.[40]

[35] Schiess, I, 268, ff.

[36] So summed up by Bucer in his letter to Blaurer, Sept. 21, 1531, Schiess, I, 268.

[37] Bucer *et al.* to Grynaeus, Dec. 30, 1531, Epistolae Buceri, I, 44; copy in the Thesaurus Baumianus, III, 370-373.

[38] Grynaeus to Bucer, Epistolae Hist. Ecclesiam, G, 250.

[39] Grynaeus to Bucer, Thesaurus Baumianus, III, 368-369.

[40] Bucer *et al.* to Grynaeus, Epistolae Buceri, I, 44.

What Grynaeus requested from Bucer was a purely
theoretical opinion on the validity of a marriage with a
dead brother's wife, but he evidently wished the reformer
to keep in mind the practical aspects of the case and to
return a favorable answer which would allow the king to
make a new marriage.[41] Praising Henry for his opposition to the pope, he dangled before Bucer's eyes the in-
ducement that a friendly attitude by the Protestants of
Germany might assist in the complete conversion of England, and be influential in effecting a league with her in
the near future.[42] All these considerations he requested
the Strasbourg theologian to weigh carefully, and then
to send in his reply as quickly as possible.[43]

Bucer took great pains in forming an opinion on the
case, and although he was busy preparing and publishing
the apology for the *Confession of the Four Cities*,[44] he still
found time to correspond extensively with Grynaeus so as
to gather all the information possible.[45] It soon became
evident that their opinions were widely divergent, Bucer
ruling, for example, that marriage with a dead brother's
wife was not contrary to natural law, while Grynaeus
contended that it was.[46] Each composed lengthy and involved epistles to convince the other, while refusing himself to move an inch.[47] About the middle of August Bucer's
first opinion was brought to Grynaeus, who immediately
informed Oecolampadius of the contents,[48] and sent a copy

[41] Grynaeus to Bucer, Thesaurus Baumianus, III, 368-369.

[42] *Ibid.*

[43] *Ibid.*

[44] Schiess, I, 255.

[45] Many of the letters exchanged between them have been lost, but a
great many still remain in the archives of Strasbourg and Basel, most of
which are undated. Grynaeus very seldom dated a letter completely, and he
could rival Bucer in bad handwriting.

[46] Grynaeus to Bucer, Epistolae Hist. Ecclesiam, G, 250.

[47] *Ibid.*, Bucer *et al.* to Grynaeus, Dec. 30, 1531, Epistolae Buceri, I, 44.

[48] Grynaeus to Bucer, Thesaurus Baumianus, XXIII, 104-105.

of the letter to Zwingli.[49] Since the text has been lost, little
is known of what the letter contained, but it is evident
from remarks made by Oecolampadius and Grynaeus,
that Bucer thought bigamy permissible because it had
been permitted to David.[50] Oecolampadius declared that
such an opinion savored more of Mohammed than Christ
and expressed the wish that Zwingli's opinion might
effect a change in Bucer's attitude and so avoid offence
to the church.[51]

Zwingli, and also Oecolampadius, judged that the Le-
vitical law was still binding, thus invalidating Henry's
marriage with Catharine and allowing him to put the
queen away.[52] Though Zwingli's opinion, which reached
Strasbourg during the first week in September,[53] had the
outspoken approval of Grynaeus, Bucer's attitude remained the same.[54] Grynaeus not only praised the answer
given by Zwingli and requested the reformer of Strasbourg to agree with it, but he went further and asked that
if Bucer could not agree he would give some indication
that he did not disapprove of Zwingli's statement.[55]

In response to this request Bucer wrote to Zwingli that
he would do nothing to oppose his opinion even though
he could not agree with him, and regretted that his conscience forced him to give different advice.[56] Grynaeus

[49] *Original Letters relative to the English Reformation written during the
reigns of King Henry VIII, King Edward VI, and Queen Mary, chiefly
from the archives of Zurich*, II, 553.

[50] Grynaeus to Bucer, Thesaurus Baumianus, XXIII, 104-105; cf. *Zwingli
Opera*, VIII, 634.

[51] *Zwingli Opera*, VIII, 634.

[52] *Zwingli Opera*, VIII, 634; *Original Letters*, II, 551; P. Smith, ''German Opinion of the Divorce of Henry VIII,'' *English Historical Review*,
XXVII, 678.

[53] Grynaeus to Bucer, Epistolae Hist. Ecclesiam, G, 253; *Original Letters*,
II, 553.

[54] Grynaeus to Bucer, Thesaurus Baumianus, XXIII, 104-105.

[55] Grynaeus to Bucer, Thesaurus Baumianus, IV, 215.

[56] *Zwingli Opera*, VIII, 644.

also wished Bucer to give him a copy of the apology for the *Confession of the Four Cities,* to be sent to the king along with the answers on the divorce question, for he felt that it would help in gaining the king's support for the doctrine of the German Protestants.[57]

When it came to forming a final opinion on the divorce of Henry VIII, Bucer hesitated. Grynaeus, on the other hand, found the delay irritating, and in the first part of September requested Bucer to send in a statement at once, since he could wait no longer. It would be best for Capito, Hedio, and Zell to write separately, he thought, so as to increase the number of replies.[58] On September 5, 1531, Bucer sent in a second opinion, subscribed by his colleagues at Strasbourg,[59] whose text seems to have perished like that of the first, which he had sent in August. Bucer himself characterized it as incomplete and rudimentary, because it was written in haste and under the impression that it could be supplemented later.[60] Among other things he expressed the belief that it was not necessary for Christians to observe certain external precepts of the Old Testament.[61] Lamenting the fact that his opinion could not be approved by the Zurichers, he said he preferred not to submit any statement. He asked Grynaeus to remember that the document was sent to him alone and begged him to return the personal letter which accompanied it.[62]

Almost as soon as he had received this opinion, Grynaeus returned it to Bucer and requested him to despatch

[57] Grynaeus to Bucer, Thesaurus Baumianus, IV, 215; Grynaeus to Bucer, Thesaurus Baumianus, IV, 76; Bucer to Grynaeus, Sept. 5 (1531), Epistolae Buceri, undated, 14.

[58] Grynaeus to Bucer, Thesaurus Baumianus, IV, 215.

[59] Bucer to Grynaeus, Sept. 5 (1531), Epistolae Buceri, undated, 14.

[60] *Ibid.*

[61] Bucer *et al.* to Grynaeus, Dec. 30, 1531, Epistolae Buceri, I, 44.

[62] Bucer to Grynaeus, Sept. 5 (1531), Epistolae Buceri, undated, 14.

it at once to Henry VIII. Since he himself did not have a copyist at hand, he asked that Bucer employ someone to copy into an "elegant volumne" his own letters and also certain letters about the same matter from Zwingli, Oecolampadius, Phrygio, Capito, Hedio, and Zell, which Grynaeus had sent him. This he requested Bucer to have done immediately, so that the messenger could start the next day for Cologne.[63] To explain the letters, Grynaeus himself wrote to the king, apologizing for the fact that the answers were incomplete, and offering hope of a more decisive reply later.[64] While there is no evidence that Bucer followed the directions given by Grynaeus, it is probable that he did.

Not until after these first replies were sent in was anything heard from the reformers of Wittenberg.[65] Meanwhile, Bucer's own answer had been sent to them,[66] and sometime during the first part of October he received their replies.[67] Luther, believing that an unjustified repudiation of Catharine would only augment the sin Henry had already committed in taking her,[68] refused to sanction a divorce,[69] but ventured to suggest that the king might solve his difficulties by committing bigamy. "It might be permitted," he said, "that the king should take another wife according to the example of the patriarchs, who had many wives even before the law, but it is not right that he should exclude her from the royal family and from the name of English Queen."[70] Melanchthon was more out-

[63] *Original Letters*, II, 552-554.

[64] *Original Letters*, II, 555.

[65] Grynaeus to the Preachers of Strasbourg, Thesaurus Baumianus, XXIII, 97.

[66] Grynaeus to Bucer, Thesaurus Baumianus, V, 184-185.

[67] Bucer to Grynaeus, Oct. 9, 1531, Epistolae Buceri, I, 32.

[68] Enders, IX, 81.

[69] *Ibid.*

[70] *Ibid.*, p. 88. The texts of Luther's opinion are contained in Enders, IX, no. 1932 and no. 1933, pp. 80-97. *Cf.* the criticism of the text by Vogt,

spoken than Luther in the suggestion of bigamy.[71] Regarding the law of Leviticus XVIII as no longer binding,[72] he advised the king for the sake of the public welfare and his own conscience to take another wife, not rejecting the first, "because it is certain that polygamy is not prohibited by divine law."[73] And, what seems more curious, he suggested the seeking of a papal dispensation "that polygamy should be permitted to the king," believing that the pope would not turn a deaf ear.[74] Overtures had actually been made to Henry's ambassadors about such a dispensation, but how sincere the pope was, and whether he would actually have given one, is a matter for controversy.[75]

Bucer believed that the sooner Grynaeus sent the replies of Luther and Melanchthon to England, the better it would be, but he criticized two points which he thought might be misunderstood. The first of these was the statement that "Moses is nothing to us." This Bucer interpreted, not as referring to the moral law of Moses, but to the ceremonial law meant only for the Hebrews. The second was their denial that marriage with the dead brother's widow was contrary to natural law. Bucer himself agreed

"Uber Heinrichs VIII Ehescheidung aus Bugenhagens Handschriften," *Theologische Studien und Kritiken,* 1885, LVIII, 725-747. The best discussion of Luther's opinion is given by Rockwell, *Die Doppelehe des Landgrafen Philipp von Hessen,* p. 213, ff.

71 *Cf.* T. Kolde, "Nachrichten," *Zeitschrift für Kirchengeschichte,* XIII, 576.

72 *CR.,* II, 521-522.   73 *Ibid.,* p. 526.   74 *Ibid.*

75 On this controversy, which is too lengthy and involved to be adequately discussed here, where it is not closely enough related to the subject, see, Rockwell, p. 210, and n. 6; T. Brieger, "Luther und die Nebenehe des Landgrafen Philipp von Hessen," *Preussische Jahrbücher,* Jan., 1909, CXXXV, Heft I, 35-49; A. F. Pollard, *Thomas Cranmer and the English Reformation,* p. 32, ff.; A. F. Pollard, *Henry VIII,* p. 207, ff.; Hardy, "Papal Dispensation for Polygamy," *Dublin Review,* Oct., 1913, CLIII, 266-274; Faulkner, "Luther and the Bigamous Marriage of Philip of Hesse," *American Journal of Theology,* 1913, XVII, 219-224.

with this position but realized that Grynaeus and the supporters of Henry VIII did not. So he requested Grynaeus to send a letter to England, explaining these two points in the replies of Luther and Melanchthon.[76]

When Grynaeus sent the opinion of Wittenberg to Zurich, he added, at the suggestion of Oecolampadius, the second opinion of Bucer, thinking that Zwingli would look more mildly upon Luther's opinion when he saw Bucer's arguments.[77] That Bucer corresponded with Wittenberg about the matter is evident from a letter written him by Melanchthon on November 8, 1531, in which he refused to sanction a divorce or give his support to anyone who did.[78]

The opinion of the Wittenbergers has a most puzzling connection with the later bigamy of Landgrave Philip. Shortly after Luther had despatched his judgment to England, he received a letter from Landgrave Philip of Hesse asking how he should answer the English monarch.[79] The landgrave requested an opinion favorable to Henry, and, curiously enough, emphasized that element in the king's case which coincided with his own experience, "that in his youth and before he had reached years of discretion, his majesty was compelled by force and by obedience to his father to take his brother's widow."[80] Luther replied on September 22, 1531, that his advice was already on the way to England, but he would send a copy to the landgrave.[81] More of what happened we do not

[76] Bucer to Grynaeus, Oct. 9, 1531, Epistolae Buceri, I, 32; cf. Enders, IX, 97.

[77] Grynaeus to Bucer, Thesaurus Baumianus, IV, 77.

[78] CR., II, 552.

[79] F. Gundlach, "Nachträge zum Briefwechsel des Landgrafen Philipp mit Luther und Melanchthon," Zeitschrift des Vereins für hessische Geschichte und Landeskunde, NF., XXVIII, 64.

[80] Gundlach, op. cit., p. 64; cf. Lenz, I, 353; CR., III, 852.

[81] Enders, IX, 105; Lenz, "Nachlese zum Briefwechsel des Landgrafen Philipp mit Luther und Melanchthon," Zeitschrift für Kirchengeschichte,

know. The version of Luther's opinion existing today in the Marburg archives, does not contain the reference to bigamy;[82] yet the puzzling fact is that when Philip sent Bucer to Wittenberg in December, 1539, to seek Luther's approval of his own desire to have two wives at the same time, he said, "Likewise, his princely grace knows that Luther and Philip have advised the king of England that he should not leave his first wife, but should take another along with her, as undoubtedly the *Rathschlag* reads."[83] Evidently the landgrave had heard of this feature of Luther's opinion from some written source, but there is no information to show what it was. Rockwell has suggested that Bucer told him at Melsungen in 1539,[84] which is possible, though there are serious objections which make it improbable. The phrase, "wie ungefährlich der Rathschlag gelautet," indicates a written, not an oral source,[85] and it is improbable that Bucer would have given the landgrave any such encouragement to commit bigamy, as will appear from the consideration of his attitude later.

Bucer's final opinion on the divorce of Henry VIII is dated December 30, 1531, and is subscribed by Capito, Hedio, and Zell, who did not write out separate statements this time.[86] It is prolix, very carefully phrased, and, most important of all, treats the subject in a practical and political way, over-riding the request that they should give a purely theological and exegetical opinion. Instead of simply deciding whether or not the law of Leviticus XVIII forbade anyone to marry the wife of a

---

IV, 136 (in referring to this work both title and author will be given to distinguish it from Lenz' chief work).

[82] Rockwell, p. 8, n. 4; p. 214, n. 1; Enders, IX, 91, n. 15.

[83] *CR.*, III, 854.   [84] Rockwell, p. 8.

[85] *Cf.* the landgrave to Luther, July 17, 1540, "Daneben hab ich zu sochem grundt auch wollen und halten von uch und anderen gelerten hiefur ausgangene schrifften und auch die ratslagen, die irr dem kunig von Englandt geben mit ein geprofft und einige" (Lenz, I, 383).

[86] Original text in the Epistolae Buceri, I, 44.

deceased brother, Bucer told Henry what he deemed the wisest mode of procedure to advance the monarch's own welfare and that of his kingdom. That the king had sufficient theologians at hand and yet came to Germany for theological advice was good reason, Bucer asserted, why an abundance of political advisers in England should not deter him from giving political advice. Content with mentioning casually that Zwingli and Oecolampadius were mistaken in their opinion, Bucer did not attack them. This reply Grynaeus sent to the king during January,[87] and never afterwards did he trouble Bucer about the matter, except to request him to preserve all the correspondence, that it might be on hand in case of trouble between himself and the English court.[88]

A mere statement of Bucer's opinion is not sufficient for a complete understanding of it: his general attitude toward the problem must first be considered.[89] Fearful of an unfortunate issue of the affair and anxious to be released from giving an opinion,[90] Bucer apologized for submitting a judgment different from that desired by Grynaeus,[91] and implored him to return his letters.[92] The opinion of the universities found little favor in his sight, for he claimed that they were not so zealous for the law of God and the purity of life, as they wished to appear to be against marriage of the dead brother's widow.[93] His deep distrust of the royal pangs of conscience

---

[87] Grynaeus to Bucer, Jan. 26 (1531), Thesaurus Baumianus, IV, 23.

[88] Grynaeus to Bucer, Epistolae Hist. Ecclesiam, G, 249b.

[89] Bucer to Grynaeus, Oct. 9, 1531, Thesaurus Baumianus, IV, 146. The admiration for Henry expressed in this letter later turned to disgust (Lenz, II, 273, ff.).

[90] Grynaeus to Bucer, Oct. 21 (1531), Thesaurus Baumianus, IV, 156-157.

[91] Bucer to Grynaeus, Dec. 30, 1531, Epistolae Buceri, I, 44.

[92] Bucer to Grynaeus, Sept. 5 (1531), Epistolae Buceri, III, undated, 14; also Bucer to Grynaeus, Oct. 9, 1531, Epistolae Buceri, I, 32. Grynaeus to Bucer, Oct. 21 (1531), Thesaurus Baumianus, IV, 156-157.

[93] Bucer et al. to Grynaeus, Dec. 30, 1531, Epistolae Buceri, I, 44.

prompted him to inquire of Grynaeus four times in succession whether Anne Boleyn had borne any children to the king,[94] until the Basel theologian was forced to reply that she had no acknowledged ones.[95] He told Grynaeus plainly, that the king yielded too much to his weak and faulty conscience;[96] that Catharine's good reputation was of more value than the peace of the king's conscience, which could easily be restored if put into the hands of the physician Christ;[97] and that Henry should trust in God, read the Scriptures, and pray over the matter until he was freed from his error.[98] So deeply was he concerned about the danger of a revolution in England,[99] even approving the solution of a divorce with the consent of the queen,[100] if such a catastrophe might be avoided, that Grynaeus accused him of exaggerating the importance of this consideration.[101]

From Bucer's various statements about the divorce of Henry VIII, one thing is clear: he regarded Henry's marriage with Catharine of Aragon as valid, and thought a divorce would be wrong. This opinion he based on three subordinate beliefs. First, he held that the law of Leviticus XVIII against marrying a brother's wife did not apply after the brother's death.[102] In support of this posi-

---

[94] Bucer to Grynaeus, Sept. 5 (1531), Epistolae Buceri, III, undated, 14.

[95] Grynaeus to Bucer, Sept. (10) 1531, *Original Letters*, II, 552, ff.

[96] Bucer to Grynaeus, Oct. 9, 1531, Epistolae Buceri, I, 32. Bucer *et al.* to Grynaeus, Dec. 30, 1531, Epistolae Buceri, I, 44.

[97] Bucer *et al.* to Grynaeus, Dec. 30, 1531, Epistolae Buceri, I, 44.

[98] Bucer to Grynaeus, Oct. 9, 1531, Epistolae Buceri, I, 32.

[99] Bucer *et al.* to Grynaeus, Dec. 30, 1531, Epistolae Buceri, I, 44.

[100] Schiess, I, 269.

[101] Grynaeus to Bucer, Oct. 21 (1531), Thesaurus Baumianus, IV, 156-157. *Cf. Zwingli Opera*, VIII, 635.

[102] Bucer to Grynaeus, Dec. 30, 1531, Epistolae Buceri, I, 44. *Cf.* Burnet-Pocock, *The History of the Reformation of the Church of England by G. Burnet*, I, 160. On Nov. 1, 1529, Pistorius wrote to Bucer requesting an explanation of the matrimonial law of Leviticus, since he found that Luther and Zwingli did not agree (Thesaurus Baumianus, III, 173).

tion he advanced four arguments: (1) before the law
was given by Moses the patriarchs had married the dead
brother's widow.[103] (2) The law of Deuteronomy not only
shows that marriage with the dead brother's widow was
required, but that the validity of such a marriage was
never questioned.[104] (3) Christians, living under the new
dispensation, are no longer bound by the law of Moses,
but are impelled in all things to do what is good, honest,
and pleasing to God. To those living in this liberty, marriage with the dead brother's widow cannot be less fitting
than when the law of Deuteronomy was given.[105] (4) The
law of Moses may be abrogated in special cases, as when
David ate the sacred bread and Christ's disciples plucked
grain on the Sabbath.[106]

Secondly, Bucer held that Henry's marriage with
Catharine was not opposed to natural law, and on this
point he differed sharply from Grynaeus, who held the
contrary.[107] In accordance with this belief, he asserted
that such a marriage was not a thing inherently evil.[108]

Thirdly, he thought it would be wrong to annul the
marriage after it had been entered into with the consent
of the church and the magistrates. He said plainly,
"keep the wife of your dead brother, who was taken with
the consent of the church and the magistrates, not only
is it a permitted but a necessary thing,"[109] for he claimed
that after the marriage had once been contracted it would
be wrong to break it.[110]

[103] Bucer *et al.* to Grynaeus, Dec. 30, 1531, Epistolae Buceri, I, 44. *Cf.*
Thesaurus Baumianus, XXIII, 104-105; Schiess, I, 269; *Zwingli Opera,*
VIII, 635.

[104] Bucer *et al.* to Grynaeus, Dec. 30, 1531, Epistolae Buceri, I, 44.

[105] *Ibid.*

[106] Grynaeus to Bucer, Epistolae Hist. Ecclesiam, G, 250.

[107] Bucer to Grynaeus, Oct. 9, 1531, Epistolae Buceri, I, 32; Grynaeus to
Bucer, Oct. 21 (1531), Thesaurus Baumianus, IV, 156-157.

[108] Bucer *et al.* to Grynaeus, Dec. 30, 1531, Epistolae Buceri, I, 44.

[109] *Ibid.*   [110] *Ibid.; cf. Zwingli Opera,* VIII, 635.

The most interesting thing about Bucer's advice to
Henry VIII, when it is considered in connection with the
later bigamy of Landgrave Philip, is the opinion he expressed about the permissibility of bigamy. In brief, he
thought that bigamy would be a permissible solution, but
not an advisable one. It appeared to him to be the only
solution besides a divorce by mutual consent, and he did
not hesitate to say that it would be better than an unjust
condemnation of the queen, as if she had lived in an immoral relation for so many years.[111] Though he defended
this opinion that bigamy was permissible by the claim
that God had permitted it to the saints such as David,[112]
he thought the possibility of injury to the church made it
inadvisable for the king to commit bigamy,[113] and no
mention of it is to be found in his last opinion. It is a
serious error to say, as Paulus has done, that Bucer preferred bigamy to divorce.[114] Undoubtedly Bucer thought
that bigamy from a theoretical point of view would be
more just than a divorce without the queen's consent;
but as a practicable solution of the difficulty he refused
to suggest it.

Bucer's opinion was in closer harmony with that of
Wittenberg than that of Zurich, for he agreed with
Luther that Henry's marriage should be respected as
valid and that bigamy was permissible. The greater
emphasis which he placed upon the personal aspects of
the affair and his deep concern for Catharine's reputation distinguished him from the other reformers and
reflected favorably upon his character. King Henry was
not at all pleased with his judgment, as Bucer was in-

111 Schiess, I, 269; Bucer to Grynaeus, Oct. 9, 1531, Epistolae Buceri, I,
32.

112 *Ibid.*   113 Schiess, I, 269.

114 N. Paulus, ''Die hessische Doppelehe im Urteile der protestantischen
Zeitgenossen,'' *Historisch-politische Blätter für das katholische Deutschland,*
1911, CXLVII, 512.

formed by the Bishop of Hereford four years later,[115] and he himself felt in after years that he had erred in the way he had given his opinion,[116] for Henry's later conduct increased his distrust of the monarch[117] so greatly that after the king had run his long course of matrimonial experiences, Bucer expressed the opinion that Catharine of Aragon had received worse treatment than Anne of Cleves.[118]

When the landgrave's condition and proposals in November, 1539, are considered in the light of the teaching and application outlined above, it is hard to see how Bucer could have consistently decided in any other way than he did.[119] His teaching on divorce was the same in 1550 as in 1530, and those elements in it which were closely related to his attitude toward bigamy were just as prominent ten years after, as ten years before he was called upon by Philip of Hesse to give his opinion on the righteousness of bigamy. As far as bigamy itself was concerned, he had already admitted that because God allowed it to David it was not wrong in itself, and only his dread of giving offence to the church restrained him from counseling Henry VIII to employ this expedient. When Philip later decided to commit bigamy, Bucer had to decide, not on the scripturalness of the act, but upon the need: whether, by refusing to give his consent, he would deprive Philip of the "means of a pure life,"[120] and so "force him into sin."

[115] Schiess, II, 823; Baum, p. 504.
[116] Schiess, II, 826.
[117] He wrote to the landgrave in Oct., 1539, "Dieser kunig ist ja alles ungluckes wert" (Lenz, I, 107).
[118] Lenz, II, 274.
[119] See below, p. 63, ff.
[120] *Cf.* above, p. 26.

CHAPTER III

PREVIOUS RELATIONS WITH
THE LANDGRAVE

Long before Landgrave Philip committed bigamy, Bucer had made his personal acquaintance at the Marburg Colloquy. There the two men found themselves in agreement in their common desire for concord, and under this banner they united their efforts in the years that followed. Starting with a preliminary conference with the Saxon chancellor Bruck,[1] while at the Diet of Augsburg, Bucer continued the conciliatory effort inaugurated at Marburg, and was so far successful that he overcame Melanchthon's repugnance to a personal meeting.[2] The landgrave's religious zeal at the Diet evidently inspired Bucer with admiration, for he characterized him as ''that most pious prince,''[3] and at the Coburg conference with Luther a few weeks later, he supported Philip's policy in dealing with the political situation.[4]

After Bucer had conferred with Luther, Zwingli, and their followers, he drew up a statement of the Supper Doctrine, in the form of a letter to Duke Ernest of Lunenberg, which he hoped would be acceptable to both parties. This attempt the landgrave supported by writing to Luther in favor of Bucer's effort, with the result that Luther expressed his desire for peace, but would not approve a formula which could be so easily misunder-

[1] Obtained by the landgrave's assistance on July 22, 1530 (Lenz, I, 21).
[2] *Ibid.*
[3] Schiess, I, 212.
[4] *Politische Correspondenz* . . . *Strassburg*, I, 514.

stood. Since Luther objected that no statement was made concerning the reception of the sacrament by unbelievers, on which subject he had conferred with Bucer at Coburg, the landgrave suggested that Bucer draft a series of articles expressing his opinion more comprehensively.[5] In return Bucer informed the landgrave of his negotiations with the Swiss, and explained that he had intentionally kept silent on the question of the participation of unbelievers, because he disagreed with Luther on this point, and wished to avoid any controversy.[6]

After the defeat of Zurich at the second battle of Kappel, Bucer interceded with the landgrave on behalf of the Swiss, and the "princely reply" which he received[7] aroused an admiration which was still further increased when he learned that Philip opposed any statement by the Schweinfurt Conference that would exclude Zwinglians, esteeming it better to have a league with the Zwinglians who disagreed only on the Eucharist, than with the papists who erred on the whole of religion.[8] That he had become intimate with the landgrave is shown by the fact that he complained to him of certain Hessian preachers who attacked Zwingli, and in particular of Erhard Schnepf.[9] Not only with the Hessian preachers did he find fault, but he also boldly reprimanded the landgrave himself for spending too much time in gaming and hunting, and advised him to pay more attention to the needs of his subjects. To a warning that Philip should not look too much upon the "flesh-pots of Egypt," he added admonitions to a sober manner of life.[10]

In 1534 Landgrave Philip conducted a successful war to restore Duke Ulrich of Würtemberg. The landgrave did not inform Bucer of his plans, which may indicate a

5 Lenz, I, 26-27.
7 Schiess, I, 321.
9 Lenz, I, 31.
6 Ibid., pp. 27-31.
8 Ibid., p. 338.
10 Ibid., p. 35.

lack of intimacy, but more probably a want of sympathy,[11] for later when they were most intimate they were far from agreed, and at this time he opposed an alliance between the landgrave and the French,[12] and condemned the use of force.[13] From the first Bucer regarded the expedition with disfavor, judging that the advantages of a possible victory were not as great as the danger of political complications.[14] Five years later he wrote to Philip that if the princes would only exhibit the same zeal in promoting the cause of Christ, that he had shown in the cause of Duke Ulrich, they would help the whole German nation with despatch and facility.[15]

The easy victory of the landgrave and Duke Ulrich was a surprise to Bucer, who had so confidently expected and greatly feared a horrible war, that he hoped Christ would intervene to stop the conflict,[16] and was glad to see peace although it did not satisfy his desires.[17] When the victory was won, Bucer lost no time in sending to the landgrave recommendations for the conduct of the Reformation in Würtemberg,[18] proposing a conference of the pious, godly people; a meeting of all the men who would not obstruct the establishment of the gospel; the employment of Ambrose Blaurer and Simon Grynaeus in the work, because of their conciliatory attitude on the Supper; and

[11] As Lenz thinks (Lenz, I, v).   [12] Schiess, I, 469.

[13] In the spring of 1528, when Philip had been led by the pseudo-revelations of Otto von Pack to mobilize an army against the Catholics, Bucer had condemned his action by writing to Farel, "Patientia scio propagari evangelion, et legitimis populorum principibus ad Dominum conversis, non armis subactis aut ditione pulsis" (CR., XXXVIII, pt. II, 2). At the same time he wrote to Zwingli, "Armis numquam est propagatum feliciter evangelion" (CR., XCVI, 121). Cf. H. Eells, "The Correct Date for a Letter to Zwingli," Revue belge de Philologie et d'Histoire, July, 1922, pp. 514-519. Perhaps this attitude was due to his experience under Franz von Sickingen.

[14] Lenz, I, 37, n. 2; Schiess, I, 494.

[15] Lenz, I, 75.   [16] Schiess, I, 494.

[17] Ibid., p. 508.   [18] Lenz, I, 36-37.

the exclusion of all Anabaptists.[19] Bucer notified Blaurer
that he had recommended him,[20] and after he was called,
gave him minute and detailed instructions for his conduct
in the newly-conquered duchy.[21] Unfortunately Schnepf,
who had opposing views on the Supper, was also called.
When he and Blaurer were unable to agree, Bucer, who
kept in close touch with the situation, complained to the
landgrave that Schnepf was an obstacle to peace,[22] urging
Philip to exert his influence to have Blaurer treated fairly
and Schnepf forced to be peaceful.[23]

If Bucer was ready to ask favors from Philip of Hesse,
he was equally ready to serve him. Thus, when the dispute
arose between Ulrich and Philip over the terms of peace,
he used what influence he had in the landgrave's behalf,[24]
condemning Ulrich as selfish and ungrateful when he
refused ratification.[25]

No greater service could the landgrave have rendered
his Strasbourg friend and the cause of the Reformation
than the calling of the Cassel Conference between Bucer
and Melanchthon in December, 1534. On September 16,
1534, Melanchthon wrote the landgrave that he would be
glad to have a conference with him about ending the
sacrament-strife, and suggested that Bucer's concord
would be a good starting-point.[26] Within a month the
landgrave arranged to have Bucer and Melanchthon meet
with him at Cassel, to talk over plans for conciliation;[27]
requested Jacob Sturm to allow Bucer to come; and
temporarily selected January 1 as the date for the conference.[28] Sturm replied that the Council of Thirteen at
Strasbourg was perfectly willing to allow their ecclesi-

---

[19] *Ibid.*   [20] Schiess, I, 501.
[21] *Ibid.*, pp. 509-513.   [22] Lenz, I, 40.
[23] *Ibid.*, pp. 42-43.   [24] Schiess, I, 629.
[25] *Ibid.*, p. 631.   [26] *CR.*, II, 788.
[27] Schiess, I, 583, II, 811.
[28] Schiess, I, 585; *Politische Correspondenz . . . Strassburg*, II, 225.

astical leader to participate,[29] and the landgrave, adopting the opinion that a private conference with Melanchthon would be most fruitful,[30] and delighted by the prospects of success, now made brighter than ever before, because of the favorable attitude of Melanchthon and Luther toward concord,[31] called the meeting definitely for December 26.[32]

En route to Cassel, Bucer held a preliminary conference at Constance with the preachers of Upper Germany, in order that he might be able to represent them correctly, and know what conciliatory measures they could be relied upon to support.[33] The result was favorable, and thus encouraged Bucer met Melanchthon at Cassel on December 26, 1534,[34] discussed the manner in which Christ's body is present in the sacrament,[35] and drew up a statement of the doctrine, which was despatched to the churches of Ulm, Esslingen, Biberach, Memmingen, Constance, Kempten, and Isny.[36] As a result of this conference at Cassel, Bucer's claim that "there was never greater hope for a strong and pure concord,"[37] proved to be correct, for Luther regarded the result with favor,[38] and assumed an amicable attitude toward Bucer and his colleagues.[39] Thus with the aid of the landgrave, an agreement was reached which made it possible to bring about the Wittenberg Concord of 1536.

In October, 1538, Landgrave Philip requested Bucer

---

[29] *Politische Correspondenz . . . Strassburg*, II, 225, 226.

[30] *Ibid.*, pp. 228, 232.

[31] *Ibid.*, p. 228; *CR.*, II, 788.

[32] *Politische Correspondenz . . . Strassburg*, II, 291.

[33] Bucer to Capito *et al.*, Dec. 23, 1534, Thesaurus Baumianus, VII, 313; Schiess, I, 613, 617. The conference came on Dec. 15, 1534.

[34] Bucer to Capito *et al.*, Thesaurus Baumianus, VII, 313.

[35] *CR.*, II, 807.

[36] Bucer to Frecht, Jan. 2, 1535, Thesaurus Baumianus, VIII, 2.

[37] Bucer to Frecht, Jan. 2, 1535, Thesaurus Baumianus, VIII, 2.

[38] *CR.*, II, 837.   [39] *Ibid.*, p. 841.

to come and help him control the spread of the Anabaptists in his lands. To understand how this happened, it is necessary to review briefly Philip's previous relations with this sect. The first leader of the Hessian Anabaptists was Melchior Ring, one of the leaders in the Peasants' Revolt, who settled in Hersfeld in 1528.[40] Here he lived for at least three years, and then moved to Münster, where he was still one of the inhabitants in 1533.[41] Hardly had the uproar in that city subsided, before the number of Anabaptists in Hesse increased so rapidly that special legislation became necessary to control them. The first ordinance, issued in 1536, was so inadequate because of its mildness, that the landgrave sought advice from the leading theologians of Germany in adopting a new plan of action.[42] As a result of the Synod of Ziegenhain, upon whose decision he consulted Bucer,[43] he issued the still less effective Ordinance of Visitation (1537),[44] and then being convinced that the Hessian theologians were unable to make any impression upon the unchangeable convictions of the imprisoned leaders of the Anabaptists,[45] he finally sent a call to Strasbourg for help.

Thus it came about that in the summer of 1538 the landgrave despatched a request to Jacob Sturm, asking that Bucer's services be loaned him for a time to assist in subduing the Anabaptist movement.[46] Evidently the authorities were willing, for on August 23 Bucer accepted the invitation, adding characteristically, "I am entirely

[40] K. W. H. Hochuth, "Landgraf Philipp und die Wiedertäufer," *Zeitschrift für die historische Theologie*, XXVIII, 541, ff.

[41] *Ibid.*, pp. 551-553.

[42] *Ibid.*, pp. 554, 557; Gundlach, *op. cit.*, p. 69.

[43] Hochuth, *op. cit.*, p. 595.

[44] *Ibid.*, p. 597. The Visitation Ordinance forbade polygamy as well as the desertion of the unconverted consort (Rockwell, p. 18).

[45] Hochuth, *op. cit.*, p. 610; Lenz, I, 320.

[46] Lenz, I, v, 45, n. 1, 322.

ready and willing to serve your princely grace under all circumstances.''[47] The landgrave suggested that Bucer come on either September 20 or October 13-19, and though the reformer chose the latter date,[48] he actually left Strasbourg on October 11, 1538.[49] To accept this invitation from Hesse[50] demanded a real sacrifice on Bucer's part. Already worn out by his many journeyings, struggling with a painful disease,[51] and overwhelmed by his multifarious duties in Strasbourg[52] he had little time to spare for a mission which involved a wearisome journey, especially difficult at that time of the year.[53]

Upon his arrival in Hesse, Bucer discovered that his task was not to organize the Hessian Church, but to assist an already completed organization which was powerless against the Anabaptists.[54] His first undertaking was a conference with the Anabaptist prisoners at Marburg: Bastian, already half-converted, Schnabel, Lenhart, and Losen.[55] For three days he discussed with them various points of theology, chiefly concerning the nature of the church and of baptism,[56] and on Saturday, November 2, was able to report to the landgrave that after he had patiently listened to them and had pointed out the disgrace which they had brought upon the church, they had agreed to take the matter into consideration.[57]

[47] Ibid., p. 45.   [48] Ibid., pp. 45-46.
[49] Politische Correspondenz . . . Strassburg, II, 522.
[50] Anrich, p. 77.
[51] Original Letters, II, 523. He wrote to A. Blaurer about three years before, ''Caput vertigine vexatur graviter, et ex pituita hepatis ventriculus ita exagitatur, ut totum corpus tantum non enecet'' (Schiess, I, 794).
[52] Lenz, I, 345.
[53] CR., Calvini Opera, X, 279; Herminjard, V, 145.
[54] W. Diehl, ''Martin Butzers Bedeutung für das kirchliche Leben in Hessen,'' Schriften des Vereins für Reformationsgeschichte, no. 38, p. 45.
[55] Lenz, I, 323.
[56] Hochuth, op. cit., p. 626. This writer prints the official record of the conference, which contains no mention of polygamy.
[57] Lenz, I, 46-47.

The next day Bucer preached on the unity of the church,[58] a subject which was one of his favorites and upon which he had been thinking for some time previous to leaving Strasbourg.[59] The sermon was so convincing that before evening three of the leading Anabaptists were converted: Hermann Bastian, Peter Losen,[60] and, most important of all, Peter Tesch.[61] The last named thought that it would be best not to demand a complete change at first from the Anabaptists, but only "that they abstain from their baptism and teaching, cast off the articles in which they err, and again go to church and help the pastors, although they cannot go to the Lord's Table right away."[62] In general Bucer agreed with this opinion, and on Monday, November 4, he sent Tesch to the landgrave, begging the prince to listen to him, for the number of Anabaptists in the land far exceeded his expectations, and "among them many well-disposed" were to be found. Punishment would only offend the pious and make them intractable, he thought,[63] but a compromise, supported by a strong disciplinary system, would gather up the good features of this sectarian and individualistic movement and unite it with the church.[64] Long after this episode Bucer continued to have an interest in the Anabaptists of Hesse. In February, 1540, he sent to the landgrave an Anabaptist whom he had almost persuaded to return to the church,[65] and again in March he interceded in behalf of some imprisoned Anabaptists.[66] On April 19, 1540, he

[58] *Ibid.*, p. 47.
[59] *Cf.* Herminjard, VI, 61.
[60] Lenz, I, 51.
[61] *Ibid.*, p. 49.
[62] *Ibid.*, p. 50.
[63] *Ibid.*, pp. 50-51.
[64] Diehl, p. 47. Bucer's tolerant treatment of the Anabaptists in Hesse is a sufficient reply to the attack made by Paulus, claiming that he had a grossly intolerant spirit (N. Paulus, "Die Strassburger Reformatoren und die Gewissensfreiheit," *Strassburger Theologische Studien*, II, Heft II, 1-28). This charge has been answered by Doumergue, II, 336, n. 4.
[65] Lenz, I, 134.
[66] *Ibid.*, p. 156.

wrote to the prince, "The baptists have been almost converted. Some, clinging tenaciously to their belief—they say fifty, but, as Hermann Bastian counts, there are not so many—will emigrate to Moravia, yet even from these a few will be converted."[67]

In addition to the conversion of the Anabaptist leaders, Bucer made three important contributions to the life of the Hessian Church: a form of church-discipline,[68] the institution of evangelical confirmation,[69] and the Cassel Catechism.[70] The results of his work were not very great at first, even in the number of Anabaptists converted,[71] but in later years it became evident that he had wrought an important change in the organization of Hessian church-life. The official gave place to the congregation as the unit in the care of the individual's soul,[72] and out of the catechism developed an ordered *Landeschulunterricht,* later replaced by the *Volkschulen,* which did not appear in other lands until two centuries later.[73] The purifying influence of the *Seniorates,* instituted by Bucer, uplifted the moral life of the principality and sustained it even through the awful trial of the Thirty Years' War.[74]

At the Synod of Cassel, convening a little over a month after Bucer's arrival in Hesse,[75] the Hessian theologians, under his leadership, drew up a remarkably severe *Rathschlag* concerning the treatment of the Jews.[76] It is sufficient to note here that the landgrave disagreed with Bucer and thought a more tolerant attitude advisable.[77]

[67] Lenz, I, 168.

[68] Anrich, p. 78; Diehl, pp. 47-53; Paulus, p. 24.

[69] Anrich, p. 78; Diehl, pp. 50-51; Wolf, *Quellenkunde der deutschen Reformationsgeschichte,* I, 535.

[70] Anrich, p. 78.

[71] Hochuth, *op. cit.,* p. 182; Diehl, p. 55.

[72] Diehl, p. 54.   [73] *Ibid.,* p. 56.   [74] *Ibid.,* p. 57.

[75] Lenz, I, 53, 54, and n. 1.

[76] M. Bucer, *Von den Juden,* etc., p. Aii (Mentz, no. 43b).

[77] Lenz, I, 59, ff.

When Bucer left Strasbourg in October, 1538, Sturm wrote to the landgrave that he might profitably confer with the reformer on the question of ecclesiastical property.[78] Moreover, just before his departure, Bucer expected that his journey might take him not only to Hesse, but also to Wittenberg, there to confer with Luther and others on the problem of church-organization.[79] The question of ecclesiastical property was a crucial one for the progress of the Reformation. Nothing hindered the progress of the movement so much as the question of the disposition of the secular possessions of the church in Protestant territories and in states ruled by ecclesiastical princes. The views of Bucer and the landgrave did not coincide on this problem for the landgrave thought that a complete reformation of the clergy and church-property would drive the bishops to war, and cause divisions among the Protestants themselves, while Bucer held that the adoption of a plan which was clearly for the benefit of the church and the advancement of the general welfare, without any encroachment upon individual property rights, would enlist the support of the secular princes.[80]

It was George von Carlowitz, chancellor of ducal Saxony, who began the movement resulting in those colloquies of 1539-1541, which were crucially influential in their futility and lack of accomplishment. Carlowitz hoped that a religious conference of several learned people might result in an agreement between Protestants and Catholics. Well pleased with this project, which offered an opportunity to win Duke George of Saxony to the evangelical cause, the landgrave laid upon Bucer the task of journeying to Wittenberg to secure the consent

[78] *Politische Correspondenz . . . Strassburg,* II, 522.
[79] Schiess, II, 7.
[80] Lenz, II, 505.

of Luther, Melanchthon, and the elector.[81] Luther and Melanchthon, to whom he first proposed the matter, doubted the possibility of gaining the consent of the elector, who answered indefinitely that Bucer should go back to Hesse, until a date had been arranged for the proposed conference.[82]

Bucer rode back to Hesse, met the landgrave in a private interview, probably at Melsungen, November 29, attended the Synod of Cassel,[83] and waited anxiously for the conference to convene, for he was impatient to return to Strasbourg that he might re-engage in the administration of his school and church,[84] and it was probably to satisfy this desire that the landgrave wrote to the elector asking for a date before January 1.[85]

No official report of these negotiations was sent to Strasbourg until December 8, when the landgrave informed Jacob Sturm of Carlowitz' proposals,[86] nor did the preachers at Strasbourg receive full information even then, for Calvin understood that Bucer was called to the proposed conference while on his way back to Hesse in December.[87] The meeting took place at Leipzig during the first week in January, 1539. The events, of which Bucer sent a detailed report to the landgrave,[88] are not as important here as is the fact that Bucer and the Hessian prince cooperated in promoting this conference, which laid the basis for the subsequent religious colloquies between the Protestants and Catholics. Six years later,

---

[81] *Ibid.*, p. 52; *cf.* Calvin to Farel, "Itaque clanculum eo uterque profectus est; si quid transiget, plerosque alios exemplo suo trahet" (Herminjard, V, 277).

[82] Lenz, I, 52-53.   [83] Lenz, I, 54-55.

[84] *Ibid.*   [85] *Ibid.*, p. 54, n. 1.

[86] *Politische Correspondenz . . . Strassburg*, II, 532.

[87] Herminjard, V, 277; *cf.* F. A. v. Langenn, *Christoph von Carlowitz*, p. 64; C. G. Neudecker, *Urkunden aus der Reformationszeit*, p. 339.

[88] Lenz, I, 63-68; *cf.* Bruck's report, *CR.*, III, 624-635.

in 1545, Bucer published the articles agreed upon at Leipzig, with his own interpretation of them,[89] and because some of his readers claimed that he accepted the papist mass and other ceremonies, he wrote another book defending himself, in which he showed just what kind of a mass he thought was right.[90]

It was in the middle of November, 1539, that Bucer was first informed of the landgrave's plan of bigamy. During the preceding summer his relations with Philip had concerned chiefly the proposed Nürnberg Colloquy and the sending of an embassy to England. Again and again he urged him to exert himself to the utmost that the promised Nürnberg Colloquy might be held,[91] and that William Langey might be sent as the representative from France.[92] While Bucer was convinced that more would be gained if the Protestant princes took a firm attitude in making their demands,[93] and lamented the concessions which had been made at Frankfurt,[94] the landgrave thought that they could not have done better under the circumstances.[95]

In September, 1539, when the Reformation in England did not seem to be progressing favorably, Bucer's cosmopolitan interest in the people of that country outweighed his distrust of the Tudor monarch,[96] and induced him to propose to the landgrave that the German Protestants should send to Henry VIII an embassy accompanied by Melanchthon.[97] The landgrave's approval of the plan, however, was unable to prevent its inevitable veto by the elector, who wisely rejected it and absolutely refused to throw before the English monarch such a valuable pearl

---

[89] M. Bucer, *Ein Christlich ongefährlich Bedenken* (Mentz, no. 59).
[90] M. Bucer, *Wider Auffrichtigung der Messen* (Mentz, no. 67).
[91] Lenz, I, 68-80.   [92] *Ibid.*, pp. 80-82.
[93] *Ibid.*, pp. 90-94.   [94] *Ibid.*, p. 76.
[95] *Ibid.*, pp. 83-90.   [96] *Ibid.*, pp. 107-108.
[97] Lenz, I, 99-105.

as Melanchthon.[98] More feasible but equally barren of accomplishment was Bucer's additional suggestion that Philip write a private letter to England, hoping that the king's reply would give a basis for further negotiations.[99] Since a choice had to be made between the emperor on one side and the alliance of Gulich and England on the other, he thought Gulich and England ought to be preferred.[100]

Such were Bucer's relations with Philip of Hesse during the decade that followed the Marburg Colloquy. Year by year there was a growing intimacy resulting from common interests and mutual admiration, until in the period from October, 1538, to October, 1539, they were in constant communication. Bucer found in the landgrave a territorial prince of great power, who, in spite of many immoralities in private life, was sincerely desirous of the success of the evangelical movement. Since his own interests extended beyond Strasbourg, the reformer frequently called to his assistance the powerful influence of the nobleman. Thus, the landgrave's prestige opened many doors for him in his exertions for sacramental concord. Though he felt free to express contrary opinions, he was also under an honorary obligation to render the prince any service he could, while the landgrave, on the other hand, discovered in Bucer a political and religious adviser, endowed with a rare combination of sagacity, candidness, and freedom from false flattery and selfish designs. Overcome with admiration for the energy and determination with which the Strasbourger worked to attain his high ideals, and for the skill with which he was able to persuade other men to accept his own beliefs, the landgrave was preeminently qualified to perceive that the Wittenberg Concord, though far from perfect, was the

[98] *Ibid.*, p. 108.
[99] *Ibid.*, pp. 109-113.
[100] *Ibid.*, pp. 117-118.

result of the most adroit maneuvering in the face of stubborn opposition by both Lutherans and Zwinglians, who neither desired nor appreciated the reconciliation which he himself had failed to accomplish at Marburg. An eyewitness of the failure of the Hessian clergy to cope with the Anabaptists, and of Bucer's instantaneous success, he did not permit his disagreements with the reformer on many questions to blind his eyes to the realization that here was an adviser whom he could trust to speak fearlessly and wisely, and a persevering servant upon whom he could rely to handle the most delicate situations with a cleverness that few of his contemporaries possessed. When he summoned Bucer to undertake difficult negotiations in the interests of the Reformation, he found him reliable and efficient. It is not strange, therefore, that he was equally ready to seek aid from him in such an important matter as the bigamy.

CHAPTER IV

THE PLAN OF BIGAMY

Philip the Magnanimous, Landgrave of Hesse from 1520 to 1555,[1] was married at a very early age[2] to Christina, the daughter of Duke George of Saxony.[3] The marriage proved to be an unfortunate one,[4] since, as he later said, " from the time when I first took her, I neither desired nor wished her because of her unattractive appearance, disposition, and reputation, and besides she was subject to spells of excessive intemperance, as her court-mistress, maids, and many other people know."[5]

The result was that the landgrave soon became unfaithful to his wife,[6] and sank into a life of such profound immorality[7] and self-indulgence that he felt forced to commit adultery, "oder bossers bei dem weibe treiben."[8] Victimized by his vices he contracted syphilis,[9] a disease from which his father had also suffered, although it is probable that Philip did not inherit it from him.[10] By 1538 his condition had become very serious,[11] and during 1539 he suffered two especially severe attacks of his sickness, one in April and one during the summer.[12] Evidently Bucer

[1] G. Wolf, *Quellenkunde der deutschen Reformationsgeschichte*, I, 527.

[2] *CR.*, III, 852; Lenz, I, 353.

[3] Rockwell, p. 1; *cf.* J. P. Kuchenbecker, *Analecta Hassiaca*, I, 32, who gives the marriage another date.

[4] *CR.*, III, 852.

[5] *Ibid.;* Rockwell, p. 2 and n. 1.

[6] *CR.*, III, 852.

[7] *Ibid.*, p. 851.

[8] Lenz, I, 353.

[9] Rockwell, p. 3 and n. 5.

[10] *Ibid.*, p. 4, n. 1.

[11] F. Koldewey, "Heinz von Wolfenbüttel," *Schriften des Vereins für Reformationsgeschichte*, no. 2, p. 8.

[12] Rockwell, p. 4. The attack in April weakened the position of the Protestants at Frankfurt (Schiess, II, 23).

was well acquainted with Philip's condition, for in May
he congratulated him on his recovery, urged him on that
account to be more zealous in the service of Christ,[13] and
added the assurance, "to that end many prayers arise
from all believers, for they all recognize that your
princely grace is the chief instrument in this work."[14]

When, in the summer of the same year, Bucer learned
that the landgrave had suffered a relapse, he advised him
to secure the services of a certain German physician, re-
nowned for the complete cure which he had effected upon
the chancellor of France by means of mercury, and at that
moment on his way back to Germany to visit his friends.[15]
It is noteworthy that Bucer did not express the opinion
that the landgrave's illness was any more a visitation
upon his sexual sins than any other disease would be.
Philip did not secure the services of this famous physician, but under the care of Dr. Gereon Sailer he took the
"wood-cure" at Giessen and gained a partial recovery.[16]

One result of Philip's sickness was a troubled conscience which developed a desire to free himself in some
way from his immoral habits. Being a zealous Bible student,[17] he began to fear that he would suffer the fate of
those shut out of the Kingdom of God for fornication and
similar sins.[18] For many years he had not partaken of the
sacrament for fear that he would eat and drink "judg-

---

[13] Lenz, I, 70.   [14] *Ibid.*, p. 71.

[15] *Ibid.*, p. 98, ff. Who this physician was it is impossible to state definitely (*ibid.*, p. 99). It may have been Ulrich Geiger (Chelius), although
Lenz says it was not, and suggests that it was an acquaintance of Geiger
(Lenz, I, 212, n. 8. But *cf.* Schiess, I, 526 and *CR., Calvini Opera*, Xb,
425).

[16] Rockwell, p. 4.

[17] Rockwell, p. 5. At the Diet of Speier, 1526, the landgrave showed a
better knowledge of the Scriptures than did the prelates (Dyer and Hassall,
A History of Modern Europe from the Fall of Constantinople, 3rd edition,
II, 69).

[18] *CR.*, III, 851.

ment to himself,'"[19] and only the most skeptical mind can
doubt the reality of his pangs of conscience which begin
at the first and run all through the history of the case.[20]
Unless he had been afraid of damnation he would not have
kept away from the sacrament, nor have gone to it so
joyfully after his marriage. No doubt it was only after the
disease became so serious as to threaten his life that his
conscience stirred him to action, and so, in a sense, his
anxiety may be called the result of a physical ruin.[21]
Forced to the decision that somehow he must behave himself in a manner worthy of a Christian husband, and unable to overcome his dislike for his wife Christina, Philip
resorted to the extraordinary plan of controlling his pas-
sions by taking another wife so attractive to him that
adulterous conduct would offer him no inducements.

It is not likely that the landgrave decided upon the plan
of bigamy before the early fall of 1539,[22] although many
previous incidents have led historians to believe that he
was thinking of it before that time. At the Diet of Worms
he joked Luther for permitting bigamy to the consort of
an impotent person,[23] and in 1526, when he was re-organ-
izing the Hessian church, he asked the oracle at Wittenberg whether bigamy might be permitted to Christians.[24]

19 *Ibid.;* Rockwell, pp. 5, 44; Lenz, I, 353; *cf.* I Corinthians XI: 29.

20 W. Köhler, ''Die Doppelehe Landgraf Philipps von Hessen,'' *Historische Zeitschrift,* 1905, XCIV, 392.

21 *Ibid.,* p. 393. But it is only by ignoring the evidence that an anonymous
writer has said, ''Viel wahrscheinlicher ist es, das der verhärtete, indiffer-
entische Politiker, dem es bei dem gesammten 'evangelischen Handel,' wie
schon oft gezeigt, um ganz andere Dinge, als um Glauben und Gewissen
zu thun war, einer solchen Beruhigung nicht im Mindesten bedurfte''
(*Historisch-politische Blätter,* 1846, p. 231).

22 Rockwell, p. 19.

23 Cordatus, *Tagebuch über Dr. Martin Luther,* pp. 88, 257; *cf.* Rockwell,
p. 7; Rady, p. 2.

24 Luther returned an unfavorable answer. Text in Enders, V, 412;
Heppe, ''Urkundliche Beiträge zur Geschichte der Doppelehe des Landgrafen Philipps von Hessen,'' *Zeitschrift für die historische Theologie,*
1862, XXII, 265.

In this case he was only inquiring about the permission of bigamy in general, so as to decide how to treat it in his ecclesiastical settlement of Hesse.[25] His interest in Luther's refusal to condemn the polygamy of the patriarchs in his commentary on Genesis;[26] his knowledge of Luther's advice to Henry VIII;[27] his publication of the *Halsgerichtordnung* (1532) which punished bigamy with death;[28] and the interview between the imprisoned captives from Münster and his theologians, in which the unscripturalness of having two wives at once was emphatically asserted,[29] all indicate that Philip may have thought about bigamy in an indefinite way before the summer of 1539,[30] but it was his meeting at that time with Margaret von der Sale, a lady-in-waiting to his sister Elizabeth, that first gave him an incentive to reach a clear decision on the matter.[31]

The landgrave was very much attracted to Margaret,[32] but there is no good reason to suppose that he had had any

[25] Rockwell, p. 8.

[26] Lenz, I, 181; *cf. CR.*, X, 161, for Bucer's attitude on the same question; T. Brieger, "Luther und die Nebenehe des Landgrafen Philipp von Hessen," *Preussische Jahrbücher*, Jan., 1909, CXXXV, Heft I, 43. Philip often used this judgment of Luther's as an argument against him in their later controversies (*cf.* Lenz, I, 369, ff., II, 70, 75, n. 2, etc.).

[27] See above, p. 37, ff.

[28] This was the first great *Halsgerichtordnung* and was given the name *Carolina* (i.e. *Constitutio Criminalis Carolina, C. C. C.*). It was passed at the Diet of Regensburg, 1532, and codified criminal law for the whole empire. The law dealing with bigamy was known as *Neminem. Cf.* Rockwell, pp. 8-9; Janssen, *Geschichte des deutschen Volkes seit dem Ausgang des Mittelalters*, III, 413.

[29] Rockwell, p. 12, ff. On bigamy in Münster *cf.* B. Rothmann, *Restitution rechter und gesundher christlichen Lehre;* L. Keller, *Geschichte der Wiedertäufer und ihres Reichs zu Münster*, p. 210. The chief argument of the Münsterites was the divine command, "Increase and multiply" (Rothmann, p. 77). The landgrave made no use of this argument (Rockwell, p. 14, n. 3).

[30] Rockwell, p. 6.   [31] *Ibid.*, p. 19.

[32] Lenz, I, 160, 181.

immoral relations with her.[33] During the negotiations
which he had carried on with her mother, Anna von der
Sale, he decided to take Margaret as a bigamous wife, to
which Anna agreed upon condition that it should be a
real, honorable, Christian marriage.[34] In order to be sure
of this, she demanded that the union should be sanctioned
by Duke Maurice, the Elector John Frederick, and several
nobles and scholars.[35] Although the landgrave later declared that the peace of his conscience was sufficient to
assure him that he was doing right,[36] he too desired the
approval of the leading theologians to uphold him before
the public,[37] and the assurance of the elector to assist him
in case of prosecution for his breach of the imperial law.[38]
He could not depend upon conscience alone in the face
of possible attack by the emperor; he needed something
more substantial to rely upon in proving the righteousness of his act,[39] and for this reason he sought the approval of Luther, Melanchthon, and the elector.

The man best fitted to obtain this assent from Wittenberg and the elector was Bucer himself, one of the fore-
most theologians of Germany. Endowed with skill as a
diplomat since recognized by both Protestant and Catholic historians,[40] his demonstrated ability in the negotiations for the Wittenberg Concord, and in the conversion
of the Hessian Anabaptists no doubt influenced the landgrave to select him as the man most likely to gain a favorable opinion from Luther.

[33] *Cf.* the accusation in Janssen, III, 413; refuted by Rockwell, p. 55,
n. 3; *cf.* Enders, XIII, 72.

[34] ''Aufzeichnung des Landgrafen über die von Frau Anna von Sale . . .
Versprechnungen,'' printed by Rockwell, p. 316.

[35] Rockwell, p. 21.

[36] Lenz, I, 354; *cf.* Rockwell, p. 25.

[37] Rockwell, p. 23.

[38] Lenz, I, 356.

[39] *Cf. ibid.*, p. 235.

[40] Rady, p. 13, and Rockwell, p. 23, for example.

Late in the night of November 4, 1539, there arrived at
Strasbourg after a difficult journey, Gereon Sailer, the
landgrave's trusted physician.[41] Without waiting to rest
from his travels, he hurried as fast as possible to Bucer's
house and arranged for an interview the next day. Bucer
was busy with his pastoral labors at Strasbourg and with
diplomatic service for his lords, yet because of his good-
will toward the landgrave, and his desire to be of assistance, he agreed to meet Sailer the next morning and talk
with him about his master's affair.[42]

For several reasons Sailer came at an inopportune
moment with the request that Bucer sanction the landgrave's plan of bigamy and secure the assent of the
Saxons. Bucer had just reformed the Anabaptists, and
though polygamy was not discussed in his conferences
with them, it was regarded as peculiarly an Anabaptist
and Münsterite sin, and for him to sanction it would savor
of hypocrisy and hurt his influence. Only three years before he had gained a promise of success in his attempts
at theological unity, and now were he to countenance
bigamy and also gain the consent of Luther and Melanchthon, the young evangelical church would again be perplexed with discord even worse than that over the sacrament. Furthermore, Bucer had difficulties and troubles
enough already. The English situation in the autumn of
1539, due to the publication of the Six Articles, did not
offer pleasant prospects, and he was exerting his energies
to remedy matters.[43] The landgrave's proposed action, if
made public, would extinguish the glimmering of hope in
Germany that a reconciliation, such as was discussed later

[41] Lenz, I, 345.

[42] Lenz, I, 345. Sailer also came to carry on political negotiations with
the Council of Strasbourg concerning the relations of the states and the
emperor (Lenz, I, 404, 432; *Politische Correspondenz* . . . *Strassburg,*
II, 641).

[43] *Cf. Original Letters,* II, 526; Lenz, I, 96, ff.; Herminjard, VI, 72.

at the great religious colloquies of Hagenau, Worms, and Ratisbon, might be effected with the Church of Rome.[44] To all this was added the personal consideration of overwhelming local demands upon his time and energy. How heavily the thought of home duties continually weighed upon his mind is evident from the request he submitted to the landgrave about a month later on December 3, ''so that I will not have to ride around through many villages, and can get back to the necessary work at home.''[45] Sailer reported to the landgrave two days after his arrival that Bucer's overworked and exhausted body, combined with the unwillingness of his lords to dispense with his services, would have made it impossible to gain his release had not the possibility that he might promote the cause of the Reformation availed to overcome these objections.[46] To a request that the landgrave accelerate Bucer's journey to Wittenberg and return, as much as possible, he added the observation, ''the good man works too hard; anxiety will bring him to nothing good with his giddiness from a plenitude of work.''[47]

The conference between Sailer and Bucer extended over three days.[48] Practically all information about what happened is contained in three letters which the Augsburg physician wrote to Philip during November, 1539, and as he seems to have been a very keen observer, his statements may be relied upon, especially since later events confirmed many of the prophecies he made.

It was not the justification of bigamy on Scriptural

---

[44] *Cf.* Lenz, I, 94-95.

[45] Lenz, I, 119; *cf. ibid.*, p. 120.

[46] *Ibid.*, p. 346.

[47] *Ibid.*, p. 347. This is a reference to Bucer's disease. *Cf. Original Letters*, II, 523, and above, p. 50, n. 51.

[48] Sailer arrived on the evening of November 4, and wrote this information to the landgrave on November 6, so he cannot mean three full days. *Cf.* Lenz, I, 329, 345; Rockwell, p. 23.

grounds, but the landgrave's need, which Sailer probably emphasized in his interviews with Bucer, perceiving that this was the point on which he was at the same time most vulnerable and needed most persuasion. His task was not easy, for the reformer was ''hard set'' against the affair, and Sailer needed to use all his powers of argument. Above all Bucer objected to the offence which the bigamy would give both to friend and foe,[49] for it was not doubt concerning the permissibility of bigamy on Scriptural grounds which caused him to hesitate, but whether the landgrave's condition justified such an action. Without making any decision upon the latter question, Bucer consented to go to the landgrave, to examine the arguments of the prince, and to act as a mediator with Luther and Melanchthon, provided Philip supported his request by convincing arguments. In order to preserve secrecy it was declared publicly that his journey was concerned with certain matters of the Reformation.[50]

There were three reasons why Bucer gave this quasi-consent to the landgrave's request. The first was the service of the landgrave to the church, and particularly his strenuous endeavors to promote unity.[51] Ordinary gratitude and appreciation demanded that Bucer should render the prince all the aid possible. Secondly, Bucer as a pastor and disciplinarian[52] wanted to do all he could to help the landgrave's conscience and morals.[53] As already observed[54] he had admonished Philip to reform his habits. Long before this he had regarded divorce as a remedy to be used in rare cases for the good of the individual,[55] and for the same reason he now considered bigamy a possible remedy, dangerous to be sure, but better than allowing

[49] Lenz, I, 345, 348.

[51] Lenz, I, 345.

[53] Lenz, I, 345.

[55] See above, p. 28, ff.

[50] Ibid., pp. 118, 345, 346, 348.

[52] See above, p. 45.

[54] See above, p. 45.

the patient to die.[56] Thirdly, he thought it would be wrong
to force anyone to live in a manner which would cause
chronic distress of conscience and imperil his soul's salvation, but it would be worse to treat a "great" man that
way, upon whom so many important issues depended.[57]

Such a solution of the landgrave's difficulties he would
allow only under protection of strict secrecy; for, as Sailer
said, "Bucerus ligt nur auf dem haimlichen."[58] Margaret's mother, known as the *hofmeisterin,* had insisted
that the marriage be openly defended, and only after
urgent persuasion did she yield to the demand that it be
kept secret, at least temporarily.[59] The landgrave was so
anxious that Bucer should consent to a publication of the
affair, possibly in the near future, that in his letter to
Sailer of November 17, 1539, he made a special inquiry
about Bucer's attitude on this point.[60] Not only was Bucer
unalterably determined that secrecy be maintained, Sailer
informed the prince, but he had even converted the Augsburg physician to his own point of view,[61] for the latter
recognized that Bucer could not afford to hamper his own
service of the gospel by publicly approving such an act.[62]

How cleverly Sailer had diagnosed Bucer's mind is
evident from two prophecies he made about his attitude
and future conduct. The first was that Bucer would oppose
as far as possible but finally consent;[63] the second, that
he would not fail the landgrave.[64] Each of these observations was correct, but especially the last, for in the days
that followed, though Bucer would not consent to the landgrave's further demands, nor approve his actions, he always stood by him to advise and help in any way that he

---

[56] Lenz, I, 348.   [57] *Ibid.,* p. 345.
  [58] *Ibid.,* p. 347. Yet on Nov. 11 Sailer was in Augsburg (Lenz, I, 432)
and had revealed the secret to other men (Lenz, I, 433).
  [59] Rockwell, p. 316.   [60] Lenz, I, 348.
  [61] *Ibid.,* p. 351.   [62] *Ibid.,* p. 346.
  [63] *Ibid.,* p. 347.   [64] *Ibid.,* p. 351.

could. Never did he go further in an approval of bigamy than the opinion he gave at first; yet he always upheld it, and even declared publicly that he could not condemn the landgrave for doing "any such thing."[65]

On November 14 Bucer wrote to Philip that he was ready to meet him as Sailer had requested, and appointed November 25 as the latest day on which he would come, adding, "the Lord grant that I may serve well and fruit-fully in this journey and in everything."[66] On November 17 he left Strasbourg with a heavy heart, having written to his friend Myconius in Basel, "Tomorrow I shall go to the landgrave on account of a very serious matter. The Lord be with us. Pray for me."[67]

In his painstaking preparations for the interview with Bucer at Melsungen, the landgrave adopted Sailer's sug-gestion, placing the emphasis on his moral degradation and inability to live in a good conscience without the "remedy" of bigamy. He also asked Sailer to recommend some plan "to avoid loading all the burden upon Bucer's shoulders."[68] Before Bucer came Philip drew up with his own hand a document afterwards called the "Explanation of the Landgrave to Bucer in Melsungen," which outlined briefly his main contentions.[69] As these are the arguments which overcame Bucer's objections, it is impossible to understand his reasons for consenting without inspecting them carefully.

The landgrave planned to tell Bucer of his miserable condition, "that I am sick and the sickness has never been more serious than at present;" that he could neither go to the sacrament nor punish criminals while in this con-

---

[65] *CR.*, X, 157-158; Lenz, II, 72.   [66] Lenz, I, 117.

[67] *Ibid.*, p. 329, n. 2; Bucer to Myconius and Grynaeus, Nov. 16, The-saurus Baumianus, XIII, 117. Even the Thirteen of Strasbourg who gave their consent, did not know the real cause of Bucer's journey (*Politische Correspondenz . . . Strassburg*, II, 642).

[68] Lenz, I, 348.   [69] *Ibid.*, pp. 352-354.

dition, for people would say, "punish thyself;" that he could not go to war without a guilty conscience; that it was easy enough to say, "put it away, keep to your wife," but he had taken her when not yet seventeen years old, and had no affection for her; and that he was unable to contain himself and not commit adultery "oder bossers bei dem weibe."

As arguments why he should be permitted to take a second wife along with the first, he adduced the following. First, the example of the patriarchs who had more than one wife, and of those polygamous "saints" in Christian times, whom "God, also Christ, highly honored." Secondly, the fact that Moses gave a law for the treatment of a bigamous wife, and neither God, Christ, nor the apostles ever forbade such a thing; that no prophet or apostle ever punished anyone for having two wives, though they listed the sins which involved exclusion from the kingdom of God; that Paul neither mentioned bigamy among these sins, nor told the heathen to abstain from bigamy, but ruled that the deacon and bishop should be the husband of one wife, implying that this was not required of every man;[70] that fear of God should be the determining factor, not fear of the world, for many would leave him alone if he should commit adultery, who would not allow him to have two wives. "What God allows they forbid, what God forbids, they wink at." In conclusion he threatened to seek an understanding with the emperor and a dispensation from the pope, unless he were allowed to have what God permitted. "Which human permission I would not desire were I not certain that God has granted and not forbidden it."

The conference between Bucer and the landgrave took

[70] In this connection the landgrave continued, "und nit hie mit bossem gewissen und dort ewiglich in ungnaden Gots sein mage; ich beger und will nit mher dan ein fraue."

place at Melsungen sometime during the last week in November, for by December 1 Bucer had departed.[71] In accordance with pre-arranged plans the landgrave made at least two requests of Bucer: (1) that if he contracted the second marriage secretly, Bucer would give him "a written testimony" that he did not do wrong before God; and (2) that he would think upon a way by which in the future the affair might be defended openly.[72] Bucer consented to the first,[73] and promised to influence Luther and Melanchthon to do the same,[74] but he gave the landgrave no assurances in regard to the second request.[75] Less interested in the landgrave's arguments for the permissibility of bigamy than in the circumstances of the case and the reasons for his resolve,[76] he urged the prince to give up his evil ways and lead a more upright life.[77] Philip reported to Frau von der Sale that Bucer assured him the marriage would ultimately be given a public sanction,[78] but the fact that this was one of the demands of the *hofmeisterin*, and that there is no record in Bucer's own words of any such promise, casts suspicion on the landgrave's statement. Since Bucer's later advice to the prince was to observe the closest secrecy, it is unbelievable that he commenced his relations with plans for a

[71] *Cf.* Lenz, I, 354. It is possible that other theologians may have been present at the conference (*cf.* Lenz, I, 193: "in den oberstuben vor euch dreien"). But, as Rockwell suggests (p. 24, n. 2), this statement may apply even more fittingly to the conference at the wedding in Marburg. See below, p. 104, ff.

[72] Lenz, I, 207.　　　　　　　　　[73] *Ibid.*

[74] *Ibid.*, p. 354.　　　　　　　　[75] *Ibid.*, p. 207.

[76] *Ibid.*, p. 354.　　　　　　　　[77] *Lenz*, I, 354.

[78] *Ibid.* Later, in his negotiations with Anna, he repeated this claim that Bucer had promised to think upon a way in which the affair might be published (see below, p. 103). "Aber, wi wir ir auch angeczeigt, das der Poczeri s. f. g. zugesagt, das er ein wenig gedult tragen sol, als dan mit der czeit wolten si wol di weg finden, das er mer leutten zugelassen sal werden, domit si alsdan zufriden gewesen" (Rockwell, p. 318).

public defense in the future. As he himself said, he could discern no possibility of granting any but the first of the landgrave's requests.[79]

At the Melsungen conference Bucer suggested that Philip could help to preserve secrecy by replying to any inquiries, ''look to it how you may justify your own deeds.'' It is hardly credible in view of his later conduct, that Bucer would have belied Sailer's warning, ''Bucer insists only upon secrecy.'' But that the landgrave would misrepresent Bucer in order to gain the consent of the *hofmeisterin* to his scheme, is far from improbable.[80] A good proof of this is that he misrepresented his own plan to Bucer, leading him to believe that he was considering bigamy only in the abstract and that he had no particular person in mind.[81] He did not tell him Margaret's name,[82] and Bucer was not led even to suspect that his consent was required to satisfy a definitely-chosen, future mother-in-law. He was told that the landgrave only wanted the assurance for his conscience.[83]

Immediately after the conference Bucer departed for Saxony, taking with him written instructions for his interview with Luther and Melanchthon.[84] This document is in general much like the ''Explanation to Bucer in Melsungen,'' but there are certain additions which are worth noticing. Among the arguments upholding polygamy, there was one asserting that polygamy was permitted to the patriarchs for the fulfilment of the promise

[79] Lenz, I, 207.
[80] See below, p. 120, ff.
[81] Lenz, I, 193.
[82] *Ibid.*, p. 354.
[83] *Cf.* Lenz, I, 193.
[84] The ''Instructio Buceri,'' *CR.*, III, 851, ff.; Enders, XII, no. 2799, pp. 300-311. It is partially translated by Faulkner in the *American Journal of Theology*, XVII, 209-210, and a poorer translation, evidently from the text of Arcuarius, is to be found in Hook, *An Ecclesiastical Biography*, III, 190-218.

to Abraham and the provision of the Messiah.[85] Philip
appealed to the case of Valentinian, and to the belief
that at that time many Christians in oriental lands prac-
tised polygamy. A papal dispensation for polygamy had
been granted during the Crusades to a certain Count von
Gleichen, he said, and there was far more reason why it
should be allowed to him for the avoidance of fornication than to Henry VIII for the sake of a male heir, a
reason which had influenced Luther and Melanchthon. He
begged them to devise a scheme by which in time the
affair might be defended openly, and the "Person"[86]
might have an honorable position before the world. Probably Bucer approved of all the arguments in the instructions which he bore to Wittenberg, but there is no
authority for claiming that he was responsible for any
one of them.

In order to understand why Bucer agreed to act as the
landgrave's mediator, in obtaining the written testimony
of Luther and Melanchthon that Philip would not act
against God in taking a second wife, his own statements
must be first considered. Soon after the wedding he wrote
to the landgrave, "God knows how hard the affair has
been upon me, and how gladly I would have turned your
princely grace away from it. But because I saw at once
that without certain offence or real evil[87] and that which
cuts off from the kingdom of Christ, this affair could not
be avoided or even postponed, I praise God that he has

[85] This was Bucer's own opinion which he taught in the classroom at
Cambridge ten years later (M. Bucer, *Praelectiones Doctiss.*, p. 179; *cf.*
Mentz, no. 89).

[86] So Margaret was often referred to in the landgrave's letters. Evidently
this last assertion was made in response to an objection by Bucer, *cf.*
Argumenta Buceri, p. 12, ff. The landgrave regarded these instructions to
Bucer and the other reformers as a confession (Lenz, I, 304).

[87] These words were underlined by Bucer (Lenz, I, 159, n. 1).

provided this solution and method so quickly; . . . Only, your princely grace should keep quiet and humble.''[88]

In a letter written on July 3 from the Colloquy at Hagenau, ''Bucer is still of the opinion that the landgrave should not be held for unchristian (since God granted such a permission to his saints under similar circumstances), provided he was convinced that by this means only could he extricate himself from his disorderly way and continue to keep it secret. The landgrave should bear witness that he and the others would gladly have turned him from it, since they did not recognize the necessity, and placed the entire responsibility upon his own conscience. 'For I afterwards regarded it not as a necessity but as an infirmity and weakness, that your princely grace could not get help from the Lord without this means, as I have pointed out sufficiently in my *nebenbedencken und disputation.*'[89] But as little as before did he consider it a *Todsünde.*''[90]

Probably Bucer never spoke more frankly to the Hessian prince than in a letter written on July 18, 1540, in which he said, ''Yet I have not advised a strong lie, or the dishonorable breaking of your word of honor, for nothing is more true than this, that when I asked if anyone was had in mind, I was plainly told no,[91] and I was assured at the same time that nothing definite was contemplated because everyone's opinion was not known, etc. In truth, if your princely grace had not daily used the kind of lies which I advise, the marriage would long ago have caused much embarrassment.''[92]

To this accusation, in which Bucer charged the land-

[88] Lenz, I, 159.

[89] Probably a reference to the *Argumenta Buceri pro et contra.*

[90] Lenz, I, 176.

[91] This refers to the conference in Melsungen before Bucer's journey to Wittenberg (Lenz, I, 193, n. 3).

[92] Lenz, I, 193.

grave with having intentionally deceived him and in
which he was correct according to the landgrave's own
statement,[93] may be added others showing that he honestly
sought the landgrave's welfare;[94] that he had no idea of
any such marriage ceremony as the landgrave had already
planned with Frau von der Sale;[95] and that he realized
that the landgrave had had "more causes than people
knew."[96]

From the statement made on July 3 it is clear that
Bucer gave his consent at Melsungen, not that the landgrave should commit bigamy, but that it would be right
before God for him to use such a means, provided his
conscience assured him that he needed it, and he did so
in strict secrecy.[97] In order to understand Bucer's reasons
for giving such a consent and also promising to secure
a similar consent from Luther and Melanchthon, certain
important considerations must be borne in mind.

First, Bucer was concerned about the landgrave's immorality before this conference took place. He had warned
Philip years before to mend his ways,[98] and Sailer's
report of the interview at Strasbourg shows that this
was the aspect of the affair with which Bucer was most
impressed.

Secondly, Bucer decided on bigamy in the abstract and
had no idea that the landgrave had already chosen a person to marry, had entered into negotiations for marrying
her, and desired the consent of the theologians and
elector to satisfy the demands of Frau von der Sale. Not
only was Margaret's name kept from him,[99] but he was

93 *Cf. ibid.*, p. 354.
94 *Ibid.*, p. 121.
95 Lenz, I, 140; *cf.* Rockwell, pp. 21, 316.
96 Lenz, II, 65.
97 *Ibid.*, I, 176.
98 *Ibid.*, p. 35. At Strasbourg adulterers were drowned (Schiess, I, 503).
99 Lenz, I, 354.

clearly told that no person in particular had been selected.[100] So Bucer lacked definite and complete information regarding anyone in particular[101] and consented not to what the landgrave did, but to what he thought the landgrave was going to do. He expected that before Philip decided upon anything definite he would argue the matter with various theologians and prominent people.[102] Perhaps if the landgrave had been more truthful, Bucer would not have given his consent.

Thirdly, Bucer insisted upon absolute secrecy. This is so evident from his correspondence that it is hardly necessary to cite instances.[103] The only statement to the contrary was made by the landgrave,[104] and is unreliable. Of course this does not affect the question whether Bucer did right or wrong, but it does help to explain why he gave his consent, because he would never have given it unless the landgrave had agreed to secrecy.[105]

Fourthly, the whole arrangement was made in such haste that Bucer did not have time to consider the matter sufficiently. He was very busy when Sailer came to Strasbourg; he made the trip to Hesse and Saxony as quickly as possible;[106] and his decision had to come quickly in order to satisfy the landgrave's anxiety.[107]

It is now clear why Bucer gave his consent. Of the three

---

[100] *Ibid.*, p. 193.

[101] *Cf.* Rockwell, p. 61.

[102] Lenz, I, 177. Bucer expected a secret marriage which would be ostensibly a concubinage, *cf. Argumenta Buceri*, p. 52, ff.; see below, p. 99, ff.

[103] *Cf.* Lenz, I, 121, 174, 175, etc.; see below, p. 229, ff.

[104] Lenz, I, 354.

[105] *Ibid.*, pp. 166, 360.

[106] *Cf. ibid.*, pp. 119, 120.

[107] He wrote to Frau von der Sale immediately after Bucer's departure, telling about the conference (Lenz, I, 354), and he did not wait for his return from Wittenberg before he demanded his wife's consent (*CR.*, III, 864).

chief reasons the most important was his desire to help the landgrave's conscience and morals.[108] For many years he had watched Philip's disorderly life and wished to have it corrected. In his commentary on Matthew he had said, "For nothing can be done anywhere forcing one to sin, or depriving him of the means of a pure life if he desires it."[109] He saw that the landgrave sincerely wanted to reform; so far as he knew, passion for any particular woman played no part in this desire; and so he told him that it would not be wrong for him to take a bigamous wife, if his own conscience assured him that he could not control himself in any other way.[110] This was not a justification of the means by the end, because Bucer did not regard bigamy as forbidden to those who needed it, nor did he regard it as perfect conduct, but a weakness.[111] To him it was an imperfect form of marriage, still permitted, as in Old Testament times, to those who could not avoid fornication without it.[112] Nor, for the same reason, was it intentionally the avoidance of the greater evil by choosing the lesser. It was rather the choosing of the lesser perfection in preference to the certain evil of fornication,[113] assuming that there are grades of perfection. The important point in this connection is not the correctness

[108] Kolde says, "Wir wissen nicht, ob er noch einen ernstlichen Versuch gemacht hat, den Fürsten unzustimmen, und damit grosses unheil abzuwenden" (T. Kolde, *Martin Luther*, II, 487). But as shown in the pages above, and in all of Bucer's correspondence, he did his best to turn the landgrave aside from immorality and bigamy. It is because Kolde ignores this that he attributes to Bucer such grossly political motives in consenting to the bigamy.

[109] *In sacra quatuor Euangelia, Enarrationes perpetuae*, p. 150; see above, p. 25; *cf*. Schiess, II, 106.

[110] Lenz, I, 176; *cf*. Schiess, II, 106.

[111] *Cf. CR.*, X, 167, III, 858; *Argumenta Buceri*, pp. 34, 51, 53.

[112] *Cf*. Bucer's advice to Henry VIII (see above, p. 30, ff.); Schiess, II, 106; *CR.*, X, 167; see below, p. 127.

[113] Lenz, I, 348.

of Bucer's attitude,[114] but what his attitude actually was. The landgrave himself admitted to Bucer in July, 1540, "We admit that the desire to free us from an evil conscience influenced you mightily and may have driven you to the dispensation."[115] This desire to help the landgrave's morals was increased by the fact that the prince had rendered great aid to the evangelical church, and being a man of such prominence, it was above all necessary that he should lead a moral life.[116]

Bucer's zeal for the unity and strength of the Protestant movement made him anxious to avoid forcing the landgrave into an alliance with the emperor. Since he desired above all to unify the Protestants, it is not strange that he dreaded, and did all he could to avoid, a break with the landgrave. He looked beyond Philip to the interests of the church, and saw that by serving him he also promoted the principles of the Reformation. But it must be remembered that while Bucer was without doubt influenced by the landgrave's threat to seek help from the emperor, if he could not get it from the Protestants, he was not at the same time granting him anything which he himself considered wrong.[117] Long before this he had

---

[114] *Cf.,* "It is easy from our high vantage-ground to fling hard words at the reformers for this reluctant quasi-consent—if it could be so called—to the bigamous marriage of the landgrave, yes, easy but cheap. It would be better and juster for us to go back to 1539, stay for a little while with men born in the Middle Ages, and try to understand the forces which lay back of the ill-fated Beuchtrat, and this not to defend or even excuse them, but historically to judge them" (*American Journal of Theology*, XVII, 217).

[115] Lenz, I, 202.

[116] *Ibid.,* p. 345.

[117] This is what Paulus would seem to imply when he writes, "Wie daher Butzer in der Sorge, Philip könne sonst der evangelischen Sache verloren gehen, der Doppelehe zugestimmt hatte, so gaben auch die Wittenberger aus demselben Grunde ihre Zustimmung" (*Historisch-politische Blätter*, CXLVII, 514). Hartmann Grisar goes even further and says, "Butzer erklärte Philipp könne sonst der evangelischen Sache verloren

used arguments for divorce that could also be used to prove the permissibility of bigamy, which in the case of Henry VIII he had actually admitted. Besides, later, when Philip insisted on open support, Bucer let him go over to the emperor rather than yield to his wish, so that the danger of losing the landgrave did not influence him to do what he thought was wrong in this case, and there is no reason to suppose that it did so in the first instance.[118] Probably Bucer would not have given his con-

gehen, habe er selbst der Doppelehe zugestimmt,'' which is merely a different arrangement of the same words that Paulus uses (Grisar, *Luther*, II, 433). But there exists no statement by Bucer in which he declared this. Grisar's three references to secondary authorities do not support the claim. (1) First, he refers to the *Realencyclopaedie für protestantische Theologie und Kirche*, XV, 310, which says that the anxiety that the landgrave would be lost ''mag seine letzen Bedenken zerstreut haben,'' and gives as authority the ''Explanation of the Landgrave to Bucer'' (Lenz, I, 354), in which nothing is said as to Bucer's reasons for consenting but the landgrave threatens to go over to the emperor. (2) Kolde (*Martin Luther*, II, 475) says nothing about Bucer's reasons for consenting on the page to which Grisar refers, but on II, 486, he asserts without giving any authority, or a quotation from Bucer, that Bucer consented for political reasons (*cf.* above, p. 75, n. 108). (3) Köstlin-Kawerau (*Martin Luther*, II, 475) contains no such statement by Bucer, but only the opinion of the author that ''Butzer verstand sich, in der Sorge Philipp könne sonst der evangelischen Sache verloren gehen, dazu, auch in dieser Sache als Unterhändler und Vermittler zudienen; er erhielt eine schriftliche Instruktion, mit der er zu Anfang Dezember nach Wittenberg reiste.'' This does not support Grisar's statement and it is impossible to find an authority which does. The verbal similarity of the statements shows that both Grisar and Paulus have derived their information from Köstlin-Kawerau, and Grisar has used his source in a most unjustifiably loose manner. Whether Bucer consented for purely political reasons or not, certainly no statement exists in which he declared that he did so.

[118] Bucer said even more frankly in the following July, ''I am sorry that your princely grace should be ungracious to me, yet more sorry that you should break away from the union and give yourself to other people, and this does not make me less sorry for your sake than for ours. Yet let this make me as sorry as it will, still I must on that account above all see how everything looks before God and in itself, how it pleases or mispleases him'' (Lenz, I, 196). If he had feared losing the landgrave enough to do what he thought was wrong, he would not have said this. Such statements

sent had not the landgrave's threat to contract a bigamous marriage served to convince him of Philip's determination and need. There is no evidence that he was in
any way dependent upon the landgrave for his position
at Strasbourg, or that he was influenced by financial considerations in making his decision.[119]

Bucer's literalistic interpretation of the Bible did not
cause him, in the strict sense of the term, to allow the
landgrave to commit bigamy, but provided a basis upon
which he could justify such a permission. He exalted un-
duly the importance of the patriarchal examples and declared that anything once permitted by God and not
clearly forbidden in the Scriptures was permitted to
Christians. This literalistic attitude made it possible for
him to declare that bigamy under certain circumstances
was theoretically permissible. The only thing that he
needed to decide was whether the actual need existed, and
this decision he left to the landgrave.[120]

As soon as the conference at Melsungen was over, Bucer
rode away, probably on the last day of November, 1539,[121]
to secure the approval of Luther, Melanchthon, and the
elector. From Arnstadt, where he arrived on December
3, he wrote the landgrave that he had been questioned
about the purpose of his journey, but had returned an

as the following by Moses, fail to recognize the fact that theologically
Bucer already considered bigamy permissible, and so did not change in this
respect to please the landgrave. Moses said that Bucer agreed to the plan,
"so sehr ihm auch derselbe widerstehen mochte; die Gefahr gerade jetzt
einen der mächtigsten evangelischen Fürsten durch eine Weigerung auf die
kaiserliche Seite zu drangen, überwog bei ihn alle theologische Bedenken"
(R. Moses, *Die Religionsverhandlungen zu Hagenau und Worms, 1540-
1541*, p. 52, ff.). Philip's threat no doubt influenced Bucer to make his
decision the way he did, but it did not make him do anything which his
conscience told him was wrong, so far as may be ascertained from the existing evidence.

[119] See below, p. 198.
[120] Lenz, I, 176.
[121] *Cf. ibid.*, p. 354.

evasive answer.[122] The cold weather made his trip even harder than he had feared. Again he warned the prince of the danger of giving offence and the necessity for strict secrecy ''until the counsel of the Lord was ascertained more definitely.''[123] On the next day, December 4, he stopped at Weimar and may have seen the elector, although the letter he wrote from there offers no clear evidence of it.[124] It is more likely that while passing through on his way to Wittenberg, he gathered from others the information imparted in his letter that ''the elector complains greatly about the Treves articles.''[125]

It was not until December 9 that he reached the gates of Wittenberg, where he conferred until the following day with Luther and Melanchthon.[126] For Luther to be asked for advice by the landgrave was no new thing,[127] but the matter upon which his opinion was now solicited was far more serious than any which had yet been submitted to his consideration. Little is known about what passed between the three reformers, the only sources being a letter from Luther to the elector in June, 1540,[128] a brief statement by Bucer in his Christmas letter, 1539,[129] and another reference by Luther at the Eisenach conference.[130]

Naturally Bucer would give to the Wittenbergers all the information he had gained at the Melsungen confer-

---

[122] Even his colleagues at Strasbourg did not know the real cause for his journey (*CR.*, *Calvini Opera*, Xb, 430).

[123] Lenz, I, 118-119.

[124] As Lenz seems to think (Lenz, I, 119, n. 1).

[125] Lenz, I, 119.

[126] *Cf.* Rockwell, pp. 25, 29; *CR.*, III, 848.

[127] *Cf.* Cordatus, p. 88; Gundlach, p. 60; P. Smith, *The Life and Letters of Martin Luther*, p. 377.

[128] Published by Seidemann, *M. Anton Lauterbachs, Diaconi zu Wittenberg, Tagebuch auf das Jahr 1538*, p. 196, note; Enders, XIII, 79, ff.

[129] Lenz, I, 121.

[130] *Ibid.*, p. 372.

ence, as well as that contained in his instructions.[131] It is quite probable that in his oral presentation of the case he placed the emphasis upon the landgrave's stress of conscience.[132] Luther was not told of the public marriage which the landgrave had in mind, and which later took place,[133] for the simple reason that Bucer himself had not been told of it.[134] It was not necessary to persuade Luther and Melanchthon that bigamy in itself was permissible, for they had so advised Henry VIII,[135] but the thing which gave them concern, and regarding which Luther afterwards felt he had been misinformed, was the sufficiency of the landgrave's need.[136] Evidently their decision was given in great haste,[137] the conference not taking more than half as long as that between Bucer and Sailer at Strasbourg.

The opinion expressed by Luther and Melanchthon, later subscribed by Bucer and certain Hessian theologians, is contained in a famous document called the "Wittenberg Rathschlag."[138] It was a quasi-consent to the landgrave's request.[139]

The contents of the "Wittenberg Rathschlag" may be

[131] *Cf.* Luther's statement (Enders, XIII, 79).

[132] *CR.*, III, 856; Seidemann, p. 196, note; Enders, XIII, 79, ff.

[133] Enders, XIII, 81.

[134] Lenz, I, 193.

[135] See above, p. 35, ff.

[136] Seidemann, p. 196, note; Enders, XIII, 80. Melanchthon also said that he and Luther had been deceived, but not by Bucer (*CR.*, III, 1078).

[137] *CR.*, III, 857; Heppe, "Urkundliche Beiträge zur Geschichte der Doppelehe des Landgrafen Philipp von Hessen," *Zeitschrift für die historische Theologie*, XXII, 266; Enders, XII, 320.

[138] The text has been published by D. Arcuarius, *Kurtze . . . Betrachtung des . . . Heiligen Ehstandes*, p. 220, ff.; deWette, VI, 239, ff.; *CR.*, III, 856-863; Enders, XII, 319, ff. English translations have been made by Hook, III, 203-209; Richard, *Philip Melanchthon*, pp. 274-279; Faulkner, *op. cit.*, pp. 213-216. On the origin of the text *cf.* Rockwell, p. 25, n. 6, and Brieger in the *Zeitschrift für Kirchengeschichte*, XXIX, 174-196.

[139] *Cf.* Faulkner in the *American Journal of Theology*, XVII, 217.

summarized as follows. After congratulating the landgrave on his recovery from illness, and reminding him
that the church needed strong champions, the reformers
asserted frankly that they could allow no open introduction of polygamy or any defense of it in printing, though
they would permit what was right before God should
there be sufficient need. The first marriage as divinely
instituted by God was monogamous, and although polygamy was allowed in the Old Testament, no law should
be set up against the first institution. A dispensation
might be allowed in case of necessity, but as it was one
thing to introduce a law, and another to dispense with it,
the landgrave must guarantee the secrecy of such a dispensation. Publicity would give offence, stir up notoriety,
lead to imitation, and injure his own good name. The reformers had long been anxious about his immorality,
which was a serious sin condemned in the Bible. Now his
conscience troubled him, they had been told, but he should
try to be satisfied with his worthy wife and children. If
he couldn't control himself and was firmly determined
to take another wife, he should do it secretly so that no
offence would follow. "So much we regard as right," they
concluded, "that whatever is permitted in marriage by
the Mosaic law, is not forbidden by the gospel, and . . .
it will restore once again the depraved nature."[140] In
conclusion, they urged him to conduct himself as a Christian prince and not to seek help from the emperor who was
a bad man.

The nearest approach to an approval of the landgrave's
action was the last sentence quoted, in which the responsibility was thrown upon the nobleman, who alone could
decide if his need was great enough. Granted that such
was actually the case, then they thought he would do right
to take a bigamous wife; but only on condition of strict

[140] *CR.*, III, 862; Enders, XII, 325.

secrecy.[141] From Wittenberg Bucer went to Weimar, where Elector John Frederick was staying. For this interview he bore special instructions written in the landgrave's own hand,[142] in which the following request was made, "if the wedding takes place secretly, then will he give me a testimony that he will regard it as a real marriage, and stand by me?"[143] If the elector supported him in this enterprise, the landgrave offered to help the Duke of Cleves in his affair, to promote the elector's Magdeburg affair, even if the others did not aid him; to assist John Frederick in the event of an imperial election or a religious war; and to assume a more favorable attitude in the controversy over the inheritance from Duke George, provided the elector would influence Duke Maurice to sanction the bigamy.[144] That Philip wanted this assistance to take the form of military aid, if necessary, is clear from the fact that he offered such aid in return.

After a cold and difficult journey Bucer arrived in Weimar on the evening of December 13, bringing back a decision from Wittenberg to the landgrave which was

[141] On Bucer's interpretation of the "Wittenberg Rathschlag" see Schiess, II, 106. The statement made by Moeller and Kawerau, *History of the Christian Church*, III, 144, that "they assented and expressed themselves ready to take upon themselves his public justification," is evidently based upon ignorance of the facts, for no authority is given or can be. Luther is reported to have said at Eisenach in the following July that "he would keep silent how Bucer had proposed the business, but it was not so negotiated with them that they should recognize the matter openly" (Lenz, I, 372); *cf.* Bucer to the landgrave, Dec. 25, 1539, "In regard to your princely grace's affair, as my gracious lord the elector and those at Wittenberg begged me, so I most humbly beg your princely grace that you would keep it quiet" (Lenz, I, 121). *Cf.* Luther to the elector, June 10, 1540, "wo es s. f. g. . . . nicht anders zu thun wuste, s. f. g. woltens doch heimlich halten" (Enders, XIII, 80).

[142] Lenz, I, 356, and n. 2.

[143] *Ibid.*, p. 356.

[144] Lenz, I, 356.

very much what he expected to procure.[145] The next morning he was received graciously by the elector, who read his instructions and the "Wittenberg Rathschlag." He then dismissed Bucer with the general answer that he would take the matter into consideration, saying nothing more about it than that he felt a deep sympathy for the landgrave.

At an audience given him on the morning of Tuesday the fifteenth, Bucer received the elector's answer. First, John Frederick apologized for his delay in answering.[146] Secondly, he requested that his reply be kept secret, and expressed a desire that the landgrave be untroubled. Thirdly, he reminded him of the difficulties and dangers involved in the plan, as the "Wittenberg Rathschlag" had already pointed out so well. Fourthly, he begged him in an entirely brotherly way to consider well the obstacles, to call upon the Lord for help to overthrow his evil habits, and to abide with his wife. If he could not do this, the elector thought he should not hasten in carrying out his resolve, "but should take the matter into close examination, while the Lord would show further counsel and help. If this also is impossible for your princely grace," he wrote, "then his electoral grace would entirely truly and fraternally beg, that your princely grace would not undertake the proposed matters in any other way than that prescribed in our answer, Dr. Luther's, Philip's and

[145] *Ibid.*, p. 120. The assertion that the elector's anger was thoroughly aroused when he read the "Wittenberg Rathschlag" (H. E. Jacobs, *Martin Luther*, p. 334), is evidently based upon a misinterpretation of some quotations made by Seckendorf (V. L. Seckendorf, *Commentarius Historicus et Apologeticus de Lutheranismo*) from what the elector said two days after his interview with Bucer (*cf.* Seckendorf, III, 278; Köstlin, II, 471). So also there seems to be no foundation for the idea that Bucer presented the consent of Christina to the elector (Jacobs, p. 334; see below, p. 102), as Seckendorf asserts (Seckendorf, III, 278).

[146] The delay was due to having waited for his chancellor, Dr. Bruck, who arrived Monday evening (Lenz, I, 356).

mine, which their electoral grace does not know how to improve.'' Fifthly, he assured the landgrave of his friendly spirit and desire to help him both in soul and body.[147]

As rapidly and directly as possible Bucer returned to Strasbourg,[148] and even on the way back engaged with joy in the actual work of the Reformation.[149] He was glad to have finished his task, and nothing can be more incorrect than to say with reference to the gaining of the ''Wittenberg Rathschlag,'' ''Bucer, glad of his success, at once departed with it to the Elector of Saxony,''[150] for Bucer foresaw the offence[151] and would gladly have turned the landgrave from his purpose.[152]

Sometime before December 23, 1539, Bucer had put in written form his opinions on the permissibility of bigamy to Christians, stating both the arguments for and against it. Within recent years this document has been given the name of *Argumenta Buceri pro et contra*.[153] The date of its composition is unknown. Certainly not begun before November 6, 1539, the completed manuscript was in the

[147] Given in Bucer's report to the landgrave (Lenz, I, 356, ff.) written from Hersfeld on December 16, 1539 (Rockwell, p. 30, n. 2). Bucer also received a *Credenz* from the elector to the landgrave, dated Dec. 14, 1539 (Lenz, I, 358).

[148] Ambrose Blaurer wrote to Capito on December 8, 1539, from Augsburg, ''Butzer soll noch nicht zurückgekehret sein'' (Schiess, II, 39). Bucer reached Strasbourg shortly before Jan. 12, 1540 (Lenz, I, 125, n. 2).

[149] E.g., the interview with Hadamar of Wetzlar. *Cf.* Lenz, I, 119, 120, 125, 131, 137, II, 429.

[150] Grisar, II, 389; cf. J. K. Hergenrother, *Handbuch der allgemeinen Kirchengeschichte,* 5th edition, III, 478.

[151] Lenz, I, 159.

[152] Lenz, I, 176. On Jan. 4, 1540, the landgrave wrote to Sailer, ''Bucer has brought us a good answer from Wittenberg and the elector in the known affair . . . strongly of the opinion which Bucer expressed to you'' (Lenz, I, 449).

[153] It was published by Löwenstein in 1878 (F. Küch, *Politisches Archiv des Landgrafen Philipp des Grossmüthigen von Hessen,* I, 3, n. 6). On the full title see above, p. 29, n. 24.

hands of the landgrave on December 23. That such a large
work could have been written during the journey to Wittenberg[154] is incredible. At least the general outline must
have been made out before Bucer left Strasbourg, even if
the manuscript had not yet been put into final form.[155]

The hand-writing proves beyond doubt that Bucer was
the author of the monograph.[156] In a paragraph of his
instructions to the envoys to Frau von der Sale, the landgrave said that they should give her a *Rathschlag* composed by Bucer, "which reads like the enclosed copy
marked F. This advice will satisfy her daughter's conscience that it can take place with God's approval and will
demonstrate to her that in spite of the secrecy which must
be maintained for a time she will be our wife, and on that

[154] Kolde's supposition that, "'noch auf der Reise fand er Zeit die gründe
für und gegen die Doppelehe in einem erst neuerdings gedrückten Büchlein
zusammenstellen,'" is a wild flight of the imagination in view of the fact
that the *Argumenta Buceri* is the result of careful thought and investigation, and Bucer had more time both before and after his journey (Kolde,
Martin Luther, II, 489).

[155] Bucer could not have left Weimar before Dec. 16, 1539, the day on
which he received the elector's *Credenz* (Rockwell, p. 30, n. 2; *cf.* above,
p. 84, n. 147). The *Argumenta Buceri* was composed before Dec. 23, because on that day it was in the landgrave's hands (Lenz, I, 331, n. 1). On
Dec. 25, Bucer was at Marburg where he had stopped for an interview with
Hadamar of Wetzlar (Lenz, I, 120, 121). It would have taken at least one
day for him to have traveled from Weimar to Hersfeld, from which place
he sent to the landgrave an account of his interview with the elector (Lenz,
I, 356, n. 4), and probably three because Weimar was about halfway
between Wittenberg and Hersfeld, and it took him three days to reach
Weimar from Wittenberg. Moreover, a letter written by Bucer to the landgrave from Weimar, Dec. 14, reached him at Friedewald on Dec. 18 (Lenz,
I, 120). A letter from the elector to the landgrave, written on Dec. 16, did
not reach him till Dec. 19 (Rockwell, p. 30, n. 2). It may have been that
Bucer carried this letter. The fact that it took four days for a letter to
go from Weimar to Friedewald, would indicate that it took Bucer at least
three days to reach Hersfeld, and so if the *Argumenta Buceri* was composed
after Bucer's journey to Wittenberg, it must have been written between
Dec. 18 and 23, 1539. This is possible, but not so likely as that he wrote it
before he left Strasbourg.

[156] Küch, I, 3, n. 6.

account she must bear a cross temporarily but will thereby suffer no injury to her good reputation."[157]

In the following July Bucer referred to "my observations and disputations,"[158] and all historians have accepted without question his sole authorship of the *Argumenta Buceri*.[159] In the list of documents given to the envoys to Frau von der Sale,[160] the *Argumenta Buceri* is crossed out;[161] but their letter saying that they had received it[162] shows that it was in their possession, though they may not have given it to the *hofmeisterin*. At any rate she had it among her papers in May, 1540, for she then delivered it to the Duke of Saxony by mistake, thinking it was a copy of the "Wittenberg Rathschlag."[163] Her opinion of the book was far from favorable, for, when she discovered her mistake, she wrote the landgrave that "she wished she had laid before them the combined answer of Luther, Philip, and Bucer, rather than the *Verzeichnus*, which she had given them through an oversight, for it was only *ein argumentische und disputerisch Verzeichnusz gewesen von argumentis pro et contra*, but the Wittenberg answer was a conclusive *Bedenken und Antwort*."[164] Because of this mistake, Duke Henry sent it to the elector,[165] and on June 12, 1540, the elector, thinking it had been subscribed by Luther and Melanchthon, sent to the landgrave a copy of this advice which Anna had given to Duke Henry. On July 7 the landgrave returned it to him, pointing out the mistake.[166]

The landgrave's sister, Duchess Elizabeth of Rochlitz,

---

[157] Lenz, I, 331, n. 1; *cf. Argumenta Buceri*, p. 54.

[158] Lenz, I, 176.

[159] Except Hausrath (A. Hausrath, *Luther's Leben*, II, 396).

[160] On these negotiations see below, p. 102, ff.

[161] Rockwell, p. 34, n. 1.

[162] On Dec. 31 (Rockwell, p. 34, n. 1).

[163] Lenz, I, 338.   [164] Lenz, I, 338, n. 1.

[165] *CR.*, III, 1046-1047.   [166] Lenz, I, 338, n. 1.

was even more disgusted with Bucer's "writing," for when it was sent to her in March, 1540, she had hardly begun to read it before "she began to weep and cried, 'O Lord God, my brother is going to take another wife'; and lost all self-control and made a great outcry and scolded Luther and Bucer, declaring that they were the worst of idiots, and carried on so excitedly that I was anxious lest she would hurt herself, since she said that she herself was somewhat to blame."[167]

After the bigamy affair had quieted down, the manuscript was not published till Löwenstein in the nineteenth century found it in a private library, and in 1878 gave it a place among Bucer's printed works.[168] The contents of the book, which in its printed form covers only a little over fifty-five pages, may be summarized as follows:

May any Christian man be allowed more than one wife?

So far as this question may be answered from divine Scripture, we will first set forth the reasons why polygamy may be granted to no man, secondly, the reasons why it may be permitted among Christians,[169] thirdly, how those whose consciences assure them that they may take more than one wife, should serve them to holiness and piety.[170]

First, nothing is granted to any Christian by which anyone may be severely offended, yet to take another wife along with one who is still faithful and capable can bring nothing but severe offence. Therefore such a dispensation is granted to no one. Our nature is inclined to serve dis-

---

[167] *Ibid.*, p. 335.

[168] *Cf.* editor's introduction to the *Argumenta Buceri*, p. iii; Mentz, p. 163. The manuscript is now in the Landesbibliothek at Cassel, and is written on folio-size sheets in Bucer's hand (no. -4° Ms. Hass. 282). It was presented to this library in 1905, and before that was in the private library of Judge Wöhler of Cassel. It is composed of 190 pages or 95 leaves of paper.

[169] See below, p. 94. [170] See below, p. 99.

orderly lusts, and such a permission would be abused. It is the "ornament" of Christianity that marriage has been restored to the first divine institution of having only one wife, "for in the beginning God created man one husband and one wife, and united the two together, not the three or four or more, that they might be one person." It cannot be said that the rule declaring that "these two shall be one flesh," is fulfilled between the man and each wife, for any woman may be one flesh with one man as St. Paul points out of the whore (I Corinthians VI). The Lord in the beginning ordained that one woman and one man should be one flesh. If the need of increasing the race is a valid reason for polygamy, then God should have given Adam more than one wife.

Even the corrupt heathen recognized instinctively that it was better for one man to have one wife. The animals who entered Noah's ark two by two had this instinct implanted by the Lord in their nature. Besides, the first bigamist, Lamech, was also a murderer. It was for the increase of God's people that Abraham took many wives, though he was evidently satisfied with one, for in his youth he took no more; at least the Scriptures do not record it, and so it cannot be argued in a Christian disputation that he did. If it is said that Abraham did not take his concubines for the increase of the children of God, since that was promised him through Isaac; yet because he drew all his servants to God, he increased the godly through his concubines, and not the godless. Sarah's answer to the angel, that it was not fitting for her to have a child in her old age, shows that Abraham had taken his concubines to increase the godly.

Isaac, who was a special type of Christ, married only Rebecca. If it is said that his marriage is merely a type of the marriage of Christ and the Church, and does not show that Isaac preferred monogamy; yet, the true marriage is rightly fulfilled between Christ and the Church (Ephesians V). If anyone will carefully observe what the Scriptures report of all those who took more than one wife, and also of the law of bigamy, then he will see that the Holy Spirit, by continually pointing out the mischances which arose out of plural marriages,[171] makes polygamy a horrible example: for instance, Hagar provoked her mistress, Leah failed in sisterly love toward Rachel, and Esau, who took two wives, troubled his parents.

That God blessed the plural marriages of Jacob and others does not show that God was pleased with such a marriage in itself, for God has often adapted for the good of his people what was openly against his will—as in the case of David and Bathsheba, whose son Solomon he blessed. It is said that evil results often followed single marriages, yet the misfortune flowed not out of monogamy but out of evil causes. The Scriptures and nature show that true love to one wife is injured when a man takes another, and then the anger of the Lord and all kinds of evil must follow. Therefore the apostles and holy fathers have advocated marriage as it was first instituted and as it was implanted in man's nature, perceiving that unnecessary divorce was wrong for the same reason as polygamy. The first institution of marriage showed them that polygamy was wrong, because God gave Adam only Eve. Married people should have such love as to be one flesh, which culmination of love is never found if more than one and one are joined in marriage.

Evil love demands that one should cleave to one only— matrimonial love should not be less complete. Though the apostles did not command polygamists to put away all

[171] This argument against bigamy was used by Bucer ten years later in his lectures on Ephesians at Cambridge (M. Bucer, *Praelectiones doctiss*, etc. p. 179).

but one wife before joining the church, yet they taught
those who were already Christians that each one should
have only one wife, as may be seen from the fact that they
ordered all bishops and deacons not to have more than
one wife. With this ordinance was subjoined the admonition that a bishop ought to be blameless, which shows that
bigamy was a culpable thing.[172]

If it is said that the apostles rejected polygamous
bishops from church service because they were too much
laden with household affairs, and not because such a marriage was reprehensible in itself; yet it would seem that
a man with two wives would be freer from household cares
than a man with one. Paul, where he speaks of things
which are a hindrance to church service, though irreproachable in themselves, has mentioned things which are
more of a hindrance than the oversight of two wives: as,
service in war, and craft-work. Truly, the Spirit of God
has urged in this passage nothing more than the cultiva-
tion of greater virtue, the rejection of all evil, and the
exclusion of the bigamist from church service because
bigamy was an evil and punishable thing. Because both
the Lord and Paul said that the church-servant should be
an example whom the people should follow with all diligence, marriage was soon restored in Christendom to its
first institution, and polygamy became abhorrent. God's
grace having been bestowed in fullest measure upon
Christians, they should live in the most irreproachable
manner.

The diligent reader of Scripture will see that "the
having of more than one wife at one time is an evil, and a

[172] Bucer held that I Timothy III:2 referred to bigamy and not to
marriage after the death of the first wife (*Scripta Duo . . . Latomi*, p. 77;
Was in Namen . . . Bonn, p. Fiii). From this passage in the *Argumenta
Buceri* it seems that he regarded this prohibition as referring only to the
clergy.

departure from the first and best institution of the Lord.'' Christians, more than Jews, are obliged by their abundant grace and high calling to prevent plural marriages. Because marriage has been restored to its first institution, and confirmed by ecclesiastical and imperial law, we should regard it as an "ornament" of Christianity, and turn aside from whatever may take it away, and from all who would take it away. It is not believable that to grant a man, and especially a prominent one, to take more than one wife, would not soon give occasion for great evils. Such a permission would be a great reproach to the Christian Church, for so she would lose her ornament of single marriage. For this cause no one "should be allowed to make this innovation.'' This is the first chief reason against such an allowance.

The second chief reason is that such an allowance would injure true matrimonial love, and become a shame to Christianity. For it is contrary to nature to show matrimonial love to many, as each may see in himself, and in the examples of Hagar and Sarah, Leah and Rachel, the wives of Helcan (Elkanah), and the law about the first-born. Christians must guard against anything which will cause any falling away or weakening. Because it cannot be denied that having more than one wife injures true matrimonial love, it is wrong to allow anyone to introduce such a departure. This is the second chief reason: because the Scriptures teach that in marriage there should exist the highest type of love, and this cannot be bestowed on more than one at the same time.

The third chief reason is the bond and duty of marriage. It is clearly a great evil to introduce anything by which the marriage-bond suffers infringement, and its promises are not fulfilled to the highest extent. Since Christianity has restored marriage to its first institution, so that monogamy is the common practice among Christians, whoever takes a wife tacitly promises not to marry any more wives while united to her. He may not vow it with expressed words, but only by the implication of customary usage. If Christians ought to keep good faith in all things, and "most faithfully, truly and completely, carry out and fulfil all their promises, which they can hold with God," then all who marry according to common understanding and usage promise to give matrimonial love and service to no one besides the one to whom it is promised. To allow any exception from the custom of monogamy, and especially to people of prominence, can result in nothing else than a deterioration of the effectiveness of marriage vows as they are taken according to common usage, and observed "according to divine, natural, and ancient law."

The fourth chief reason is this, "the shame and reproach which is cast upon the gospel whenever anyone, and especially a person of high rank, is allowed to take more than one wife." As Christians pray, "Hallowed be thy name," so they must act in a way which will promote the sanctification of the divine name. Paul urged good works that thereby the teaching of the holy gospel might be ornamented. In I Corinthians X: 31-33 he has written, "whether you eat or whether you drink, or whatsoever you do, do all to the glory of God, and give no occasion for stumbling." The Lord himself has commanded, "Let your light so shine," etc.

Many burdensome restraints must often be endured by Christians that people may be attracted, not repelled by the holy gospel. For this reason Paul and Barnabas did not take their wives with them, as did the other apostles, nor accept support from the churches. To no man may be allowed a permission of polygamy which would bring Christianity into disrepute, lower the standard of matrimonial love, and infringe upon the sacredness of matrimonial vows. Such a radical innovation, added to the recent abolition of celibacy and fasts, would cause the public to condemn us as Turks and libertines who renounce all religious discipline. Our failure to follow the example of the patriarchs in the observance of general, moral precepts would deprive us of all just basis for appealing to the example of their polygamy.

Someone may object that the same public which is horrified at polygamy such as God permitted to the patriarchs, allows men to practice adultery without punishment or even condemnation. But this is the way of the world. That weak Christians, who do not fully understand what is permitted by God, may not be offended, care must be exercised in the use of such liberties, and for this reason Paul would not accept material support, even from those who owed it to him. In the matter of polygamy the offence would be worse, because the divine permission is not only unrecognized by the weak, but it is even in doubt among the pious. Monogamy has been the common practice for so many centuries that the divine approval of polygamy among the patriarchs is not sufficient excuse for an infraction of the law in modern times. In fact the rule of monogamy is so firmly established, that people regard the prohibition of plural marriages as divine. It is, therefore, vain to argue that because polygamy was right for the patriarchs, it is right for us. Anyone who would take more than one wife must consider his duty to the weak, "and there is little doubt that any man can easily abstain from it."

"For if any man has a wife who is capable of matrimonial service, it being the duty of a Christian to hold his flesh in subjection, that man can find one wife sufficient. . . . It is easy to serve those who comprehend, but every Christian must serve those who do not comprehend." Even a thing permitted by God is not allowed to a Christian, if thereby the weak are offended, and it is plain that to allow a man to have more than one wife would give severe offence.

Next, let us consider the answers to these four reasons given by those who think plural marriages may be allowed among Christians just as righteously as among the patriarchs.

First, the advocates of polygamy recognize; that it was God's first institution that marriage should be a union of only two people, since this is best and advisable for all Christians so far as it may happen without fornication; that St. Paul condemned plural marriages for church servants as an imperfection in itself, and not alone because of the multiplicity of church business laid upon them; that true matrimonial love cannot be shown as completely to two or more as to one; that marriage vows presuppose single marriage; and, finally, that bigamy would give offence to many people. But still they consider that what God has granted to the Ancients must also be granted among Christians. And this is their chief argument, "what God grants to men in general, that cannot be intrinsically evil or unlawful in the sight of God, but must comprise some serviceable quality, conducive to true piety and holiness, and if the same causes exist may be used with God at all times." Observe that David took extra wives by divine permission, not only to produce children, but also through love, and he was not punished for it. Likewise, the law that the king should not take too many wives,[173] shows that love was often the reason why the Ancients took more than one wife.

Whatever God grants must promote holiness, otherwise it would not be a gift of God. The giving of more wives than one advances holiness by removing fornication; for, though Paul is thinking of only one wife in what

[173] This law is found in Deuteronomy XVII:17, ''Neither shall he multiply wives to himself that his heart turn not away.''

he says about this matter, still this passage[174] means that
God regards the avoidance of fornication as one reason
for taking a wife, and "it could also by God's grace be
the reason for taking plural wives in modern times as
well as in the days of the ancients." Likewise, in the command to take the dead brother's wife the Lord has in
mind the maintaining of the race. But in general there
was no other reason for the permitting of polygamy to
the Ancients than the suppressing of fornication. To be
sure Paul presents this reason as a concession, but as a
holy concession. If, then, God permitted bigamy among
the Ancients, surely, they say, it should be granted to all
pious people for whom single marriage does not suffice.

Experience does not support the claim that there are
not as many men among us Christians who with one wife
are unable to avoid adultery, as among the Ancients. It is
true that Christians today are more inspired by the Holy
Spirit than were the Jews, but the discipline of faith has
fallen into such disuse, that there are as many people
weak in chastity among us as among the Ancients. "If
then, there is the same sickness among us, perhaps to a
greater extent, why should not the same medicine be
used?" Divorce for other reasons than adultery has always been against the primitive usage of marriage, yet
the Lord allowed it to the Ancients on account of the
hardness of their hearts. Just as God has granted to men
marriage and all his ordinances, and instituted the Sabbath for man, so, in order to avoid the greater evil of
people living in adultery and hardness of heart, he has
granted divorce, which is out of harmony with the first
institution of marriage and wrong in itself.

"Now this one God is also our God, and he never
changes, but, finding among us the same weakness, he can
use the same medicine which he himself has given and

[174] I.e., I Corinthians VII.

prescribed.'' The standard should be the system established by God in the beginning. As we are not able to
conform to that standard, the Lord will make a large
allowance for our weakness in marriage as in other
things. Since the Fall we have a distorted nature. In the
beginning there was no need of marriage to avoid fornication; since then there is. It is a deficiency that God will
pardon.

There are two kinds of good works; first, those which
serve to the sanctifying of God's name and the widening
of his kingdom; secondly, those which promote the first,
and although of no use in themselves, add to the comfort
of the body, as do more desirable food and drink, amusements, etc. By such good works people are guarded from
evil and helped to do the good works which are useful in
themselves, for if done in moderation then they are ''truly
good works and a service of God.'' Because then, God
allows so many of these works to be of value, which had
no existence in the beginning and are only good because
''they either help to avoid some evil or promote some
measure of good,'' so it cannot be established as a rule
that because ''this was not so in the beginning, therefore
it cannot be granted to Christians,'' or that what existed
in the beginning may be demanded in the same measure
from Christians. We still await the age of the perfect
man.

Thus, the advocates of polygamy, believing that with
God's permission the men of ancient times employed
polygamy as a device to prevent fornication, reach the
conclusion[175] that recourse may be made among Christians
to the same medicine, since God always remains the same
and is as ready now, as in ages past, to bless whatever
avoids sin. Not only do they fail to find in the New Testament any statement contradictory to this conclusion, but

[175] According to Bucer.

they contend that polygamy, far from being a special dispensation granted to the Israelites, is a general ordinance promulgated by God for the benefit of the whole human race. Though Christians should strive to attain the perfect state of monogamy, which is obligatory for all servants of the church, great noblemen, being more sorely tempted—because of their greater power and immunity from punishment—to commit fornication, should be permitted to indulge more freely than most men in the medicine of polygamy.

Having made this statement of the argument in favor of polygamy, Bucer then proceeds to outline the replies given by its advocates to the defenders of monogamy. To the first argument, that a permission of polygamy would take away the "ornament" gained by Christianity through the restoration of monogamy, they reply that a complete prohibition of polygamy is no "jewel" of the Church. There are so many Christians who are unable to attain the excellence of monogamy, so many who need the medicine of polygamy, that to refuse them the expedient of having more than one wife at the same time would not add lustre but disgrace to the reputation of Christianity, since it would cause all kinds of immorality. Not compulsory monogamy is the "ornament" of Christianity, they declare, but so to hold and promote single marriage that no occasion is given for immorality. For those who are unable to attain the heights of excellence and purity which she holds forth as the ideal, the church "knows how to use the medicine given by God for each and every evil, rather than attempt a higher purity than the Lord has granted for all her children."

Of a similar nature is the reply given to the second argument of the monogamists: that to permit polygamy would cause an impoverishment in the quality of love bestowed upon the first wife. Candidly admitting that such would be the result, the advocates of polygamy are represented as answering that even this undesirable situation would be preferable to a prevalence of immoral relations, certain to be brought into existence by compelling men to live in a state of matrimony beyond their abilities. Though the perfect form of monogamy should be urged upon all, none should be caused thereby to fall into immorality; for those who remain within the lower grades of marriage remain within the grace of God, but those who fall into fornication fall outside of his grace. The weakening of a husband's love for his first wife, which would be caused by marrying a second, should not be regarded as such a serious evil, for in its practical working out the trouble will rectify itself. The recognition that he has fallen short of the perfect ideal will impel the polygamous husband to seek recovery from his abasement by striving to develop complete love for both wives. Certainly this would be better than the complete extinction of matrimonial love caused by an immoral life, since there are many weak people among us who are beyond doubt unable to avoid fornication otherwise than through the expedient of polygamy.

As for the third argument, that polygamy would be an infringement upon the tacit promise of monogamy, made by the implication of custom and usage when the vows of marriage are taken, the advocates of polygamy admit that such a promise is made, and a Christian should keep all his promises. But they contend that no man has a right to demand that another shall hold to a promise whose fulfillment requires him to do evil, for a man belongs to God, soul and body, and he has no right to bind himself by a vow which will make his body unacceptable to the Lord.[176]

176 Bucer himself had taken the vow of celibacy when very young and had asked to be released from it because he had taken it before reaching years of discretion (see above, p. 2).

The fourth argument against a permission of polygamy is the familiar admonition of Paul, that a Christian should deny himself many things in order to avoid giving offence to weaker Christians. To this the answer is made, that a Christian, though he might offend others by committing bigamy, should not place himself in danger of disinheritance from the kingdom of God through deference to the mistaken beliefs of weaker brethren.

In the last part of the *Argumenta Buceri* is given a series of suggestions for anyone who wishes to commit bigamy without giving offence to other Christians. "Should a man take another wife as a concubine," Bucer wrote, "this would give less offence to the gospel than if she were given the name and state of a married wife."[177] For a time he must forego the divine permission of full polygamy and submit himself to the ignominy of concubinage. The disgrace of living with a concubine might be mitigated, however; first, by keeping the concubine secluded as closely as possible; secondly, by taking a "God-fearing person" and regarding the marriage, privately before the Lord, as valid; thirdly, by cultivating a Godly manner of life in the attempt to gain the forbearing approval of Godly people. The marriage service should be performed secretly before a few trusted persons, the bride agreeing to bear the shame of concubinage with patience. If the pair appeal to the Word of God for justification and live a blameless life, the offence will be finally overcome.

The man who intends to use the permission of polygamy may reassure his conscience in the following way.

---

[177] This and the remainder of the *Argumenta Buceri* is evidently intended as Bucer's proposal of the way in which the landgrave should commit bigamy. The contrast with what actually happened shows that Bucer was not thoroughly acquainted with Philip's plans when he wrote his opinion. All the following arguments can be duplicated from passages in his letters to the landgrave.

First, he should pray to God and question himself, whether, to avoid the great offence, he may be satisfied with single marriage. Secondly, ask the advice of understanding and God-fearing people, and pray for himself that he may never do injury to the holy gospel. Thirdly, if it then appears that he cannot live without the prescribed means, he should take such a person in the presence of God-fearing people who understand the matter, keeping it secret before the judgment of God. If any offence arises, he should remain silent as if it were nothing, and live with that much more circumspection so as to drive it away. Fourthly, in nothing speaking proudly of himself, he should trust only to the dear Christ, who has supported the Ancients in such weakness as his own. So all faith and trust should be put in the Lord, who will give further help.

"The Lord grant his grace. Amen!"

The *Argumenta Buceri pro et contra* was written with the particular case of the landgrave in mind, as a statement of Bucer's attitude on the general question of the permissibility of bigamy for Christians in the sixteenth century. Perhaps he wrote it primarily to clarify his own thinking, for he employed the same method to which he had resorted long before in formulating his belief on the manner of Christ's presence in the Supper.[178] The two parts of his work, one opposed to such a permission and the other in favor of it, were not meant to be inconsistent, and evidently Bucer held firmly to both of them. The most remarkable feature was the way in which he tried to harmonize monogamy and polygamy. A permission of bigamy given only to a few people who were unable to live righteously without it, he did not regard as a contradiction to the law of monogamy. It is significant that he represented the arguments against polygamy as his own,

---

[178] Bucer to Martinus, Thesaurus Baumianus, II, 213; *cf.* above, p. 13.

and those in favor of it as advanced by other people. And perhaps Sailer's influence may account in some degree for the figurative description of such a permission as a medicine against immorality,[179] although this view of marriage was a prevalent one at the time, and had been advocated by the apostle Paul.[180] Bucer's most serious objection to the special permission which he allowed, was not the lack of spiritual sanction, but the offence which it would cause.[181]

The second half of the book, which is largely composed of arguments in favor of bigamy, is distinguished from the first part by its repetitious nature; and the line of reasoning is by no means so clear and systematic. Two fallacies are especially prominent. The first is the assumption that polygamy was granted to the patriarchs that immorality might be avoided.[182] The second is the setting up of two moral codes, one for the man who can be continent with one wife, and one for the man who needs more.[183] In citing Paul's injunction that everyone should have his own wife to avoid fornication, he forgets that Paul said that every woman should have her own husband for the same reason. If this injunction would allow a man to have more than one wife, it would also allow a woman

---

179 *Argumenta Buceri*, p. 26; Lenz, I, 348.

180 Rockwell, p. 227, n. 4; see below, p. 224, ff.

181 Kolde says of the arguments in the *Argumenta Buceri*, ''Sie lauten doch wesentlich anders als die der Wittenberger und sind ein klägliches Zeugnis dafür, wie bei diesem Manne die politische Rücksichtnahme auf die Grossen den Sieg über die bessere Erkenntnis davontragen konnte'' (Kolde, *Martin Luther*, II, 489). This is misleading because the attitude taken toward bigamy in the *Argumenta Buceri* was in essential agreement with that of the Wittenbergers in Dec., 1539, even to the prospect of an ostensible concubinage (*cf.* Enders, XIII, 81). Nothing is said in the book about political motives, and as shown above (see p. 76), political motives were not the only ones which made Bucer consent to the bigamy, nor did they outweigh any of his moral or religious convictions.

182 *Argumenta Buceri*, pp. 25, 28.

183 *Ibid.*, pp. 37, 40, ff.

to have more than one husband, and for this Bucer would find no precedent in the Old Testament, nor does he mention it. The Bible everywhere presupposes one moral code for all men, and to set up such a double code would create an impossible situation, for only a man's conscience would be the judge of which applied to him, thus causing an individualism which would be essentially anarchy. How absurd this situation would be, is clear from the fact that it is necessary to assume that the man who found himself requiring two wives, would be humbled so much by discovering this shortcoming that he would remedy it by living a scrupulous life. But it is impossible to imagine how a man unable to control himself with one wife, could ever have the moral ability to gain the respect of society by his conduct.

In spite of the landgrave's assurance to Bucer that he had no definite plan,[184] he could not wait until Bucer had returned from Saxony before he began to crystallize the arrangements already made, and to complete the final preparations for the wedding. In November he bought the wine through the agency of Sailer, who seemed to enjoy the task.[185] On December 11, he influenced his wife Christina to draw up a document, in which, under condition that he should in no way discriminate against her children, she gave her consent to the bigamy.[186] Perhaps he did this at Bucer's demand, for Bucer emphasized the sanctity of the marriage vow, which by common understanding tacitly implied a promise of monogamy.[187]

With the beginning of the new year, when he had received the reply from Wittenberg and the elector, Philip re-opened negotiations with Frau von der Sale, sending

---

[184] Lenz, I, 193.   [185] *Ibid.*, p. 347.
[186] The text is printed in the *CR.*, III, 864, ff.; *cf.* Lenz, I, 358-359; Rockwell, p. 31.
[187] *Argumenta Buceri*, p. 12, ff.

her some of the documents which he had collected.[188] She
objected to the secrecy which the reformers demanded,
but upon being reminded of Bucer's alleged promise of
a public defense in the future, she agreed to let her
daughter marry the landgrave.[189] To protect Margaret's
honor she demanded that the wedding should be witnessed
by the elector, Duke Maurice, Bucer, Melanchthon, certain Hessian counselors and theologians, and her brother,
Ernst von Miltitz; also, that the secret be revealed to
Elizabeth of Rochlitz as her daughter's mistress.[190] The
landgrave agreed to gain the consent of Duke Maurice,
although it cost him his claim to the Saxon inheritance,[191]
but he refused to allow Ernst von Miltitz to be present
on the ground that he was a papist, and so "was not well
enough grounded in the Scriptures to understand the
legality of bigamy before God."[192] The *hofmeisterin* gave
up her demand for the presence of her brother and Duke
Maurice,[193] who were told about it after the wedding;[194]
and the secret was not revealed to Elizabeth till afterwards. Margaret herself offered no objections, and soon
after the middle of February she and her mother started
on their way to Hesse.[195] By March 2 they had arrived
at Rothenburg.[196]

The landgrave lured Bucer to the wedding by false
pretences, not even informing him of the geographical
end of his journey when he started, and the best which
can be said for the landgrave is that he did not tell the
reformer the purpose for which he called him to Hesse.
After seeking the permission of Bucer's lords, Philip

---

[188] Rockwell, pp. 318, 34, n. 1, 320; Lenz, I, 160, 330, 354.
[189] Rockwell, p. 318.
[190] Lenz, I, 331.
[191] Worth about 20,000 thalers (Lenz, I, 331, n. 2).
[192] Lenz, I, 331.   [193] Rockwell, p. 36.
[194] Lenz, I, 331, n. 3.   [195] Rockwell, p. 36; Lenz, I, 333, ff.
[196] Lenz, I, 334.

asked that while on the way to Smalkald he would stop
to confer about several important matters.[197] This was a
convenient excuse, though by no means an empty one,
for drawing Bucer away from Strasbourg. When he
started out he understood that he was to meet the landgrave at Giessen.[198] Greatly perplexed at not finding him
there, and wondering what the prince could want of him,
he followed further directions to Ziegenhain, where he
was again sent on to Friedewald. But on the journey
thither he stopped at Hersfeld for the night, on Wednes-
day, March 3, 1540. While there he learned that the landgrave was at Rothenburg, and so he sent a messenger
to Simon Bing, the Hessian secretary, asking if he should
not come to him directly, instead of going on to Friedewald.[199] Nothing can be clearer from this letter to Bing
than that Bucer did not know on the eve of the wedding-
day, where, or why, the landgrave wanted to meet him.
The next day he came directly to Rothenburg, where
Melanchthon had arrived on the day before.[200] There the
landgrave's purpose was explained to them by the Hessian preachers, Melander and Lening.[201] Even then Bucer
was not told Margaret's name,[202] but was informed that
his presence was needed to witness that it was a true
marriage. Nor was the landgrave entirely honest in his

[197] *Ibid.*, p. 139, and n. 1; *Politische Correspondenz . . . Strassburg,*
III, 3, 14; Lenz, I, 131. Bucer was already planning to go to the Smalkald
convention, and requested the landgrave to have Frecht sent from Ulm
(Lenz, I, 134). He assured the prince that he himself would certainly come
(Lenz, I, 136).

[198] Lenz, 1, 140. Bucer left Strasbourg before Feb. 20, 1540 (*CR., Calvini Opera,* XI, 10).

[199] Lenz, I, 140.

[200] Rockwell, p. 41. Eberhard von der Thann, the electoral representative,
rode up the same morning (*ibid.*, pp. 42, 62).

[201] *Cf.* the "Landgrave's Confession to Bucer and Melanchthon" (Lenz,
I, 360).

[202] Lenz, I, 360, n. 1.

confession to Bucer, for he said, "after that I may hold it as secretly as I will and she will be satisfied."[203] Yet he had told Margaret through the person of her mother, that Bucer would find a way to give up secrecy, and the *hofmeisterin* had not been satisfied till she heard this.[204] Just as inconsistent was his further assurance, "as far as their request that the matter be kept secret is concerned, they need have no anxiety."[205] Evidently Bucer now heard for the first time of the consent of Philip's wife.[206] At two o'clock on the afternoon of Thursday, March 4, 1540, the marriage was performed by Melander,[207] in the presence of Melanchthon, Bucer, Eberhard von der Thann, certain Hessian counselors and theologians, and others.[208] The landgrave had no twinges of conscience, but was happier if anything.[209] In the presence of a notary he made out a marriage contract whose wording was unknown to Bucer,[210] and if, as there seems good reason to believe, he gave any advice as to the way in which it should be composed,[211] yet he was not intimately

[203] Lenz, I, 360.   [204] Rockwell, p. 318; Lenz, I, 354.
[205] Lenz, I, 360.

[206] *Ibid.*, p. 361; *cf.* Jacobs, p. 334. With Melanchthon, Bucer helped to persuade von der Thann of the propriety of the wedding (Rockwell, pp. 64, 68, n. 1).

[207] On the so-called wedding sermon of Melander, see Heppe, *op. cit.*, pp. 272-274; Köstlin, II, 469; and Janssen, III, 418. Each one of these writers gives to this opinion by Melander a different date. *Cf.* Rockwell, p. 43, n. 4.

[208] Rockwell, p. 42, ff.

[209] Lenz, I, 361; Hassencamp, I, 476; Rockwell, pp. 44-46. On the subsequent moral conduct of the landgrave see Köhler in *Die Christliche Welt*, Aug. 30, 1906, no. 35.

[210] Lenz, I, 194, 203; see below, p. 117. The text has been published also by Arcuarius and an English translation is given by Hook, III, 210-212.

[211] The landgrave wrote to Luther on July 18, 1540, that he would not acknowledge the marriage as an immoral relation, "wie ich dan auch nit gethan, wie das eur schrifften, und das instrument, das mit Philippi und Butzeri ratt und wissen gemacht, answeisset" (Lenz, I, 385; Enders, XIII, 129, and note 37).

acquainted with the contents of the document, and he may not have read it at the time.

So was brought to pass what has been fitly called "one of the most unhallowed incidents in the history of the Reformation."[212]

[212] E. F. Henderson, *A Short History of Germany*, I, 372.

CHAPTER V

THE EXPOSURE OF THE BIGAMY

Long before December, 1539, the landgrave had frequently discussed the permissibility of bigamy, and as a result rumors of his intention to take another wife had already begun to circulate[1] before Bucer returned from Wittenberg with a *Rathschlag* enjoining secrecy. On Christmas Day Bucer wrote him, begging that the matter be kept quiet, for at Marburg some devoted followers of the prince had hinted that they knew a great secret, and repeated a slanderous report that Philip would make some great innovation.[2] After the prince had gained what he sought, there would be time enough to reveal the matter to a few trusted persons, Bucer said. Then, as an antidote against suspicion, he recommended that the landgrave improve his government, adding, "it is truly high time that your princely grace should bestir himself to employ his great princely power earnestly in the Lord's service. Your princely grace has God-fearing people everywhere who will point out all that is needful and can also prescribe the right medicine. Your princely grace will consider this with all earnestness for it is truly of the highest importance. And especially your princely grace should confer with Henry von Luther, Master Adam, and other people of understanding, about how conditions and affairs in your principality might everywhere be improved. For truly, truly, gracious prince and lord, where there is a strong contempt for God and the

1 Rockwell, p. 49.
2 Lenz, I, 121.

government, there the devil is by that much mighty and
the people have no confidence in good things.' ''[3]

Soon after the wedding the landgrave sent to his sister
Elizabeth an announcement of what he had done,[4] with
the consequence that she flew into a violent fit of passion
and would listen to no one.[5] So boundless was her anger
and so long did it rage, that she disregarded all secrecy
and started several rumors of what had happened.[6] The
landgrave requested the elector to pacify her, but the
latter discreetly refused to play the rôle of peace-maker.[7]
Turning in his habitual way to Bucer for advice and assistance, Philip received from him a letter on March 18, only
five days after Hundelshausen's embassy, saying, ''Your
princely grace should seek comfort from the Lord on
account of his sister's anger, and try to force her with
no further arguments than that your princely grace is
her gracious brother, to whom she owes sisterly trust and
affection. . . . I will send, I will do, as a faithful servant
of the truth through God's grace; God knows how irk-
some the business has been on me, and how gladly I would
have turned your princely grace away from it. . . . If
evil words are spoken about me I am accustomed to them.
If they slander your princely grace, I know well that it
is said, 'let the other side be heard.' ''[8]

In a letter written the next day, March 19, 1540, the
landgrave instructed Bucer to write to Duchess Elizabeth
of Rochlitz; to ignore her accusations against Frau von
der Sale, because the *hofmeisterin* had refused him her
daughter until he showed her the *Rathschlag* of the
scholars; to say that if the landgrave could not have
secured Margaret, he could have had another beautiful

[3] Lenz, I, 121, ff.
[4] Rockwell, p. 50. It was delivered by Marshal Hundelshausen.
[5] Lenz, I, 335.   [6] Rockwell, p. 51.
[7] Lenz, I, 335.   [8] Lenz, I, 159.

and honorable young lady who had been offered him;[9] and to assure Elizabeth that no general innovation would be made by the bigamy. "If I would not allow it to remain secret for the sake of you scholars, then certainly I would make her no promises. I have no timidity about recognizing it openly. For I have done it before God with a good conscience. . . . It is on that account our gracious request that you show tireless diligence in quieting our sister's spirit as much as possible."[10]

Bucer's letter to the duchess was dated April 19, 1540, and was enclosed in a letter written to the landgrave on the same day.[11] Probably the reason why Bucer did not write sooner and directly to the duchess was because he knew of her anger against him, and judged it best to let it be assuaged by time. In a letter to Elizabeth, Bucer begged her to leave the matter in quietness; to pardon him; and to disbelieve the accusation that he and others had carried away many presents from Rothenburg, for he had received only one hundred gulden for his family in return for his many services.[12]

Meanwhile the news of the bigamy had been spreading, and in this letter of April 19, Bucer informed the landgrave that he had heard shortly before (at Hersfeld) of a public sermon in which Melander proclaimed that it was not wrong for a man to have two wives.[13] Although

[9] *Cf.* Lenz, I, 193.   [10] *Ibid.*, p. 160.   [11] Lenz, I, 168, n. 5, 335.

[12] *Ibid.*, p. 168, n. 5. 100 gulden was barely enough to pay Bucer's expenses, although it was more than equal to his yearly salary (*cf.* Rockwell, p. 44, n. 5; and see above, p. 19).

[13] Lenz, I, 166. Justus Jonas heard reports of such a sermon by Melander, as late as the middle of June, 1540 (G. Kawerau, *Der Briefwechsel der Justus Jonas*, I, 396). This report may have been caused by the sermon that Bucer heard in April, because Jonas reports that the landgrave also partook of the sacrament, which happened for the first time after the wedding on March 28 (deWette, VI, 258; Enders, XIII, 23, ff.; Rockwell, p. 44). But since the landgrave went to the sacrament again on May 16 (Enders, XIII, 23, ff., n. 5), the report which Jonas heard may have been caused by a later sermon, and in that case Bucer's advice was not heeded.

he promised to write to the Hessian preacher, Bucer also demanded support from the landgrave, for "Dionysius ought to think that he agreed at Rothenburg to keep this affair secret as a dispensation in the highest 'need of conscience.' Our church is yet too weak and is so overburdened by our infirmities, that each one should refrain above all from anything by which it may be slandered. Very few Christians can approve of the dispensation. Especially to the women must it be a pain to hear such words. Although your princely grace's sister may be of an excitable disposition, yet there is no doubt that among a thousand pious and kind women, not one may be found to whom it would not be mustard to hear such a dispensation." Fervently Bucer urged upon the landgrave the value of silence to curb the spreading rumors; the virtue of showing more affection for Christina; the need of a better government with the suppression of drunkenness and other evils; and the obligation incumbent upon him as a ruler to do more work and less hunting.[14]

So anxious was Luther to keep the affair secret, that he burned to ashes the letter in which the landgrave thanked him for his advice.[15] But without this there was no lack of fuel for the flames of rumor which mounted ever higher. About the middle of May Philip wrote to Bucer that he was afraid to go to the Diet for fear the secret of the bigamy would be disclosed, and he would be attacked on account of it.[16] Corvinus, a Hessian preacher who had signed the "Wittenberg Rathschlag," wrote to the landgrave on May 25, "a horrible report is spread abroad that your princely grace has taken another wife." He also

[14] Lenz, I, 166-167.
[15] Lenz, I, 361, n. 1; Köstlin, II, 514. The landgrave's letter, written on April 5, 1540, is also printed in Enders, XIII, 23. In his reply, April 10, 1540, Luther requested the landgrave to keep the matter secret (Enders, XIII, 30). In May the landgrave sent him a cask of wine (Enders, XIII, 67).
[16] Lenz, I, 171.

heard a rumor that the landgrave would send Luther a cask of wine,[17] and so he begged him to deny the slander. In order to preserve secrecy, he urged that the advice of Luther and Bucer be sought, and claimed that the building activities at Weissentein had aroused suspicion.[18] In the last part of May, Anton Lauterbach wrote to Luther for further information about some rumors which he had heard, but received an evasive answer.[19] When Duke Henry of Saxony heard of it, he began to fear complications in the Hessian claim on the Saxon inheritance, and to secure definite information he arrested Frau von der Sale. From her glib and willing tongue he learned what had occurred and also secured copies of some of the documents, including the *Argumenta Buceri pro et contra*.[20] Naturally, Duke Henry did not keep the secret, and during the month of June the report of the landgrave's bigamy was widely circulated. Duke Maurice heard of it in the first part of June,[21] as did also Christopher von Ebleben[22] and Justus Jonas.[23]

Out of this rumble of rumors one came to Bucer's ears which he reported to the landgrave on June 15.[24] "Your princely grace's other affair is unfortunately so greatly exposed, and is everywhere so openly discussed, especially at the court of Mainz, that it is a great trial to all your friends.[25] John von Hulich has said to Margrave Ernst

[17] *Cf.* Enders, XIII, 67.

[18] P. Tschackert, *Briefwechsel des Antonius Corvinus,* p. 79, ff.

[19] Enders, XIII, 72; deWette, V, 290; Rockwell, p. 55. On other rumors see Lenz, I, 336, n. 1; Rockwell, p. 50, ff.

[20] Rockwell, pp. 52-53; Lenz, I, 338.

[21] Lenz, I, 367; Rockwell, p. 54.

[22] Rockwell, p. 58.

[23] Justus Jonas wrote to Prince George of Anhalt on June 9, 1540, and showed considerable knowledge of the secret. *Cf.* Kawerau, I, 392, 395, 396, 397, II, 82. One source of his information was a report spread by the Abbot of Fulda (*ibid.,* I, 396).

[24] Lenz, I, 174.   [25] *Cf.* Rockwell, p. 59, n. 4.

of Pfortzen [Pfortzheim] that two of the nobles have
written to him, and told in such a confidential manner,
when the thing happened, who was present, etc., that, if
there was nothing in it, it must be the greatest lie he had
ever heard.''[26] For the sake of the church and the "bitter
sufferings and death of our Lord Jesus," Bucer begged
him to exert himself actively to keep it secret. Again he
recommended that Philip show more affection for Christina, punish the insolent prattlers in his land, and appoint
one or two counselors to defend his deeds with writings.[27]
In another letter, written seven days later from Strasbourg, he repeated the request that whoever was telling
the secret should be quieted.[28] But this it was no longer
possible for the landgrave to do, and during July the
rumors spread to France, England, the emperor, and even
to the ears of the curia in Rome.[29]

When Philip heard of the arrest of Frau von der Sale,
he excitedly wrote a number of letters trying to remedy
matters.[30] This they failed to do and his condition became
even more unpleasant when he received from Melanchthon a new opinion unfavorable to bigamy,[31] and a letter
from the elector on June 20, which afforded him little
satisfaction.[32] On June 22, 1540, the chief Hessian theologians gathered at Cassel with Chancellor Feige to talk
over the situation and what could be done. Holding fast
to the requirement of secrecy they recommended that any
further legal inquiries should be evaded with ambiguous
expressions, such as calling Margaret a concubine, since
in the Old Testament such concubines had been wives.[33]

26 Lenz, I, 174.　　　　　27 Ibid.
28 Ibid., p. 175.　　　　　29 Rockwell, p. 60.
30 Ibid., p. 67. On June 9, 1540, he wrote to Luther asking him to restrain
Duke Henry (Enders, XIII, 75).
31 Rockwell, p. 61. It was sent on June 15. Cf. below, p. 179.
32 Rockwell, p. 69. On the elector's attitude, see below, p. 134, ff.
33 Rockwell, p. 70.

Luther and Melanchthon they requested to stand by their *Rathschlag*,[34] and also wrote a letter to Bucer on June 23, in which they asked him whether certain of the nobility and magistrates should be taken into their confidence, and if he would influence the Würtembergers and Swiss so that in case of an open defense of the bigamy they would not attack it with tongue or pen.[35] Bucer, who regarded secrecy as vitally important, did not agree to any kind of public defense, and Feige said of his answer, "It read sour to me, and besides I could not completely understand it. I am sending it to your princely grace, since the illegibility of certain words prevents me from making a satisfactory copy."[36]

Not only did the landgrave fail to preserve secrecy, he now expressed himself willing to acknowledge the bigamy publicly, if Luther would stand back of him.[37] In fact, Philip had always looked forward to a time of publication, and the wedding itself would be more accurately described as private than secret.[38] Had it not been for the open offence, so he said, he would have acknowledged the "Wittenberg Rathschlag" in the first part of the summer of 1540.[39] Perhaps he was also restrained by the unencouraging attitude of Luther and the elector, but the fact remains that as far as the landgrave's conscience was concerned, he did not dread publication. More accustomed to autocratic despotism than to ascetic self-examination, he easily exalted his conscience into an unquestionable authority.

From numerous statements it appears that the land-

[34] Enders, XIII, 98.   [35] Printed by Rockwell, p. 322.

[36] Lenz, I, 378, n. 3. Evidently the chancellor found Bucer's notoriously bad hand-writing difficult to read (*cf.* facsimile in Ficker and Winckelmann, I, 58).

[37] Rockwell, pp. 69, 77.

[38] W. Walker, *A History of the Christian Church*, p. 377.

[39] Lenz, I, 181.

grave was proud rather than ashamed of what he had
done. After the wedding he said, "I have done it with
God and a good conscience, and do not doubt I have not
done wrong before God."[40] And in December, 1540, he
declared that he could not forbid bigamy to his subjects,
"for if the dispensation was correct, it was valid not for
him alone, and he could therefore not forbid it with a
good conscience."[41] It is quite clear that not only did the
landgrave's desire to acknowledge the bigamy openly
become continually stronger and stronger, but his confidence in the infallibility of his tender conscience
mounted so high that he placed it above the authority of
all public opinion and scholarly advice, fearing only the
physical punishment for his crime.

With the exposure of the bigamy by well-founded
rumors, the affair entered upon a second phase in which
the landgrave sought protection against the possible
imperial prosecution for his deed, and the reformers
advised various precautionary measures to preserve the
veil of secrecy. It was Bucer's conduct at this time which
is most discreditable. From Hagenau, where he was attending a religious colloquy, he wrote four letters to the
landgrave during July, which contain his chief suggestions for preserving secrecy.[42]

In general, Bucer suggested that the landgrave could
improve his situation and win the favor of the public by
a better conduct of his government. Reminding the nobleman that although he had always been trustworthy in
public matters, yet he had often neglected his people, he
urged him to give less time to hunting and other amusements, while devoting himself more actively to petitions,

[40] March 19, 1540 (Lenz, I, 160).   [41] *Ibid.*, p. 272.
[42] Bucer went to Hagenau about June 23, 1540 (*Politische Correspondenz
. . . Strassbourg*, III, 67). For an "important reason" Philip did not go
to Hagenau (*ibid.*, p. 173). This reason was evidently the bigamy.

judicial cases, the oversight of officials, and the details of government business. In undertaking such a reform he counseled him to seek the advice of Feige, Nordeck, Lerschner, and other nobles.[43]

Bucer suggested four methods by which the landgrave might take precautions against the exposure of the bigamy. First, he should guard the secret by hiding Margaret in a secluded place, and demanding that her relatives and those who were telling of the marriage should keep quiet. Particularly against the wagging tongues of his sister and Duke Henry of Saxony did he warn the prince, suggesting that the latter might be induced to say that it was only a matter of concubinage.[44] Secondly, it seemed to the reformer that it would be well for Philip to confide in some of his most trusted noblemen, explaining to them that the desire for a clear conscience had driven him to the act. This might be done by sending to them a private writing, declaring that whoever said he had broken the imperial law, and had taken a bigamous wife, lied falsely; for he had not forsaken God, and believed that the restoration of monogamy was an "ornament" of Christianity which should not be lost, and he begged the prince receiving the writing not to believe the report against him.[45]

Bucer's third suggestion was a most curious one. The landgrave should enter into a new contract with the "Person," by which all previous contracts would be nullified, and according to which she would be a concubine such as God had granted to the patriarchs. By such an action the landgrave would be no longer liable to prosecution under the existing laws, which only forbade the having of two wives with equal rights, and not the having of one wife and one concubine. Philip's conscience need

[43] Lenz, I, 176.   [44] Lenz, I, 175.
[45] *Ibid.*, p. 179, ff.

present no obstacle, Bucer thought, "for that the rights of the Person would remain uncurtailed, your princely grace could well see to that."[46] Thus the landgrave would treat Margaret legally as a concubine, but actually as a bigamous wife. Fourthly, Bucer advised the prince to tell a lie. But, in order to soften the harshness of this sugges- tion, he described it as a "holy lie," and referred Philip to various examples in the Bible, particularly to those of Abraham, who said his wife was his sister, and of Paul, who declared he was called into question on account of the resurrection. The reformer stated explicitly that he did not want to make *no* out of *yes,* but only to conceal the *yes* from the world in accordance with examples in the Scriptures. Instead of *lie* he used such terms as *Verschweigen* and *abwenden,* and said that even God himself had protected his people by putting their enemies on the wrong track. In further defense of such advice, he argued that there were three distinct varieties of wives, "ein gleich gemahel, ein zugemahel nach dem gesetz, ein gehulff nach dem gewissen vor Gott und einigen zeugen des gewissens. Weil nun ich allein das erst hab gerathen zu verneinen sein und das dritte allein war ist, was lugen habe ich gerathen?"[47] But by far his most conclusive argument was that the landgrave had already told such a lie at Melsungen, when he said he had no definite person in mind to marry.[48]

Not only did Bucer assist the landgrave with good ad- vice, he also tried to help him with deeds. With various theologians, among them Brenz, Osiander, Schnepf, and Blaurer, he discussed the matter and tried to gain from them a favorable attitude. He found many who not only refused to defend the landgrave, but were even ready to take the opposite side because of the offence an open

---

[46] Lenz, I, 178, ff.   [47] *Ibid.,* p. 193.
[48] *Ibid.,* pp. 176-180, 192-196.

defense of bigamy would give to the Church.[49] Bucer's letters were characterized above all by frankness, and he declared that although Philip might be angry at him, yet on that account he would hold nothing as true or untrue, right or wrong.[50]

The landgrave did not receive Bucer's advice favorably. Thoroughly confident in the righteousness of his act, and finding that he had much persecution to meet, he declared that the affair was not "without" but "with" God, because "just affairs are commonly persecuted."[51] He admitted the need for an improvement in his government, but pointed out to the reformer the practical difficulties involved in applying the reform he had proposed.[52] Such a writing to the nobility as Bucer suggested, should be withheld, he thought, until Duke Henry of Brunswick attacked him on account of the affair, but meanwhile the reformer might send him suggestions for its composition.[53] The rest of Bucer's advice he rejected as unworthy of him. He refused to annul the marriage-contract with Margaret, for that would be dishonorable, and Margaret and her relatives would never agree to it. Moreover, he sent Bucer a copy of the first contract, whose wording he thought was not contrary to the law.[54] The advice to tell a lie angered Philip. Though willing to give an ambiguous answer, implying that Margaret was a concubine, he refused to deny openly his relationship with her. "For lying does no one any good, and besides God has forbidden false-witness."[55] In order to elicit more definite assurances of support from Bucer, he resorted to threats, declaring that if his own allies would not help him, he would seek aid from the emperor or pope in temporal affairs,

[49] Lenz, I, 177.
[50] Ibid., p. 196.
[51] Ibid., p. 181.
[52] Ibid., p. 182, ff.
[53] Ibid., p. 202.
[54] Lenz, I, 186, 203.
[55] Ibid., p. 183.

although he would not fall away from the true religion.[56] His phenomenal conscience peacefully contemplated laying before "his imperial majesty what moved us to it, what was answered us by you, the scholars, what was preached and taught by Luther . . . and also with what words and in what manner we were advised by you, the theologians, against seeking the consent of the emperor."[57] One of his most terrible threats was to allow a general introduction of bigamy, for he said, "We will not dispute at this time, if it may be considered an indifferent matter and a general usage or not, for we leave that to you, the learned in your knowledge. Yet if anyone falls into the same lack, we would not hesitate to countenance a similar permission in his case."[58]

So Bucer's advice to the landgrave had little effect. He refused to give the prince the desired assurances of open support, and the latter in turn declined the suggestions offered him to prevent an exposure of the secret. Their interests were opposed: Bucer wanted the matter hushed up and cared little about the vindication of the validity of the marriage. But this validity was essential to the landgrave, and rather than forego it he welcomed complete exposure of the secret. He was not seeking secrecy so much as safety. Bucer saw safety in secrecy alone.

Meanwhile there had taken place at Eisenach, on July 15-20, 1540, the famous Eisenach Conference between Hessian and Saxon representatives, to answer the question whether, in case of necessity, the landgrave could count on the help of the Saxons. The landgrave had called the conference on July 3, and soon afterwards Luther had started with Melanchthon.[59] On the way Melanchthon was taken seriously ill at Weimar, and had it not been for the encouragement Luther brought him, it is probable that

---

[56] *Ibid.*, p. 204.   [57] *Ibid.*, p. 187, ff.
[58] *Ibid.*, p. 203, ff.   [59] Rockwell, p. 170.

he would have died.[60] Though the immediate cause of his sickness was "remorse over the part which he and Luther had taken in the bigamy of Philip of Hesse,"[61] the landgrave claimed that it was not so much remorse itself which afflicted Melanchthon, as the reproachful complaints of the elector.[62] This hypothesis Bucer advised him not to advance actively as if he would question the causes of Philip's sickness, especially among the Saxons.[63]

To his envoys the landgrave gave written instructions that he would in no way recognize the affair as "adultery or fornication," and repeated the assertion, "We do not intend to lie about the matter."[64] The Hessians feared prosecution by the emperor, the Saxons feared the publication of the "Wittenberg Rathschlag" and an open defense of the bigamy. Having opened with a speech by Luther,[65] the conference lasted throughout four days of hot discussion and some recrimination until July 20. The result was very unsatisfactory to the landgrave, for Luther and the electoral representatives agreed in demanding that the *status quo* be maintained. Asserting that the landgrave ought to hold by the "Wittenberg Rathschlag," and attempt no open defense of the affair, thus changing it from a question of fact to a question of law, they recommended that imperial prosecution might be forestalled by a "strong denial," ambiguous forms of reply, closer attachment to Christina, and the concealment of the marriage-contract in a safe hiding-place.[66]

This opinion, agreeing in principle with Bucer's advice, was not satisfying to the landgrave, who, feeling that

[60] Köstlin, II, 515, ff.

[61] Richard, p. 274.

[62] Lenz, I, 205.

[63] Lenz, I, 209. Melanchthon's place at the conference was taken by Amsdorf (Rockwell, p. 170).   [64] Lenz, I, 369.

[65] *Ibid.*, p. 372, ff.   [66] Enders, XIII, 134-137.

secrecy was no longer possible, and a public attack upon himself was to be expected soon, wanted definite assurances of open support. While he did not forsake the evangelical party, he could not fail to perceive that an agreement with them in this affair was impossible, and that a definite assurance against legal prosecution could only be secured from the emperor. What had before been a threat, now became a plan of action, and from this moment Philip drew further away from his religious allies and nearer to Charles V.

In view of certain inconsistencies in his conduct, the landgrave's refusal to lie is somewhat puzzling and not entirely to his credit, as it might seem to be. Bucer, as observed, advised him to tell such a lie as Abraham, or Rahab, or many other "saints" in the Bible had told, for these, he said, were holy lies and justified by their purpose to deceive the enemies of God.[67] The landgrave asserted in reply that he could not tell such a lie as Abraham, for Abraham's wife was actually his sister. "But to say, if the affair becomes exposed, that the thing is nothing, that we cannot well do, for we do not intend to lie. For lying does no one any good: also God has forbidden lying. So long as it is possible, we are quite willing to answer in a dubitative and ambiguous way, but to say that it is nothing, that should be advised to another and not to us."[68] Most emphatically he repeated, "We can and will not lie, for lying does no one any good, also God has forbidden it."[69]

But within a couple of weeks his position seems to have changed a little for on July 24 he said, "In this affair we might well tell such a lie as you in your latest writings

---

[67] Lenz, I, 193.　　　　　　　　[68] *Ibid.*, p. 183.

[69] *Ibid.*, p. 185. These two statements agreed with the instructions he gave to his counselors at Eisenach that he did not know how to lie in this affair.

have proposed to us, although we are not yet fully decided about it. But Luther desires, as you will see from the enclosed copy, a strong lie, which for all kinds of reasons is objectionable.''[70] It appears that the landgrave had changed his attitude a little on the matter, and this supposition is supported by the fact that his conduct was often calculated to deceive, and was inconsistent with any claim to strict personal honor. It was for reasons of policy more than of morals that he objected to telling a lie.

For example, he had deceived his sister in order to get Margaret away from her court in February, 1540.[71] At Melsungen he had misled Bucer, giving him to understand that he had no particular person in mind, when, as a matter of fact, he had.[72] Although the thought of breaking his marriage-contract with Margaret was repulsive to him, his desire to marry her had made it easy for him to violate his marriage vow to Christina, and demand her permission to commit bigamy. That she gave her permission would hardly excuse his conduct, especially in view of the fact that it was somewhat, if not entirely, gained by force.[73] In addition to these cases in which the landgrave transgressed the demands of personal honor, he also declared himself ready to do things equally dishonorable. The ''Wittenberg Rathschlag'' had been submitted to him as confidential advice, to say the least, and Philip himself had recognized it as given in the confessional.[74] He declared to Bucer and Melanchthon at Rothenburg that Margaret was willing to have the affair kept secret,[75] and ''as far as their demand for secrecy was concerned, they need have no anxiety.'' As a

[70] Lenz, I, 202. This was in reply to Bucer's letter of July 18 (Lenz, I, 201; cf. ibid., p. 192, ff.), in which Bucer stated more fully the kind of lie he desired.

[71] Lenz, I, 332; cf. Köhler, op. cit., p. 397.

[72] Lenz, I, 193, 354. [73] Rockwell, p. 31, ff.

[74] Lenz, I, 304. [75] Ibid., p. 360.

man of honor he should have kept confidential the advice which the Wittenbergers gave him, and yet he had hardly received it before he sent it to Frau von der Sale, and within a month after the wedding he had revealed the affair to enough people to violate any promise of secrecy. Worse than that, he threatened to publish the "Wittenberg Rathschlag,"[76] which he had no right to do, and even to tell Charles V what the reformers had said in confidence against him.[77] Again, he had promised not to start any propaganda or institute a following,[78] and yet on July 24, 1540, he wrote to Bucer that he could not deny this remedy to anyone who wished it.[79] Even more boldly he asserted in the following December that he could not forbid bigamy to his subjects, for if the dispensation was right, it was valid not for him alone, but for all those who did not have a good conscience.[80]

Though the landgrave may not have been willing to tell a lie "in this case," he was quite ready to deceive his opponents, for in his *Dritte Wahrhafftige Verantwortung* to Duke Henry of Brunswick, published in March, 1541,[81] he said he had not contracted "an unchristian marriage— for although, to be sure, we are a poor, imperfect Christian and sinner . . . still we stand in our conscience and faith before God and firmly hope to remain by him, so that our conscience judges us not to be unchristian."[82] He knew that his readers would understand by a "Christian

---

[76] *Ibid.*, pp. 182, 187, 381.   [77] See above, p. 118.

[78] Lenz, I, 360. *Cf.* the landgrave to Luther, July 18, 1540, "Item das ich woldt ein nug recht ader gewohnheit in die weldt bringen, ist mein meinung auch nit, sunder will es ein dispensation bleiben lassen" (Lenz, I, 383). *Cf.* the landgrave to Bucer, Mar. 19, 1540 (Lenz, I, 160).

[79] Lenz, I, 203, ff.

[80] *Ibid.*, p. 272.

[81] A. Dommer, *Die Aeltesten Drucke aus Marburg in Hessen*, no. 135.

[82] F. Hortleder, *Von den Ursachen des Teutschen Kriegs*, Bh. IV, Kap. 19, no. 35, p. 516. F. Koldewey, "Der Erste Versuch einer Rechtfertigung der Bigamie," *Theologische Studien und Kritiken*, LVII, 555, ff.

marriage" only monogamy, while he regarded bigamy as also Christian. It is doubtful if this statement deceived anyone, but it was certainly intended to do so.

Consequently, although the landgrave may not have been willing to tell "ein starcke lugen," it is plain that he was quite ready to deceive. Had his personal honor been the reason for his attitude, he would not have been so willing to tell what was actually a lie, so long as it was not an out and out lie. The cause of his unwillingness to tell a "straight lie" was his relation to Margaret and her relatives. First, his love for Margaret made him unwilling to deny that he had actually been married to her.[83] Secondly, he realized that it was impossible for him to tell such a lie and not be convicted of falsehood, because her relatives possessed abundant evidence of the truth.[84] No doubt the landgrave felt himself in honor bound to keep the contract he had made with Margaret, but it would have been possible for him to have done this privately, as Bucer suggested, and have denied his relation publicly, if he had not been hindered from adopting this solution of his difficulties by other, more influential reasons. According to the most charitable judgment, he could hardly lay claim consistently to a high sense of personal honor,[85] when he was willing to violate its demands on many occasions. The only honor which he had a right to claim was of a technical and superficial variety, for, as Bucer said, he daily made use of such lies as the Strasbourg reformer advised,[86] and so could not object to the advice as unfitting for him.

That Bucer was perfectly sincere in the counsel he gave to the landgrave for keeping the bigamy secret, is apparent from the fact that he acted consistently with this

[83] Lenz, I, 182-183. Yet he said she would bear the shame (Lenz, I, 194).
[84] Lenz, I, 186, 203.
[85] *Cf. ibid.*, p. 186.
[86] *Ibid.*, p. 193.

advice when he himself was questioned on the matter. This is illustrated by what may be termed the Memmingen episode. During the late summer of 1540, probably in August, Gervasius Schuler, a preacher of Memmingen, wrote a private letter to Bucer, referring in passing to the rumors about the bigamy. Whether he asked for more information is not clear but seems probable.[87] Bucer's answer did not satisfy the preachers of Memmingen to whom Schuler showed it, and they were particularly displeased because he said so little about the permission of a concubine. Unfortunately, this letter is lost, but the indications are that he wanted to pass over the matter as lightly as possible.[88] Schuler would not let himself be put off with any such evasive reply. He wrote a stormy letter to Bucer, demanding an out and out statement, whether the rumor was true, that he, Luther, Melanchthon, and certain Hessian clergymen had counseled the landgrave to take a concubine, and defended the deed in a "writing of 66 pages."[89]

To this inquiry Bucer replied on September 19 in a long letter which is of first-rate importance for an understanding of his attitude toward the bigamy.[90] Offended that they were not satisfied with his former letter, which he

[87] This letter is lost but is referred to in a letter from the Memmingers to Bucer, Sept. 23, 1540, Thesaurus Baumianus, XII, 188.

[88] *Ibid.;* Bucer to the Memmingers, Sept. 19, 1540, *CR.,* X, 156.

[89] This letter is missing but is referred to in a letter from the Memmingers to Bucer, Sept. 23, 1540, Thesaurus Baumianus, XII, 188.

[90] Printed in the *CR.,* II, 156-161. A copy, used by Bretschneider, is to be found in the Strasbourg Archives, XX, Schrif. Bucer's, II, 8. There is a note in the margin of the first page of this copy which reads, "Vide Epistolam ad Blaur. 1541, 2 Nowb. & alibi." Another note in the same place refers to "Der CXX Psalm pag. iii," while still another note at the top of the page reads, "Jac. Clerbig misit nobis." The copy is written in a beautiful and regular hand. The postcript at the end has been crossed out with a red crayon and a note added in the margin, "alibi expressi." The correct date is not March, 1541 (*CR.,* X, 156) but Sept. 19, 1540 (Thesaurus Baumianus, XII, 188).

thought should have been sufficient for those, knowing his faithfulness, seeking to avoid offence to the church, and desiring to overlook the faults of others, he said explicitly, "I declare to you in the presence of God, neither I, nor Luther, nor Philip, nor so far as I know, any Hessian preacher of this prince has given any such counsel or taught it is permissible for Christians to have a concubine while married, or undertaken to defend such a teaching. Nor have I ever understood that this prince has tried to introduce that dogma into the church either by deed or word." But if the landgrave had done any such thing Bucer preferred to pass over the offence rather than make it greater, holding that a Christian man should not inquire into the sin of another, unless to afford a remedy, and especially in the case of such an illustrious prince who had done so much for the cause of the gospel. "When thus I do not see what remedy for this evil, if any is admitted, you either wish or can offer," he asserted, "I ought to turn you aside from that investigation; not lead you into it. Thus I wrote what I knew to be true, the prince has in no way done anything of that sort which the enemies of the gospel tell about him. You wish to warn me of sinister stories spread about me, I thank you, and I think you have now done your duty, and if I could do anything without fear of greater offence, now openly I would clear myself. Concerning the writing which is said to be of 66 pages, if you have anything certain, see to it that you may secure a copy of that writing and send it to me; if it shall be mine, I will by no means deny it. But that I may refute that charge: truly I have written and subscribed nothing."[91]

[91] In speaking of the *Dialogus Neobuli* (see below, chapter VII) Paulus has said, "Recht bezeichnend ist ein bisher wenig beachtetes Schreiben, das er [Bucer] im Jahre 1541 an die Prediger von Memmingen gerichtet hat. In ganz Süd-deutschland wurde er damals als Vertheidiger der Vielweiberei verschreien, auch wurde ihm ein Dialog in welchem ein gewisser Neobulus die

So much Bucer said in reply to the inquiry of the Memmingers, and then went on to state his own opinion on the
question of bigamy—an opinion identical with that expressed in the *Argumenta Buceri pro et contra*. His chief
arguments were as follows:

Monogamy has been re-instituted by God, and the dispensation of polygamy granted to the patriarchs has not
been repeated for Christians. Christians should obey
every human law which is not evil. But if anyone today
avails himself of the dispensation granted to the Ancients,
and hides his action on account of the offence to the
church, assured by his conscience that he is right, and does
not attempt to institute a following, he may not be condemned because: there is no clear word of God to condemn

Polygamie in Schutz nahm, zugeschrieben'' (N. Paulus, ''Die Hessische
Doppelehe im Urteile der protestantischen Zeitgenossen,'' *Historisch-
politische Blätter*, 1911, CXLVII, 503, ff.) Paulus, who accepts the date
given by Bretschneider without question, because he knows nothing of
the Memmingen episode except the letter from Bucer to the Memmingers,
is evidently ignorant of the fact that the *Dialogus Neobuli* was not
even known to Bucer himself until a month after that date at the earliest,
and not given out to the public until six months later (see below, pp.
163-164). For many reasons the letter cannot refer to this *Dialogue;* the
letter was written in Sept., 1540, and the *Dialogue* was not seen by Bucer
until April, 1541; the *Dialogue* was a printed book with a name and had
about 200 pages, not ''66.'' So the letter to the Memmingen preachers and
the *Dialogus Neobuli* did not come at the same time, but the letter was
written long before the *Dialogue* appeared. Paulus then goes on to say that
in spite of the fact that Bucer wrote the *Argumenta Buceri pro et contra*
and another little book at Regensburg, and amended the *Dialogus Neobuli,*
''Dies alles hinderte ihn nicht in seinem Schreiben an die Prediger von
Memmingen zu erklaren, er habe nie zu Verteidigung der Doppelehe etwas
geschrieben oder unterzeichnet'' (*op. cit.*, p. 511). But since the *Dialogue*
and the little book written at Regensburg (see below, p. 151) were unknown to Bucer until long after he wrote this letter, even on the date
accepted by Paulus, it is rather unreasonable to charge him with dishonesty
for not acknowledging them. And since the *Argumenta Buceri pro et contra*
was written probably before Bucer had even discussed bigamy with the
landgrave, it can hardly be said to have been written in defense of something which happened three months later, especially since it was never
published nor intended to be (see note in the ''Cod. Palat.,'' *CR.*, III, 850;

bigamy;[92] Christ may use bigamy as a means of salvation; Leo and Ambrose did not condemn bigamy in others than church servants; Christ recalled marriage to its first institution but he did not abolish the dispensation of divorce for hardness of heart, and so also neither did he abolish polygamy;[93] and it is far more important to attack those princes and priests who are real enemies of the church, and to root out known evils, clearly condemned by the Scriptures, such as fornication and usury, and to restore true discipline, true communion of believers, true prayers, true ordination, etc.

For these reasons Bucer asked the pastors of Memmingen to suspend judgment in uncertain things. As for himself, he had indeed discussed the permissibility of a man using today the dispensation of polygamy granted to the patriarchs, if he did it secretly, and without asserting a new dogma; and had come to the same conclusion which Luther reached in his commentary on Genesis, that such a man could not be condemned.[94]

The importance of this letter from Bucer to the pastors

---

cf. Rockwell, p. 226. If it was published, Bucer did not want it to be issued in German, the language of the common people, but in Latin, the language of the scholars, so that it would not be interpreted as a defense of the bigamy, but the submission of a topic for debate). Besides, the *Argumenta Buceri* does not defend anybody, or anyone's deeds, but only states Bucer's opinion about the permissibility of bigamy. Moreover, Paulus misuses Bucer's statement to the Memmingers in which Bucer does not mention "der Doppelehe" but uses far more indefinite language and says, "Quod defendam istud faciamus, equidem nullum (scriptum) scripsi aut subscripsi" (*CR.*, X, 157).

The writing of "66" pages referred to, may have been the *Argumenta Buceri* or the "Wittenberg Rathschlag," or, more likely, a fabulous document which the Memmingers had never seen but knew only by rumor. The *Argumenta Buceri* is written on what according to the old-fashioned method of reckoning would be 96 leaves of paper.

[92] I.e., for laymen. Bucer held that bigamy was forbidden to clergymen by I Timothy III: 2 (*Scripta Duo Adversaria D. Barth. Latomi*, etc., p. 76, ff.).

[93] In Matthew XIX; *cf.* above, p. 22, ff.

[94] *CR.*, X, 161.

of Memmingen lies not in the opinion which he expressed
about bigamy, for that is only a summary of what he had
already said in the *Argumenta Buceri pro et contra,* but
in the light which it throws upon his conduct in preserving
the secrecy of the bigamy. In replying to a direct inquiry
whether the rumors about the affair and his part in it were
true, he used ambiguous language, which, though it may
be explained in such a way as to show that he was telling
the truth, was yet intended to deceive and mislead.
Though not a direct lie, it was just as dishonest, and followed out the advice which he had given to the landgrave.
For instance, Bucer said, "neither I nor Luther, nor
Philip, nor so far as I know, any Hessian counselor of
the prince, has ever given any such counsel or undertaken
to defend it.'"[95] In one sense this was true, because Bucer,
Luther, and Melanchthon all advised the landgrave not
to commit bigamy. In another sense it was not true, because they had given their opinion that it was Scriptural
and right for him to do it, if his conscience assured him
that he could not contain himself with one wife. Because
the Memmingers referred to an ostensible defense, for
which specific purpose Bucer and the others had written no
books, it is true, in one sense, that they did not undertake
a defense of the landgrave's bigamy. In another sense it
is not true, because Bucer discussed with others the permissibility of such an action as he knew the landgrave
had undertaken, with the purpose of winning a favorable
opinion toward it,[96] and besides they had defended it to
his conscience. Moreover, in this very letter Bucer resorts
to the use of the word *concubine* in an ambiguous and
confusing way, so that it is hard to know whether he
refers to a bigamous wife or a mistress.

In brief, Bucer met a direct inquiry as to the truth of
the bigamy-scandal and his part in it, with three methods

[95] *Ibid.,* p. 156.   [96] *CR.,* X, 158, ff.

of defense. First, he used ambiguous language to remove the suspicion that anything had actually been done, and to counteract the abhorrence and prejudice aroused by the deed. Thus he prepared the way for an open-minded attitude of impartial consideration, and transferred the problem from the realm of action into the realm of thought. Secondly, he discussed the theory of the permissibility of bigamy so as to put it in the best light, trying to remove the chief objections of the offence it would cause, and the danger of a general innovation. This he submitted as a question for discussion on the basis of the Scriptures. Thirdly, he recommended suspension of judgment together with a severer treatment of known evils, and a restoration of strict discipline, while reminding them of the landgrave's virtues and services to the church.

Bucer's letter to the Memmingers had the desired effect. They apologized most sincerely for Schuler's stormy epistle, whose contents he had not disclosed to them until after it had been sent. Quite candidly they admitted that the tone of the letter had been sharp but asked the Strasbourg reformer to remember that it was a very serious matter and they had not acted maliciously but simply unknowingly. The harm that the enemies of the gospel might do in case they could so defame him, must be considered. They assured him that his reply had fully persuaded them of his innocence, and they did not fail to remember what a blessing he was to the church, and his many labors in the Lord's vineyard. Finally, they said that they would obey his admonitions to brotherly forbearance and would do their best to stop rumors instead of spreading them.[97] Undoubtedly, this result was due as much to Bucer's prestige as to his method of argument, but the whole episode shows what wonderful tact and skill he displayed in handling such delicate situations, and

[97] Memmingers to Bucer, Sept. 23, 1540, Thesaurus Baumianus, XII, 188.

it is only to be regretted that his conduct in this case was not more commendable.

A very different method of defense was employed by the reformer in a letter which he wrote to his intimate friend Ambrose Blaurer in March, 1542. Blaurer had already been approached about his opinion[98] on the permissibility of bigamy, and without any attempt at concealment Bucer gave a candid explanation of his own attitude. He wrote as follows, "I am not able to condemn him, [i.e., the landgrave] from fellowship in the kingdom of God, after he swears that by this means alone he can escape condemnation—Nemo scortator, impurus, proximos defraudans, convivitator etc. habet partem in regno dei—in truth there are those today to whom that also is permitted, which was permitted to all patriarchs: I do not wish to argue the matter. We permitted him nothing except the assurance that he is not excluded from the kingdom of God, when he swears that by this means alone he can escape from that which would keep him outside the kingdom of God, and meanwhile is upheld by that permission of the Lord in good confidence in his grace. So that in truth he could not be condemned by the church, but if he would guard against the offence caused by his deed and the imitation of it, we were rightly encouraged to assure him that it seemed to us he should not doubt the grace of God. For no one ought to live in an evil conscience, and no one is able to live perfectly. If there is anyone who has tried to avoid both the deed and the writing, and with reasons which seemed most efficacious to me among all the sons of God, that we are all of the church, and our possessions and ourselves should be wholly devoted to it, lest in anything we give offence and injure the gospel of Christ, I certainly am he; Christ knows this

98 Bucer asked him to come to Worms to talk over the bigamy (Schiess, II, 57; cf. Lenz, I, 197, II, 53).

and whoever is connected with the business. I could not make him have such an evil conscience, or condemn him from the communion of Christ, when he said it was necessary for him to use the permission given to the patriarchs. As to other disputations, why it was permitted to the patriarchs and whether for similar reasons it may now be permitted to anyone, I wish no action to be taken, or only to cover all with a mantle of secrecy without offence and injury.''[99]

In this letter Bucer used an entirely different method. He was writing to a trusted friend and so he told candidly what sort of permission he gave to the landgrave; what were his motives; and, without discussing the Scriptural arguments for bigamy, relied upon the confidence of his friend. No statement from Bucer's pen exists, in which he tells more sincerely and plainly what he did and why. It is evident from this letter that he gave only a negative consent; and that he gave it because of a pastoral interest in the prince, since he could find no condemnation of polygamy in the Bible. He tried his best to avoid what came to pass, and opposed any attempt to spread propaganda in favor of the bigamy.

[99] Schiess, II, 106.

CHAPTER VI

THE LANDGRAVE'S AGREEMENT WITH THE EMPEROR

The Eisenach Conference was a turning-point in the history of the bigamy. The landgrave had sought for help from his religious allies and the Protestant theologians. The conditions upon which they offered assistance were unsatisfactory: he rejected them. The only way left for him to gain safety was to secure from the emperor an assurance that he would not be prosecuted for his deed. But before he actually resorted to this solution, he tried once more by personal correspondence to procure from the Saxons a more favorable reply to his demands.

Before the conference at Eisenach had terminated, the landgrave wrote to Luther, remonstrating against the attitude of his second speech. He repeated all his arguments for bigamy, begged Luther to uphold the "Wittenberg Rathschlag," and refused to tell a lie.[1] But the Wittenberg reformer refused to yield an inch. Neither had he counseled a public bigamy nor did he intend to do so, and asserted that Philip must continue to give an ambiguous answer, not recognizing Margaret before the world as married to him. Moreover, Luther threatened that if the landgrave started a controversy he would have reason to regret it.[2] Full well the prince knew the controversial powers of the man who had crossed swords with the pope and his emissaries, yet he could not refrain from replying angrily, "From the world we do not demand

[1] Enders, XIII, 122-132.　　　　[2] *Ibid.*, pp. 141-145.

any declaration of their attitude toward Margaret, but
we consider her our wife through God's Word and your
advice: God grant that the world may so regard the wives
of preachers in ours, yours, and other's lands.''[3] This
was as much as to say that many people regarded
Luther's wife as no more married than Margaret, and
that since the legitimacy of clerical marriages was upheld by such nobles as the landgrave, Luther ought to
return the favor by upholding the bigamy.

Of peculiar interest is Bucer's relation to this correspondence between the landgrave and Luther. Copies of
Luther's letters and speeches were sent him by Philip,[4]
and from these he judged there had been a misunderstanding between Luther and the landgrave at the Eisenach Conference, chiefly upon the importance of preserving close secrecy. ''Being such a man as he is,'' he remarked with a keen perception of Luther's character,
''I do not think it advisable to try to force him. He goes
further by himself. He lets himself be led stubbornly: he
cannot be driven at all. But when he may be shown a need
of the conscience, and a danger to Godly truth and freedom which he himself sees, then he runs of himself and
needs to be driven of no one, yea, cannot be held in. Therefore the Lord has given us this dear man, and so we must
use him rightly if we would be satisfied.''[5] Bucer advised
the landgrave not to be too hasty in his anger against
the Saxons, who, as his allies, would give him more help
than the emperor. Perfectly frank with the prince, he did
not hesitate, while seeking to encourage him, also to
tell him that he erred in urging the Saxons too hard, in
not giving up his own sins,[6] and in betraying his country
and religion by seeking the emperor's aid.[7] Above all,

---

3 Enders, XIII, 150.
4 Lenz, I, 201, 205 and n. 9, 211, 217.
5 *Ibid.*, p. 208.   6 Lenz, I, 210.   7 *Ibid.*, p. 209.

Bucer showed an irenic disposition, doing his utmost to smooth over the disagreement between the emperor and the Saxons. To some extent he exaggerated the encouraging features in Luther's attitude,[8] but time proved that he had a basis for doing so, since Luther's letters to the landgrave in the following month showed a more friendly spirit.[9] When he said the landgrave had more to expect from his religious allies than from the emperor, he was right. Philip would have done well had he listened to this advice, for Bucer was able to see the good qualities of the Saxons which were hidden from the prince by his anger. Yet with all his desire to arrange an agreement between the landgrave and his allies, the Strasbourger was firm in the position he had taken that the bigamy should not be published, thus agreeing with his own statement of Luther's attitude, although he knew that Philip was opposed to it. While desiring peace above all else, he gave to the landgrave no unjustifiable or compromising assurances.

Even more unsuccessful were the landgrave's attempts to secure from the elector any definite pledge to render aid against an attack on account of the bigamy. Long before this John Frederick and Philip of Hesse had had their disagreements. The elector had not favored the recovery of Würtemberg, and because Philip was a Zwinglian would gladly have parted from him at Augsburg.[10] Nor had he approved of the landgrave's treatment of the Anabaptists;[11] and the dispute over the Saxon inheritance after the death of Duke George gave cause for further rivalry between the two princes.[12]

---

[8] *Ibid.*, p. 211.   [9] Enders, XIII, 178.

[10] Lenz, I, 204.   [11] Hochuth, *op. cit.*, p. 546.

[12] Lenz, I, 98. On Sept. 1, 1540, Melanchthon wrote to Vito Theodoro, ''Interim metuo, nostrorum Principium discordias aliquid mali parituras Macedo hereditatem petit'' (*CR.*, III, 1079).

Just before the wedding was to take place at Rothen-
berg, the elector attempted to postpone it,[13] and, although
he later wrote to the landgrave that he was not displeased
that Thann had been present at the ceremony, he endeavored thereafter to withdraw from the enterprise.[14] When
he learned in the latter part of March the circumstances
under which the marriage was performed, he was displeased with what Philip had done, largely because of its
bearing upon the Saxon inheritance.[15] At Smalkald, in the
first part of April, John Frederick tried in vain to exact a
promise from the landgrave, that the children of the second wife should not inherit after the death of the children
of the first.[16] The rapid and ominous exposure of the bigamy aroused within the elector the fear that Philip would
resort to the publication of the "Wittenberg Rathschlag"
or introduce polygamy as a general practice;[17] and yet he
refused the landgrave's request in June for an assurance
of protection against the emperor.[18]

At the Eisenach Conference their inability to agree
became startlingly evident. To Bucer the landgrave complained that the elector had troubled him with a request
to see Margaret, and that he would "gladly have made
himself a stranger to the affair."[19] But Bucer saw that
John Frederick was too valuable a friend for the landgrave to lose, and he advised Philip not to allow his
anger to be aroused by the answers of the elector,[20] nor

---

[13] *Cf.* Rockwell, pp. 62-64.   [14] Lenz, I, 204.

[15] Duchess Elizabeth of Rochlitz requested him to prevent Margaret
from becoming *landgrafin* in case Christina should die, and any participation
by Margaret's children in the Saxon inheritance (Rockwell, p. 65). This
request agreed with the elector's own desires. He wrote to Luther on April
5, 1540, expressing his discontent with the inheritance scheme, and asking
Luther not to give the landgrave any further advice without consulting him
(Enders, XIII, 25).

[16] Lenz, I, 248, n. 8, 149.   [17] Rockwell, p. 71.

[18] *Ibid.*, p. 76.   [19] Lenz, I, 204.

[20] *Ibid.*, p. 208.

regard him as totally devoid of virtue, for the "true God will help him yet more through this man and his allies than through those of whom he has spoken so hopefully yet not in earnest."[21] The elector's attitude toward the Würtemberg expedition gave the landgrave no just cause for complaint, Bucer declared, for Philip erred in that respect, and any attempt to force promises of assistance from the elector would be unwise.[22] This was good advice, favoring the elector more than the landgrave, and rejected for that reason.

Not only the elector, but also Duke Ulrich of Würtemberg, who was more indebted to the landgrave than probably any other prince in Germany, refused to give promises of aid to Philip in his perplexity.[23] Consequently, no recourse was left the landgrave, since their advice was unacceptable, but to seek from the emperor a guarantee of protection from the penalty for his crime. Aside from the attitude of his allies there were two reasons why Philip of Hesse resorted to an agreement with Charles V; first, his threat to do so had helped to win the consent of the theologians, and he thought that now it might gain an assurance of open defense. When it failed to accomplish this purpose, he was forced to carry his threat into execution or else bring reproach upon himself as being a man of idle words. Secondly, he had every reason to expect that he would secure reasonable terms from the emperor, because his neutrality was a prize which Charles would give much to gain. The danger was, however, that Charles would break his word whenever he found it convenient or profitable. With this possibility Philip decided to take his chances.

The landgrave's first attempt to secure a favorable

21 I.e., the emperor and the pope (Lenz, I, 209).
22 Lenz, I, 210.
23 *Ibid.*, p. 249; Rockwell, p. 96, n. 2; *cf.* Schiess, I, 631, ff.

attitude from the emperor had been made in April, 1540, when he wrote to Granvelle expressing his interest in the welfare of the emperor, and requested him not to listen to the calumnies circulated by Duke Henry of Brunswick.[24] But it was not until September, 1540, that he began negotiations with Granvelle, deliberately planning to put his threat into action.[25] At the same time Philip easily secured a promise of support from his nobility, whose leaders he summoned to Marburg,[26] but he had some difficulty with the clergy, a few of whom attacked bigamy openly.[27]

Not until late in October did Bucer hear of the landgrave's action, for it was on November 3, 1540, that he first wrote to him from Worms, where he was attending the religious colloquy, begging him not to seek help from the emperor.[28] During the months that followed he did all that he could by entreaty, argument, and intercession, to turn the prince from his purpose. He declared that the landgrave need not fear the existing laws, so long as he observed a strict silence, because the imperial laws applied only to the overt act.[29] That the emperor was deceitful and untrustworthy, he showed from the fact that he was a confirmed papist, and was at that moment persecuting the Christians in the Netherlands.[30] It would be not only unchristian but also unpatriotic for him to make an alliance with the emperor, Bucer asserted, for "the court is the greatest enemy of all freedom and righteousness in the German nation."[31] It would be an unchristian

---

[24] Lenz, I, 490.

[25] *Ibid.*, p. 491; Doumergue, II, 596; Moses, p. 57.

[26] Rockwell, p. 79.

[27] *Ibid.*, pp. 81, 83.

[28] Lenz, I, 223-225. *Cf. Politische Correspondenz . . . Strassburg,* III, 109. For Feige's comment on Bucer's letter see Lenz, I, 505.

[29] Lenz, I, 236.   [30] *Ibid.*, pp. 225, 237, 243.

[31] *Ibid.*, p. 238.

thing to do, not only because Christians should maintain an unbroken unity, but also because it would show a lack of faith and trust in God.[32] Bucer begged the landgrave to picture to himself how the Protestants would be offended and the Catholics delighted, by such conduct.[33] Moreover, the reformer saw that an alliance between the landgrave and Charles might turn the king of France against the German Protestants, whereas he might otherwise be a helpful ally.[34] His allies would not desert him in time of need, so he assured the prince, but far more support might be expected from them than from the emperor. It would be a good plan for him to make an agreement with the chief Protestant states, by which he would bind himself to maintain the *status quo,* and give the assurance that he would reply to legal prosecution that he did nothing against the general Christian order. Because they could not afford to be separated from him, they should give him the counter-assurance of protection against all judicial processes, provided he did not misuse this promise.[35] In accordance with this suggestion Bucer complained to the Saxon chancellor that the landgrave was left without aid in the face of unrighteous legal prosecution, and the answer was given him, ''if the landgrave will begin negotiations with the chief states through the elector, he will find as certain a hearing as among his own people.''[36]

Though quite willing that Bucer should undertake such negotiations,[37] the landgrave found himself in such a situation that he was compelled to seek definite assurances of protection immediately. Since he could not depend upon his allies to give them,[38] he saw no other resource

[32] Lenz, I, 224, 237, 238.
[34] *Ibid.,* pp. 224, 242, 258.
[36] *Ibid.,* p. 243.
[38] Lenz, I, 235, 252.

[33] *Ibid.,* p. 242.
[35] *Ibid.,* pp. 225, 236.
[37] *Ibid.,* p. 245.

but an understanding with the emperor.[39] Even Duke
Ulrich of Würtemberg had given him a "strange answer," and allowed his theologians to attack the landgrave so sharply, that he had written a reply, which he
requested Bucer to criticize.[40] Concerning the emperor's
treachery he had no illusions, but defended his action
by saying that he sought the monarch's protection for
only a few years, and far from deserting his religious
allies would use the alliance to help them.[41] That his action
was unchristian, he would not admit for a moment, for
he beheld as much persecution in France as in the Netherlands, and he thought little would be lost if Francis did
oppose the German Protestants.[42] Curiously inconsistent
was the logic to which the landgrave opportunely resorted in defending himself. In July he had claimed that
the persecution he suffered was an evidence that he was
doing right, "since just affairs are commonly persecuted." Now he said, "We have given this affair entirely
into the hands of God Almighty, who must order it. If
it does not please him he will make the conditions so dear
and hard that they will be unacceptable to us. But if it
pleases his Almightiness and the prospects are favorable,
as we have written you, then he will doubtless grant
timely, suitable, and Christian terms and conditions."[43]
Such was the reply which Bucer received from the landgrave. It was not an encouraging one, and small indeed
was the comfort to be derived from the promise that if
Philip reached a good understanding with Charles, he
would use his influence for the advantage of his religious
allies.[44]

Perceiving that all his arguments against the folly and

[39] *Ibid.*, p. 252.   [40] *Ibid.*, pp. 249-250.
[41] *Ibid.*, pp. 235, 246, 267.
[42] *Ibid.*, pp. 246, 254-255; *cf.* p. 495 and Rockwell, p. 97, ff.
[43] Lenz, I, 254; *cf. ibid.*, p. 181.   [44] *Ibid.*, p. 267.

wickedness of seeking help from the emperor were of little avail to change the landgrave's mind, Bucer tried the other plan: namely, to gain a satisfactory assurance from the elector. On the evening of December 8, 1540, he conferred at Worms with Jacob Sturm and Chancellor Burkhardt, impressing upon the latter the chagrin which the landgrave suffered from the sharp answers of the elector and Duke Ulrich. How sorely the Hessian prince needed help, how serious would be the loss of his valuable services, especially while the emperor was imprisoned by the pope, these and other considerations, Bucer emphasized. Burkhardt, forced to admit the justice of his complaints, wrote to the elector about the situation. While all waited anxiously for a reply, Bucer begged the landgrave to delay his negotiations, and exerted his irenic abilities to the utmost to soften Philip's anger against the Würtemberg theologians, since their criticisms had been due more to misunderstanding than to evil intentions.[45]

So confident was Bucer that the Saxon chancellor's letter would be successful, that he urged the landgrave to suspend active negotiations with the imperialists. Again he suggested that Philip could ward off all legal action against himself by replying that he held the "Person" as a "Help of the Conscience," feeling confident that even if he were prosecuted, "all his allies would come to his assistance." In case of necessity he promised to draw up a brief outline of several "corollary arguments and solutions."[46]

The results of Bucer's conference with Sturm and Burkhardt were gratifying to the landgrave, but he declared it was now (December 15) too late for a "retrench-

---

[45] *Ibid.*, p. 263. This answer of the landgrave to the Würtemberg theologians, Bucer gave to Melanchthon to read (Lenz, I, 268).

[46] Lenz, I, 268.

ment.'' The only advantage which he could derive even
from a successful result of these negotiations would be
to gain better terms from the emperor, and even for that
purpose any assurances needed to arrive speedily or they
would be too late. The conversion of Charles V to the
evangelical cause; the election of a new emperor[47] who
would be more favorable to the Protestants; such were
the vapid chimeras with which he sought to comfort
Bucer. It was even possible for the landgrave to imagine
''that our dear wife Christina should die,'' in which case
he would not disinherit the children of the ''Person.''[48]

But Bucer, regardless of Wittenberg's past or future
attitude, could see no valid reason why the landgrave
should seek help from the emperor. That he had some
justification for his opinion, he proved by what he was
able to gain from the landgrave's allies. From Balthasar
von Gutlinger, Duke Ulrich's plenipotentiary at Worms,
he learned that there was no doubt ''his lord will give
help if it remains as at present.'' That the landgrave
would not be at a loss for help from his allies, Jacob
Sturm and Chancellor Burkhardt also agreed. With these
assurances Bucer waited anxiously for the reply from
the elector and begged the landgrave to be patient, warning him that should he make a treaty with the emperor,
he would still be required to keep the matter secret, thus
gaining little but danger to the ''true religion'' and
liberty.[49]

This was just what Philip was unable to do. Not the
slightest confidence did he have in Duke Ulrich, and reminded Bucer that he could not depend upon Wittenberg,
Denmark, and the Pomeranians, or the Upland Cities.

[47] Charles was now in his prime.

[48] Lenz, I, 270-272.

[49] Lenz, I, 268-269. Feige thought that Bucer's arguments showed good
prospects of assistance (Lenz, I, 519, ff.).

In his bitterness he declared (December 25, 1540) his intention to resign from the leadership of the Smalkald League, giving as his reasons the following: his body was not strong enough; he and his counselors were too busy with their own affairs; it required a large expenditure of money with no return; as the leader he would be especially subject to attack in time of war; it brought upon him the special disfavor of the emperor; it put him under an obligation to help those who had been unfaithful to him, as Duke Ulrich of Würtemberg; and it brought him no advantage but only great harm. Although he was fully decided to continue along the path he had chosen, he asked for Bucer's advice, and promised him he would be willing personally to help the Upland Cities.[50] Thus, while the day of the emperor's coming drew nearer and nearer, the landgrave became more and more determined to seek peace with him.[51]

Mere maintenance of secrecy was all that Bucer demanded of the prince, believing confidently that promises of assistance could be obtained from the leading Protestants for the protection of the *hofmeisterin,* while the refusing of similar "helps for the conscience" in time of necessity would not be demanded. Excellent opportunities for carrying on his negotiations to see what assistance could be gained for the landgrave, were afforded him by the Colloquy of Worms, and in the last part of December he gained from the preachers of Ulm and Augsburg a promise to do their best for Philip. But Bucer was working against forces too strong for him to overcome alone. The imperial party eagerly desired an agreement with the landgrave. How eagerly is indicated by the fact that neither the imperial secretary, who was very free with his words, nor anyone else, reproached

[50] Lenz, I, 282-284.
[51] *Ibid.,* p. 297.

Bucer in any way on account of the bigamy.[52] Not only against the allurements they offered the landgrave did he contend, but also against the short-sightedness of the elector and other leaders, who failed to see that they were driving Philip into an agreement with the emperor, which was fatal to their own interests.

The long-expected reply from the elector finally arrived, and on the last day of this eventful year in Bucer's life, he sent it to the landgrave.[53] John Frederick made two demands. First, "that the affair be maintained in its present condition of secrecy." For this purpose he required that the "help of the conscience" should not be called by any name of the "first or second grade." Her own birth or baptismal name might be used, but no such term as "meins g. h. gemahel" or "zugemahel." She should be maintained in a fitting manner at a quiet place, in no excessive luxury. Secondly, if the landgrave was so questioned about the affair that an answer could not be avoided, he should reply that whoever accused him of taking and keeping either "ein ordentlichen gehulfen oder ehegemahel" against general Christian order and the imperial and other laws, did him an injustice; for he "had undertaken nothing against them," neither intended to undertake or allow to another.

If the landgrave would agree to these demands, the elector said he would help him against any "unjustified prosecution." But he held that he would be freed from this promise if, through Philip's fault, it became no longer a question of fact but "juris questio in foro fori." A pledge that his preachers and scholars would not be allowed to defend the bigamy was also demanded from

---

[52] *Ibid.*, pp. 285-286.

[53] Lenz, I, 292. Bucer mentioned the elector's letter in a postcript to a long letter to the landgrave, in which he discussed the colloquy at great length (Lenz, I, 287-294).

the landgrave, and in conclusion the elector added that this agreement should not be binding on his heirs.

These uncompromising terms were accompanied by certain explanations from Bucer in which he tried to soften their harshness.[54] He thought the article of the "succession" should not be an obstacle or burden to the landgrave. The reference to the "present treatment of the Person" he understood as meaning the way in which she was treated at the time of the proposals, and that should be conceded so long as there was any danger to be feared, and any help needed. The fact that the elector made some concessions afforded him ground for thinking he might make more, nor would the landgrave need to fear any molestation so long as he kept it secret. Würtemberg, Brandenburg, and Duke Maurice gave no occasion for anxiety, so Bucer thought, and he hoped that the landgrave would accept the elector's proposals, not only because he· wished to see peace between them, but also that he might turn his full powers to the promotion of the concord, "for whose accomplishment there was never greater hope."[55]

But Bucer's sanguine anticipations were doomed to disappointment. The elector's demands only irritated the landgrave more than ever, since the longer he contemplated them, the more "weitläuftiger" they seemed to him. So sharply and "cavillationsweise" did they appear that he placed no dependence in them, and decided to have no further negotiations with their author. Indeed, he characterized them as so elastic that they could be "strained like a cowhide," and he preferred to lose a third part of his possessions rather than accept them.[56]

Although the landgrave intended to keep Margaret the same "as now," no pledge would he take in regard to

[54] Lenz, I, 292-294. [55] *Ibid.*
[56] Lenz, I, 301-303.

the name he would give her. The answer which the elector demanded in case of inquiry, he regarded as a "verba exaggerationis und einstheils neue Zusätze," and he declared it would be impossible for him to forbid his preachers to defend bigamy in cases of necessity. To show that the elector was guilty of sodomy, and to drive Duke Ulrich out of his lands, setting up his son in his stead,[57] were some of the threats he made, and though neither was ever carried out, they show how the treatment which the landgrave received from these two men had wounded his pride, and now that the prospect of aid from the emperor seemed certain, he was not only separated from them but possessed with a desire for revenge. Made bolder by the favorable attitude of Duke Henry and Margrave Joachim,[58] the landgrave's self-confidence was further strengthened by the prospect of a successful completion of his negotiations for the marriage of his daughter to Duke Maurice of Saxony.[59]

During January Philip's correspondence with Granvelle concerned chiefly the terms upon which he should come to the Diet of Regensburg. Granvelle insisted that he should come, for Philip's presence was necessary to a religious agreement of any value.[60] When the landgrave made his coming conditional upon an assurance of imperial favor,[61] this was granted him on January 24, 1541,[62] and he promised to be present at the Diet.[63] On February 10 he sent to Bucer a copy of the document, in which the

[57] *Ibid.*, p. 302. This was no empty threat, for Christopher, the son of Duke Ulrich, was a popular man, and Ulrich's subjects would have been glad to have seen the change (W. Walker, *The Reformation*, p. 192).

[58] Lenz, I, 301.

[59] *Ibid.*, p. 304. The wedding took place on January 10, 1541, at Marburg (*ibid.*, p. 312, n. 1).

[60] Hassencamp, I, 542; Lenz, I, 498.

[61] Lenz, I, 499.

[62] *Ibid.*, p. 540, ff.

[63] *Ibid.*, p. 499.

emperor promised to show him favor, and pardoned him anything in which he might have seemed to have acted against his majesty and the laws of the empire. Philip was also guaranteed a safe-conduct to the Diet, together with the safety of his possessions while he was there.[64] Bucer found little definite assurance for the landgrave in this document, and replied after he had read it, "Everything is made dependent upon the religious situation, if that fails, then everything has failed."[65]

Once more in the first part of February, the Strasbourg reformer tried to influence the landgrave to make a French alliance, even sending him word of a definite assurance of favor from Francis I. On February 4, 1541, he wrote to Philip that the king of France "has now expressly commanded his envoys, as I read in the instructions myself, to comfort your princely grace with special articles and expressions of help, if your princely grace should be disturbed on account of the affair, for he considers that your princely grace has not acted against the law of God in such matters. He has also commanded his envoys if it is necessary, to negotiate with the elector and others, so that they may equally assure your princely grace." To these friendly offers Bucer urged the landgrave to make an amicable response, reminding him that Francis was a mighty king, and also it would be to the advantage of the kingdom of Christ.[66]

But the landgrave was even more opposed to a French alliance than before,[67] because, as he said, "Should we enter into close relations with France at the present time, that would make our negotiations with the emperor fall

---

[64] *Ibid.*, p. 542.   [65] *Ibid.*, II, 17.

[66] Lenz, II, 5.

[67] Yet in 1534 Philip had been allied with Francis I through the Smalkald League, and received some support from him in his restoration of Duke Ulrich of Würtemberg (Lavisse-Rambaud, *Histoire Générale*, IV, 112, 432, 493. See above, p. 45).

through, and discredit us."[68] The news of the failure of his last attempt to save the landgrave reached Bucer a few days before his departure on February 22 for the Diet of Regensburg.[69] When the French envoys did arrive with promises of assurance, it was too late.[70] With a heavy heart Bucer rode away to the Diet, little hoping that anything would be gained there,[71] and destined not to return home for many months.[72]

The conduct of the Strasbourg reformer at the Diet did more to injure his reputation among the Prostestants of Germany than his connection with the bigamy. Chosen by the emperor to be one of the three Protestant collocutors to confer with three Catholics on the whole system of theology,[73] he showed such an earnest desire to reach an agreement with the papists that many evangelical leaders suspected him of excessive readiness to surrender essential articles of belief.[74] Yet in the Strasbourg archives there is a report sent by Bucer from Regensburg

[68] Lenz, II, 9.

[69] *Ibid.*, p. 18; *CR., Calvini Opera*, XI, 155; cf. *Politische Correspondenz . . . Strassburg*, III, 166, 175, n. 1.

[70] Doumergue, II, 596.

[71] Schiess, II, 63, ff.

[72] Anrich, p. 80; *CR., Calvini Opera*, XI, 162.

[73] Bonnet, I, 255; Doumergue, II, 596; *CR., Calvini Opera*, XI, 200; Lenz, III, 18, ff.

[74] Bucer admitted this when he wrote to the landgrave on Nov. 30, 1541, ''Mein armer dienst aber, der des herren ist, wird dadurch verschlagen, und kumet diese wunde alszbald auff die mir meine dorechte bruder, die prediger, von regenspurgischer handlungen wegen eben tieff gehawen haben'' (Lenz, II, 39). The landgrave often defended him against the charges made about him at Regensburg (Lenz, II, 45, ff.). Bucer himself wrote a copious defense of his conduct to Ambrose Blaurer (*cf.* Schiess, I, 910, 913). Among other things he said, ''Ut consilii vero mei ratio et a me—nam alii satis varia et non amice de eo sparserunt multa—vobis perscribatur, ne dubitate hanc fuisse; primum ut nobis omnis et doctrinae puritas et rituum libertas salva maneret et apud alteram partem qualecunque initium fieret'' (Schiess, II, 79). The bigamy gave considerable offence at the Diet (*CR., Calvini Opera*, XI, 179; Herminjard, VII, 55).

in which he says that he agreed with his two colleagues
"that everything shall depend upon the Reformation; if
that is not made possible, then nothing will come out of
all the negotiations."[75] So deep was the distrust which
Luther conceived for Bucer on account of his attitude,
that he wrote to Justus Menius in the following January,
"As for Bucer, he stinks sufficiently because of the
Regensburg Articles."[76]

Landgrave Philip arrived at the Diet on March 27,[77]
and after long negotiations with the emperor's ministers,[78] concluded a treaty with Charles on June 13, 1541.[79]
Though the Catholics were vociferous in their condemnation of the quasi-consent given by the reformers to the
landgrave's bigamy, no compunctions deterred their
imperial champion from breaking the laws of the empire
that he might gain Philip's neutrality by protecting his
act, and he had even proposed the abolition of sacerdotal
celibacy to the Diet.[80] In this important treaty the landgrave promised among other things: to prevent the king
of France or the Duke of Cleves from entering the Smalkald League, or making any alliance with the protesting
states; to influence Duke Maurice and Duke Ulrich not
to make any alliance with France or Cleves; and to hinder
the use of German mercenaries by France or others
against the emperor. On the other hand the emperor
agreed, to forgive the landgrave all past transgressions
of imperial law, and not to undertake any war against

---

[75] *Politische Correspondenz* . . . *Strassburg*, III, 188, n. 1.

[76] Enders, XIV, 152. *Cf. ibid.*, XIII, 288, XIV, 182, 183, n. 11; Kroker,
nos. 499, 543, 546.

[77] Lenz, II, 26, n. 5, III, 16.

[78] *Ibid.*, III, D, pp. 72-91.

[79] Many years later Calvin accused the landgrave of having yielded himself servilely to Charles (Bonnet, III, 92). The text of the treaty is printed
in Lenz, III, E, pp. 91-96.

[80] H. C. Lea, *A Historical Sketch of Sacerdotal Celibacy*, p. 431.

him on account of religion.[81] Thus, within a year after the wedding at Rothenburg the landgrave sought and gained assurance, not only for his conscience but also for his body.

The tremendous influence of this treaty upon the history of the Reformation can be only briefly indicated here.[82] It is evident that the emperor was contemplating war with France and Cleves. All the demands he made of the landgrave had a military purpose in view. Philip, on the other hand, expected an attack from the emperor, either in person or through one of his allies, on account of the bigamy, and his demands were aimed to gain protection from this. Each had a need which the other could satisfy. While the landgrave gained safety from the penalty of death to which he was liable, the emperor gained not only the neutrality of Philip in case of a war with Cleves, but, more important still, the assurance that he would make no foreign alliance against him, or allow the Smalkald League to do so.[83] For the Protestants in Germany the result was disastrous. One of their chief leaders was allied with the enemy, and to the emperor's prospects was added a gleam of hopefulness which they had sadly lacked only a year before. All chance of an alliance between France and the Smalkald League was destroyed, in spite of the fact that it would have been more advantageous than the alliance with England, because France

[81] Charles also made a similar treaty with the Elector of Brandenburg, allowing him to retain the Lutheran religion in his dominions until the assembling of a council, if he would stand by him against Cleves (Dyer and Hassal, II, 148).

[82] Grisar says, ''Und jetzt trat der Fürst, der diese allein hatte zu stande bringen können [i.e., a protestant alliance with France], von der Opposition zurück, deckte ungebeten alle Karten auf, machte freie Bahn gegen Geldern, bot seine gewichtige Unterstützung im Reiche und nach aussen Gewährung der kaiserlichen Huld'' (Grisar, II, 427).

[83] *Cf.* Doumergue, II, 596; W. Walker, *History of the Christian Church*, p. 378; Henderson, I, 372.

was more directly opposed to the emperor.[84] The defeat
of Cleves in the war for Gelders was made certain, and
so the power of the opposition to the emperor's dynastic
ambitions in Germany made weak. Greater damage was
done to the evangelical cause than anything which its
enemies could have done,[85] for the power of the Protestant league against the emperor was broken.[86]

In view of these results the landgrave might well be
called a traitor to the cause of the Reformation, since
he did it so much harm by coming to an understanding
with its enemies.[87] Yet it must be remembered that he
refused to surrender his religious convictions, and Hesse
remained a Protestant state. Moreover the treatment
which he had received from the elector, Duke Ulrich, and
others, was well calculated to drive him to this resource.
It was consideration for his own selfish interests which
led the elector to make such unbearable demands of the
landgrave. If the events of the following years are not
considered, and it is remembered that at this time the
emperor assumed a favorable attitude toward the Protestants, the landgrave cannot be blamed so severely for
resorting to an action, which did not at the time seem
so injurious to the cause of the allies as it later proved
to be. But he should have been more patient, and in rejecting the French alliance he showed a lack of wisdom.[88]
He would have done better to have followed his own
maxim, ''Believe not that man who is not of your own

[84] Lenz, I, 499.

[85] Köstlin, *Life of Luther*, p. 506.

[86] ''So war ein Zusammengehen der Protestanten nicht mehr zu denken''
(Kolde, *Martin Luther*, II, 508).

[87] ''The future was to show what he could do and what he would suffer
for the cause he now abandoned; but the fact remains that he was a traitor''
(Henderson, I, 373).

[88] The landgrave also planned to seek a similar agreement with the pope.
Cf. his plans for such negotiations (Lenz, I, 368), and Rockwell's account
(Rockwell, p. 279, ff.).

belief." With Francis he had the mutual "belief" of
opposition to the emperor but with Charles he had
nothing in common whatever. If it was right for the landgrave to seek his own selfish interests first, and be sure
that whoever suffered for his bigamy it would not be
himself and Margaret, though it might be the church
and those who, like Bucer, had helped him, then he cannot be reproached for his treaty with the emperor. But
judged by the standard of self-sacrifice, established by
many who were giving their lives for the cause which he
injured so severely, it can hardly be said that he showed
a fitting devotion to the religion which he claimed to
honor so highly.[89]

While at Regensburg Bucer wrote another book for
the landgrave about which little has been said and less is
known. On July 18, 1540 he had proposed to Philip as one
of his plans for keeping the affair secret, that, "since
absolute silence would be a confession, he should issue
not a public, but a private writing to one of his trusted
princes with contents something like this. . . . Your
princely grace will inform the prince to whom the writing
is addressed, that everywhere in the empire people talk
as if your marriage-vows and princely honor were forgotten; and against the general laws of Christendom, and
also of the imperial court, you have taken and kept an-

[89] The best comment on the nature of his action is an indirect one made
by Bucer in the "Denkschrift Bucer's für den Reichstag zu Speier" (1543,
Lenz, II, 173). Bucer discussed the power of the magistrate and all temporal
authorities, placing upon them the duty of reforming the nation. "Darumb,
wa unsere obren, fursten und andere, die bei den iren ein gantz imperium und
volkomen gewalt zu regieren haben, dazu auch glider des zeitlichen reichs
deutscher nation und uff den reichstagen mit zu rathen und handlen haben,
die sachen unser religion der krafft götliche worts also befehlen wolten das
sie, die zu befordren das ampt der oberkeit, ja all ir vermögen nit auch
darzu brauchen wolten, thäten sie wider ir götlichs ampt und pflichte und
handleten nit als Christliche obren und darzu gegeben und uffgelegt, das sie
bei den iren die gotsäligkeit vor allem befordren sollen" (Lenz, II, 175, ff.).

other wife. You will assert that anyone who repeats and spreads such reports about you lies falsely, is a coward and will have to suffer for it. For your princely grace has not so forsaken God Almighty that you do not recognize that it is a blessing of Christendom that holy matrimony is brought again to the first divine institution of monogamy, requiring that not only church officers, but also other Christians should each one have only one wife; and such a God-given ornament of Christendom[90] your grace would be unhappy to lose for himself, or deny to any other man. On that account you beg the prince to whom the writing is sent, if the accusation has been made public, that he would give no belief to the wicked, false report, brought against your princely grace through ill-will.''[91]

Again on December 12, 1540, Bucer thought of writing a statement of several ''corollary arguments and solutions'' which he intended to give to the landgrave for use in replying to the objections of the Würtemberg theologians.[92] When the landgrave, still later, sent Bucer his *Dritte Warhafftige Verantwortung*, Bucer sent back not only a profuse criticism of the passage relating to the bigamy, but he also enclosed an ''outline, which I have composed . . . agreeing fundamentally with your princely grace's attitude except that the two arguments are omitted of your princely grace's conscience and the lack of condemnation.''[93] This outline was probably a brief summary agreeing with the changes which he had made in the *Dritte Warhafftige Verantwortung*.[94]

When the landgrave informed Bucer in July, 1541, that he intended to publish a certain dialogue defending bigamy,[95] Bucer begged him not to publish either that or

[90] *Cf. Argumenta Buceri pro et contra*, p. 2, ff.
[91] Lenz, I, 179, ff.   [92] *Ibid.*, p. 268.
[93] *Ibid.*, II, 20.   [94] *Ibid. Cf.* below, p. 159, ff.
[95] The *Dialogus Neobuli*, see below, p. 163, ff.

"the writing which I prepared for you here."[96] It is evident from this statement that at the Diet of Regensburg Bucer wrote a book for the landgrave, which probably concerned bigamy, because he connected it with the other book which did. Further than this nothing is known about the work,[97] but it is reasonable to suppose that it had its antecedents in the writing sent by Bucer to the landgrave along with his criticisms of the *Dritte Warhafftige Verantwortung,* and that it also agreed in character with the book suggested on July 18, 1540, perhaps being composed for the same purpose as the writing which he promised on December 12, 1540. Long before, in the *Argumenta Buceri pro et contra* he had suggested a "form of reply" to inquiry,[98] and perhaps the little book composed at Regensburg may have been for some such purpose, and may have contained some of the ideas given in the suggestions mentioned above. Probably it was never printed and this explains its disappearance. Yet it is far from improbable that it may not have concerned the bigamy at all.

[96] Lenz, II, 26.

[97] It has been noted by Rady (p. 102), and Paulus (*Historisch-politische Blätter,* CXLVII, 511), who assume that it concerned the bigamy.

[98] *Argumenta Buceri pro et contra,* p. 54.

CHAPTER VII

THE *DIALOGUS NEOBULI*

For a long time Henry, Duke of Brunswick-Wolfen-
büttel, and Philip, Landgrave of Hesse, had been close
friends.[1] But in the year 1538 there came a coolness between them, when Henry was chosen head of the Catholic
league in northern Germany and refused to grant Philip
and the elector, who were the leaders of the Smalkald
League, free passage across his lands.[2] The ill-feeling
kindled by this rivalry was fanned into open hostility
near the close of the same year, when the landgrave
arrested a messenger of the Duke's while crossing Hesse,
and opened the despatches which he was bearing to the
Elector of Mainz.[3] The messages, permeated with enmity
toward the landgrave, reported to the Elector of Mainz
that, "The landgrave does not sleep very much, hardly
an hour during the night, has no rest, except in wood,[4]
will become insane."[5] This meddlesome and pernicious
gossip enraged Philip while the discourteous treatment
of his messenger aroused the Duke's bitter resentment.
A defense of his action, written by the Hessian prince,
followed by a reply from Duke Henry, began a long controversy in which each retaliated against the other with
all imaginable invective and contumely. Since this quarrel

[1] Koldewey, "Heinz von Wolfenbüttel," *Schriften des Vereins für
Reformationsgeschichte*, no. 2, p. 5.

[2] *Ibid.*, p. 7.

[3] Hortleder, Bh. IV, Kap. II, no. 2.

[4] A reference to the wood-cure he was taking.

[5] Hortleder, Bh. IV, Kap. II, no. 8, p. 13.

concerned Bucer only indirectly, a brief discussion will be sufficient here.[6]

When the landgrave committed bigamy, he suffered from a natural premonition that Duke Henry would hear of his action and include it in his arsenal of slanders. Realizing this peril, Bucer wrote to the landgrave only four days before the wedding, "I have spoken with Master Philip. If that wicked man[7] should smell anything and start a disturbance, we both think it would be well if your princely grace, as you can well understand, should not in any way expose himself or acknowledge anything."[8] Not merely the fear that Henry would attack the bigamy troubled the reformer, but even more he dreaded the landgrave's indiscretion, which might expose the secret should he reply, and so he assured the prince that since such matters were not within the jurisdiction of the *Kammergericht,* they were relegated to the clergy. "But it is now high time for our princes and states to revive the court in all things, because they openly write in their dialogue that we should not be allowed the benefits of the law."[9]

The landgrave, who planned before the Eisenach Conference how to answer Duke Henry in case he said anything about the bigamy,[10] wrote to Bucer on July 4, 1540, that he would prefer to let an explanation of his conduct wait until the "faithless man, Duke Henry, issues a publication about it, which he will certainly not neglect to do, if the fear of the disclosure of his own unprincely business does not somewhat hold him back."[11] No such fear restrained Duke Henry, and in his *Dritte bestendige, warhafftige, redliche, Göttliche, und ergründte, unablegliche*

[6] The best and most complete discussion of the subject is in Rockwell, p. 101, ff.

[7] I.e., Duke Henry.
[8] Lenz, I, 142.
[9] *Ibid.,* pp. 142-143.
[10] Rockwell, p. 103, and n. 2.
[11] Lenz, I, 202.

Antwort,[12] published on July 22, 1540, he said, ''Who has
ever heard of a prince of the empire, who has contracted
a second marriage during the life-time of his first wife,
for now over the whole empire it is reported that the
landgrave has contracted a second marriage during the
life-time of his first wife?''[13]

During the next three months Duke Henry collected
fuller information about the bigamy, and with it sharp-
ened the sword of slander which he flashed in his next
pamphlet: the *Duplicae*.[14] After denying emphatically the
truth of the scandalous tale of Eva von Trott, a young
lady whom the Duke of Brunswick claimed was dead,
while others asserted that this was only a pretence on
his part that he might live secretly with her in his castle
of Stauffenberg,[15] Henry turned upon his accusers, asserting that if he wished to stoop to such slanders, he could
expose the iniquitous lives of the elector and ''his
brother,''[16] how ''his brother, the landgrave, had taken

[12] Hortleder, Bh. IV, Kap. XI, p. 276, ff.

[13] *Ibid.*, p. 302. It was in the month of September, 1540, that Bucer
heard a rumor that this book contained a copy of the marriage-contract
(Lenz, I, 210). This report was false (Lenz, I, 210, n. 1), and shows that
Bucer had not seen the book.

[14] The full title is *Ergrünte, bestendige, erhebliche, warhafftige, Göttliche, Christliche, Fürsten und Adel liebende Duplicae, desz Durchleutigen
Hochgebornen Fürsten und Herrn, Herrn Heinriches desz Jüngern, Herzogen
zu Braunschweig und Lüneberg wider desz Churfürsten von Sachsen andern
ehrnrürigen, ungegrünten, unbestendigen, erdichten, ungöttlichen, unchrist-
lichen, truncknen, Gotteshessigen Abdruck, . . . Prouerbiorum xj. Der
Wein macht lose, und die trunckenheit wilde leute, welchen darzu lust tregt,
wirt nimer weise. j. Corin, vj. Die Truncknen werden das Reich Gottes nicht
besitzen* (Rockwell, p. 104).

[15] The elector had declared his belief in this accusation. *Cf.* Koldewey,
''Heinz von Wolfenbüttel,'' *Schriften des Vereins für Reformationsgeschichte*, no. 2, p. 9; Koldewey, ''Der Erste Versuch einer Rechfertigung
der Bigamie,'' *Theologische Studien und Kritiken*, XLVII, 556; C. v.
Rommel, *Philipp der Grossmüthigen, Landgraf von Hessen*, I, 441; Hortleder, Bh. IV, Kap. XVI, no. 32, p. 465.

[16] I.e., the landgrave.

a second wife, and had two wives at the same time, . . . how his theologians of the University of Wittenberg helped negotiate such things, all of which he permitted and allowed. Who then can say, or well conclude otherwise, than that it must have happened with his secret advice, foreknowledge and consent?[17] . . . And even if he did not consent to it openly, yet he did it like Nicodemus, in secret.''[18]

Luther, who was included in the attack by the *Duplicae*, responded with one of his most virulent tirades, *Wider Hans Worst*,[19] while the elector answered on April 4, 1541, with his *Warhafftige, Beständige . . . Verantwortung*.[20] Neither could the landgrave ignore Duke Henry's challenge, and in his *Dritte Warhafftige Verantwortung*[21] he replied to the charge of bigamy in a passage which is important in this connection because he submitted it to Bucer for his opinion. The passage reads as follows, ''Further Duke Henry continues, eagerly endeavoring to make us hated by everyone, and testifies to a horrible thing; saying, 'who has ever heard of a prince of the empire, who, during the lifetime of his first wife, has contracted a second marriage!' as he intimates that we

---

[17] Hortleder, Bh. IV, Kap. XVI, no. 32, p. 465.

[18] Rockwell, p. 105.

[19] Dommer, no. 139, p. 76; *Luthers Werke* (Erlangen ed.) XXVI, 1-75. Luther said, ''None had more shamefully offended against marriage than Duke Henry through his shameless relations to Eva von Trott, who to all appearances had died and been buried with all ecclesiastical ceremonies in order to live with him upon the Stauffenberg in secrecy'' (Koldewey, ''Der ErsteVersuch,'' *Theologische Studien und Kritiken*, XLVII, 556). Luther called him ''Hans Wurst'' because it was a name given to ''groben Töppeln, die klug sein wollen, jedock ungereimt und ungeschikt zur Sache reden und thun'' (Köstlin, II, 547; *cf.* deWette, V, 345).

[20] Hortleder, Bh. IV, Kap. XXII, 574.

[21] Dommer, no. 135; Lauze, the Hessian chronicler, dates this work March 4, 1541. He sums up the duke's accusations, gives the landgrave's replies, but says nothing about the bigamy (W. Lauze, *Leben und Thaten . . . Philippi*, II, 408).

have done. . . . In regard to the first point concerning the marriage, we have long before this heard evil things said of Duke Henry, . . . But for us we say, let Duke Henry or whoever he may be, say that we have entered upon or contracted an unchristian marriage, which is not fitting for a Christian prince of the empire . . . he lies about us wickedly. For, although we are a poor, imperfect Christian and sinner, as we must recognize ourselves before God our maker, begging his grace, yet we still stand firm in our faith and our conscience before God, as we certainly hope to remain by him, and our confessor recognizes us as not unchristian. We hope also that we give offence to no man. Besides, we live with the high-born princess, Frau Christina . . . in Christian, friendly, good-will and unity, to which we summon her own testimony, that of our lords, and of many others both inside and outside of our lands. But Duke Henry lives with his wife, without her guilt, in disagreement, quarreling and contention, and the condition is such that at the Diet of Brunswick, Duke Ulrich of Würtemberg, her brother's counselor, could not see her to speak to her. Likewise, Count George of Würtemberg, her own natural brother, was not allowed to speak with her except in the presence of Duke Henry's counselors and servants, as at that time was openly reported.''[22] The landgrave then repeated the accusation that Eva von Trott was not dead, and that Duke Henry had never given her relations any satisfactory proof of her decease, ''but he has seen to it that vigils and masses for her soul are celebrated just as if she were dead.''[23]

With his customary diligence Bucer wrote out a long criticism of this passage, and sent it to the landgrave.[24]

[22] Hortleder, Bh. IV, Kap. XIX, no. 35, p. 516. *Cf*. Lenz, II, 20, n. 1.
[23] *Ibid*.
[24] On March 10, 1541 (Lenz, II, 19, ff.).

Far from flattering the prince upon the nature of his defense, he criticized it severely and enclosed in his letter a form of reply which he thought would be more advisable.[25] First, he judged that Philip was indiscreet in summarizing Duke Henry's accusation. Should it be necessary to state the accusation, he thought that Philip's expression "onchristliche eh" was preferable, but the best method would be to quote Duke Henry's own words first, and omit the phrase, "that we have contracted an unchristian marriage." This sounded too much like an admission of the second marriage, because no one would accuse the first marriage of being unchristian. Secondly, Bucer thought that the words, "he lies about us wickedly," were too harsh to be included in the defense. The argument from the good-will of Christina, he considered was proper and should be used, but he objected to the arguments from the landgrave's good conscience, and the approval of his confessor, because they were not convincing, and his opponents would say that they were both "zu luck." Finally he interceded on behalf of Duke Henry's wife, not denying the truth of Philip's statements, but reminding him that the unfortunate lady was not to blame.[26]

Except the statement about his relations to Christina, there was nothing in the landgrave's reply to Duke Henry of which Bucer approved. With a keen perception of the weakness of the landgrave's answer, his suggestions were calculated to conceal the bigamy which the landgrave almost openly admitted. But Philip was not wise enough to wait for Bucer's criticism, and it came too late for any changes to be made.[27] Regretting that it had not arrived soon enough, Bucer urged secrecy and a strict discipline in the landgrave's court.[28] It is doubtful if the landgrave

---

[25] *Ibid.*, p. 20.   [26] Lenz, II, 22.
[27] *Ibid.*   [28] *Ibid.*, pp. 22-23.

was troubled by any regret, for it would seem that he
was not so anxious to hide the fact of the bigamy, as to
assert that it was not an unchristian marriage. Duke
Henry's next attack was entitled *Vierte bestendige Antwort*[29] and to this the landgrave replied on February 4,
1542, with a *Vierte warhafftige Verantwortung.*[30] Again
he denied that he had entered an unchristian marriage,
and repeated the accusation about Eva von Trott. "But
we have recognized our imperfection as a fallible Christian, while denying that we have begun any unchristian
or ungodly marriage, as his writings report."[31]

At the same time that these official denunciations were
being exchanged, there were also issued certain pseu-
donymous libels which played an important part in the
controversy. Three of these need to be mentioned here.
The first appeared in February, 1541, on the side of Duke
Henry, and was entitled, *Evangelische, brüderliche,
getreue Unterrichtung, durch Meister Justinium Warsager, Nachrichter zu Warheitsbrun, in einem Sendbriefe
an den Landgrafen von Hessen beschehen.*[32] In this pamphlet, Justinius Warsager, a hangman, asked the landgrave what reasons he had for taking another wife, since
it was forbidden in the Bible to have more than one wife
at one time, and his wife Christina had never given him
sufficient cause for committing bigamy. "As I believe and
hold, the devil must have gotten into your princely grace
and your princely grace has learned the Münster art, so
that your princely grace doubtless intends to take as many
wives as you will, as the king of Münster did."[33]

It was not long before an answer appeared on the side

---

[29] Rockwell, p. 106, ff.
[30] Hortleder, Bh. IV, Kap. 35, p. 744; Dommer, no. 51, p. 83.
[31] Hortleder, Bh. IV, Kap. 35, no. 31, p. 762.
[32] Koldewey, "Heinz von Wolfenbüttel," *Schriften des Vereins für
Reformationsgeschichte*, no. 2, p. 21.
[33] Rockwell, p. 108.

of the landgrave with the title, *Expostulation und Straff-schrift Satanae des Fürsten dieser Welt, mit hertzog Heintzen von Braunschweig, seinem geschworen diener und lieben getrewen, das er sich im pillicher weisse, in der person eyns Diephenckers wider den Landtgrauen nicht one merklich nachteyl seins Reichs, mit ungeschickten liegen eingelassen habe. Getruckt in Utopia.*[34] This tract, described by Koldewey as "The first attempt at a justi-fication of the bigamy,"[35] appeared in April, 1541, and for the first time flaunted before the public a systematic argu-ment in favor of bigamy.[36] Satan was represented as repri-manding his servant, Duke Henry, for his indiscretion in telling such monstrous lies that no one will believe them, in spreading a slander so horrible that his inability to prove it will react to the disadvantage of Satan's king-dom when the landgrave exposes its falsity, and in for-getting that had the prince committed bigamy with de-liberate intent, then he could still argue that his action was not so disgraceful as the permission of all kinds of immorality. In the same manner the landgrave set forth under the guise of a scolding by Satan to Duke Henry, the following arguments in favor of bigamy: the examples of great and honored people in the Old Testament; the absence of any attack by the Old Testament prophets upon this sin, though they inveighed against many others; the injunction of Paul that the bishop should be the hus-band of one wife, which indicates that bigamy was at that time prevalent and permitted to all but clergymen; and the bigamy of Valentinian, together with his law, which shows that bigamy was not condemned at that time since he was considered a pious emperor.

[34] Dommer, no. 144, p. 79.

[35] Koldewey, "Der Erste Versuch," *Theologische Studien und Kritiken*, XLVII, 553-562.

[36] Corvinus asked Simon Bing to send him six copies of the book (Tschackert, *Briefwechsel des Corvinus*, p. 103).

The "Explanation" made to Bucer at Melsungen[37] contained all these arguments except the one from the example of Valentinian, and that was advanced in the "Instructio Buceri" composed only a few days later.[38] Consequently, the argument for bigamy set forth in the *Expostulation of Satan* can lay no claim to originality, but is, in fact, a less complete statement of the case than the landgrave had made a year and a half before to the reformers.[39] When Luther read the *Expostulation of Satan,* he was so enraged that he wrote to Melanchthon, "That Melsungen fool retains his horrible garrulity in his mouth with more difficulty than fire."[40] This statement by Luther that John Lening, pastor at Melsungen, and so "that Melsungen fool," wrote the *Expostulation* is the only definite clue to its authorship. On this ground both Koldewey[41] and Dommer[42] assert that Lening was the author, though the evidence is hardly strong enough to prove it.

Duke Henry forthwith adopted the landgrave's method of controversy and replied with a *Dialogus oder Gespräch wider ein vermeinte, ungeschickte Expostulation oder Straffschrift Satanae,* in which the claim was advanced by Lesterle, a servant of the chief devil Lucifer, that he could tell who the priest was that gave the dispensation; what scholars assented to it; who helped perform the marriage; how the second wife's mother had given a copy of the marriage-contract to Duke Henry of Saxony; etc.[43]

---

[37] Lenz, I, 352, ff.

[38] Enders, XII, 330, ff.; *CR.*, III, 849, ff.

[39] Consequently Koldewey's statement that what was only pointed out in the *Expostulation* was further elaborated in the *Dialogus Neobuli* is not accurate if he means that there was a necessary dependence of the second on the first, and that the author of the second necessarily secured his arguments from the first (Koldewey, "Der Erste Versuch," *Theologische Studien und Kritiken,* XLVII, 560, ff.).

[40] Enders, XIII, 304.   [41] Koldewey, *op. cit.,* p. 559, ff.

[42] Dommer, no. 144.

[43] Koldewey, *op. cit.,* p. 560; Rockwell, p. 109.

It is small wonder that Melanchthon, wearied by the conflict, wrote to a friend in October, 1541, "Thus far some rage in the church, some make corrupt doctrines, some compose insulting dialogues."[44]

Even before the wedding, the landgrave, realizing the need of defending the action he contemplated, had begun to collect material for that purpose.[45] Sailer's aid was enlisted in these efforts, and on September 15, 1541, the Augsburg physician wrote to his master that he had discovered a certain "Scot" whose services he thought it would be wise to secure.[46] No one has been able to reveal the identity of this remarkable Scotchman,[47] whom Sailer described as a man of such great ability that it would be wise to make him one of the faculty of the University of Marburg.[48] At any rate, Philip failed to engage him, and so far as is known he never became connected with the bigamy.[49] Yet without him there was no lack of theologians to justify the landgrave's act, for the Hessian clergy were particularly encouraged to do so.[50] In December, 1540, the landgrave said that he could not prohibit his preachers from defending bigamy "as a dispensation from God in cases of necessity."[51] Not only did he fail to prevent them from spreading such propaganda, but it is evident that he welcomed any arguments from them which would defend bigamy, and used them in the writings which he issued.

The greatest literary defense of the bigamy published by the landgrave was a book which became famous as

---

[44] *CR.*, IV, 679. [45] Rockwell, p. 113.

[46] Lenz, III, 183, n. 1.

[47] Rockwell, p. 113, ff., and p. 115, and n. 3.

[48] Lenz, III, 183, n. 1.

[49] Rockwell, p. 115.

[50] On July 24, 1540, he wrote to Bucer to send suggestions (Lenz, I, 203); see above, p. 117.

[51] Lenz, I, 302; *cf. ibid.*, p. 272.

the *Dialogus Neobuli.*[52] It was dated March 27, 1541, and
though this date seems to be false, it was probably completed not earlier, but later, while Philip was at Regensburg, where it was taken to him by Andrew Kolbe,[53] a
printer of Marburg.[54] The latest date possible is June 13,
1541, when the landgrave left the Diet,[55] for while he was
there he showed the manuscript to Bucer[56] and Melanchthon,[57] both of whom begged him not to publish it.[58]

In July of that year Bucer again requested Philip
most humbly not to publish the *Dialogue* in such a
troubled time. Since the landgrave required no defense
to protect his reputation among believers, Bucer felt
that it would be wrong to create additional, unnecessary
difficulties for the church in such a time of distress.[59]
Evidently the landgrave had notified him that he intended
to publish the book, and this resolve he consummated in
spite of the reformer's remonstrances. On August 16,
1541, he declared that he could no longer refrain from
publishing the *Dialogue,* and either shortly before, or
after, this date the book was printed secretly,[60] and distributed privately among the people whom the landgrave
hoped to influence.[61]

To this act, which gave up practically all pretence at
secrecy,[62] the landgrave was forced by circumstances with

---

[52] Dommer, no. 138, p. 75. Baumgarten has called it, ''Eine höchst
seltene Vetheidigung der Doppelehe des Landgrafen Philipp'' (S. J. Baumgarten, *Nachrichten von merkwürdigen Büchern,* p. 103; *cf.* Baum, no. 56,
p. 601, ff.).

[53] See below, p. 181, n. 160.   [54] Dommer, p. 17, ff.
[55] Lenz, III, 97.   [56] *Ibid.,* II, 26, n. 5, and p. 78.
[57] *CR.,* IV, 798.   [58] Lenz, II, 78; *CR.,* IV, 798.
[59] Lenz, II, 26.   [60] *Ibid.,* p. 29.

[61] *Ibid.,* pp. 26, 45. Bucer sent a copy to Blaurer, saying, ''die andere
Schrifft, den Dialog, habe ich mit dem Franzosen geschickt, der wegen
Farels Eueren Rat einholen wollte; ist er nicht zu Euch gekommen so
berichte, und ich will ein anderes Exemplar senden; eines ist noch hier''
(Schiess, II, 93).

[62] P. Smith, *The Life and Letters of Martin Luther,* p. 384.

which he felt unable to cope in any other way. First, the "horrible outcry" made by his sister and the Duchess of Saxony had resulted in scandalous reports about him, and his embarrassment was increased by the attacks of Duke Henry of Brunswick.[63] Most of all Philip had been aroused by Henry's latest attack, the *Vierte bestendige Antwort,* in which he was reproached especially on account of the bigamy.[64] Fearing not so much the exposure of the fact of the bigamy as that people would be influenced to believe he had committed a sin against God, the landgrave sought to preclude such a disaster by having the *Dialogue* printed "and afterwards distributed as advantageously as possible,"[65] . . . "in order that people could have a basis for concluding that we have begun nothing without divine Scripture and good reason.'"[66] If Duke Henry had not made such shameless and bitter accusations, the book would have remained a manuscript, so the landgrave claimed.[67] Secondly, Philip thought that the nature of the book was such that printing and selling it would be a wise procedure.[68] He described it as only a disputation, "presented in mild language" so that "it would not give occasion for any embarrassment.'"[69] Thirdly, fully convinced that a secret publication would avoid the offence which Bucer feared,[70] thus removing the chief objection, the landgrave saw no reason why he should hesitate longer and refused to do so.[71]

That no time was lost in distributing this new defense

[63] Lenz, II, 68.

[64] *Ibid.,* p. 29, n. 1.

[65] *Ibid.,* p. 29.

[66] *Ibid.,* p. 45.

[67] *Ibid.*

[68] *Ibid.,* p. 29. It was probably sold in the markets at Leipzig (Kroker, no. 565), and Strasbourg (Lenz, II, 79). *Cf.* below, n. 282, and Muller, "Zur Digamie des Landgrafen Philipps von Hessen," *Archiv für Reformationsgeschichte,* 1903-1904, I, 367.

[69] Lenz, II, 29.

[70] Lenz, II, 29.

[71] *Ibid.,* pp. 29, 45.

of the landgrave's conduct, is shown by the fact that when Sailer expressed a desire on August 17, 1541, to receive a copy of the *Dialogue*,[72] only ten days elapsed before the prince sent him eighty copies[73] for distribution to "people of discernment." While not informing Sailer of the origin of the book, he made it clear that it only submitted a question for discussion and not an example for imitation.[74] One copy the physician gave to Duke Ottheinrich, another to Wolfgang Musculus, a theologian of Augsburg who had gone there from Strasbourg,[75] and who read it with "cautious reserve," and others to various preachers whom it "pleased very well."[76]

When Bucer received a notification that the landgrave would print and distribute the *Dialogue,* he again warned the prince not to fall into such an error. Believing that Philip and the elector should show more patience in enduring the attacks of Duke Henry of Brunswick, he declared that God was chastening the landgrave through Satan and his instrument Duke Henry, in order to remind him of his weakness and impel him to live more chastely.[77] "Therefore your princely grace should not be angry at him who is a rod of God, but more at that for which God uses the rod, and consider rather how the true office of prince is imperfectly exercised by him and others who oppress the poor and hinder the kingdom of God."[78] To scold so much Bucer regarded as un-German and un-princely, thinking it better to ignore the enemy's accusations.

[72] Evidently offered him by Philip (*ibid.*, III, 145, 147).

[73] *Ibid.*, p. 186, n. 1. This is an evidence that it had been printed only a short time.

[74] *Ibid.*, pp. 147-148.   [75] Rockwell, p. 123.

[76] Lenz, III, 186, n. 1. In March, 1542, Bucer found an extract from the *Dialogue* in Nidda, which was printed for general insertion in other books (Lenz, II, 64).

[77] *Cf. Argumenta Buceri*, p. 55, ff.   [78] Lenz, II, 30.

Not only would it be wrong to publish the *Dialogue* merely to reply to Duke Henry, Bucer thought, but the evil would be increased because the book itself was of such a nature that it was dangerous to distribute it. He said, "to distribute this book among the common herd will surely instigate a new sect of wild fanatics, because people will think it is intended as an example for all and the opinion aroused will be far from approval or justification."[79] By publishing the book the landgrave would only give the mad reason for more madness, he believed, and unnecessarily offend those who were faithful to him.[80]

The *Dialogue* was published under the pseudonym of "Hulderichus Neobulus," and even as late as 1900 the authorship has been attributed to Bucer. The first record of this supposition is a letter written by Luther to Justus Menius, January 10, 1542, in which he said concerning the *Dialogus Neobuli,* "It has been told me that the author is that Carthusian monster, the pastor at Melsungen. At least I can easily believe it . . . for Bucer smells bad enough on account of the Regensburg Articles."[81] While Luther evidently did not regard Bucer as the author, this letter shows that he had heard a rumor that the Strasbourger had written the book.

Corvinus, who was himself accused of writing the *Dialogue,* indignantly denied the report, of which he said, "Nothing has ever yet happened to me in my whole life more depressing than this false rumor, which is circulated so that I should be forced to bear the sins of

[79] *Ibid.,* p. 31.

[80] *Ibid.,* pp. 29-31. A little less than a year later, when he was attacked as the author of the *Dialogue,* he said, "De dialogi invidia plus satis scio; sed si scirent studiosi Christi, quae ea in re egerim ab initio et quanta molitus sim, ne quid existeret offendiculi: scio, me facile absolverent hic omni crimine" (Schiess, II, 132).

[81] Enders, XIV, 152. On Bucer's publication of the Acts of the Diet of Ratisbon, see Mentz, no. 49, ff.

others.''[82] He asked his friend Agricola to defend him
against the accusation, and expressed his opinion concerning the authorship by saying, ''For Bucer is the
author of that *Dialogue,* and a certain Lening, a Hessian
preacher, not Corvinus, that which as a friend I entrust
to the confidence of a friend.''[83]

In March, 1542, Bucer found on returning to Strasbourg, that the whole council and many good citizens had
been turned against him through the ''false accusation''
by certain disciples of Schwenckfeld that the landgrave
had paid him four hundred talers to write the *Dialogue*
for print, as was also reported generally in Nürnberg and
Swabia. The reformer asserted that he had neither instigated such a writing nor had it printed; that he was
sorry that the people were offended by it; and that he
had ''received no money from the landgrave or anyone
else for writing such or other writings.''[84] Who these
disciples of Schwenckfeld were, Bucer did not state, but
they continued to use this report as a basis for attacks
against him,[85] and with the assistance of Michael Hahn[86]
endeavored to influence the rulers of the city to compel
Bucer to write against the *Dialogue.* This last effort was
unsuccessful, but one of the Schwenckfelders said to him
in the presence of other people, that if he had composed
this writing, then he regarded him as the worst demon
upon the earth.[87] Bucer reported his reply upon this occasion as follows, ''I thereupon asserted that I had
neither given advice nor assisted in the distribution of
such compositions among the people, nor in the institution of a following of such actions; but that I would not

[82] Tschackert, *Briefwechsel des Corvinus,* p. 110.
[83] *Ibid.*
[84] Lenz, II, 65.
[85] *Ibid.*
[86] The secretary of the city of Strasbourg (Lenz, II, 78).
[87] *Ibid.,* p. 72.

write against it, for I knew no word of God that condemned the deed, as it condemned general immorality, lewdness, and the like; and, though God had not only permitted somewhat of the former among his [people] but also blessed it, he had severely punished the latter. . . . And this is their chief complaint, that in the *Dialogue* it is called a gift of God to render marriage service to many wives; understanding it in an immoral sense; and [do] not, like the Scriptures, call reproduction and the raising of children a blessing of God.''[88]

It is unlikely that this attack by Schwenckfeld's disciples was due to any personal influence by Schwenckfeld, although he was not friendly to Bucer at this time.[89] On January 5, 1542, Schwenckfeld wrote to the landgrave, sending him a copy of his *Large Confession*.[90] A month later the prince forwarded it to Melanchthon for criticism with the remark, ''Also, dear Philip, it seems to us from Schwenckfeld's book that he is somewhat opposed to Bucer, and as we are well inclined toward Bucer, so we would be unhappy to let this *primats odij* go without reply.''[91] The subject upon which Schwenckfeld was opposed to Bucer had nothing to do with the *Dialogue* or the bigamy, but concerned the sin against the Holy Spirit. This is clear from the landgrave's reply, in which he said, ''But we are very much displeased with you in that you accuse Bucer of having written that no sin is condemned except the sin against the Holy Ghost, and you attack him sharply, . . . But we must say this truthfully, that Bucer has preached often to us and others a far different teaching, and I have seldom heard a preacher, who has exhorted so earnestly to an upright life,

---

[88] *Ibid.*   [89] Lenz, II, 81.

[90] J. L. French, *The Correspondence of C. Schwenckfeld . . . and the Landgrave Philip of Hesse*, p. 18, ff.

[91] *Ibid.*, p. 33; *cf.* Varrentrapp, ''Achte Briefe Melanchthons,'' *Forschungen zur Deutschen Geschichte*, XVI, 13.

abstinence from sin, and good conduct, as he has done. How often have we heard him preach, as Paul declares, that fornicators and adulterers should not inherit the kingdom of God!''[92] The fact that the landgrave lays so much stress on Bucer's moral and disciplinary advice, requires no further explanation than that this was the virtue for which he most admired him, and affords no basis for the presumption that Schwenckfeld had attacked Bucer as lax in this respect.[93]

Michael Hahn, the secretary of Strasbourg, though later reconciled to Bucer,[94] was at this time numbered among his most persistent enemies. Recognizing in the report that Bucer had written the *Dialogus Neobuli* a fortuitous means of discrediting him in the eyes of the city magistrates,[95] he returned to Strasbourg from Speier in the following April, bringing new copies of the *Dialogue* with the report that the landgrave had commanded them to be distributed openly.[96] By marrying the daughter of the Ammeister,[97] Hahn gained considerable influence, which he used against Bucer,[98] and it is possible that he was the author[99] of an anonymous poem, published probably in 1544,[100] which satirized the reformer and ac-

[92] French, p. 29. Melander offered to let Bucer copy out the part of Schwenckfeld's book in which he was attacked, and Bucer replied that he would do so (Lenz, II, 80). Before the end of May a confutation of Schwenckfeld had been prepared by the landgrave (Schiess, II, 125).

[93] In April, 1542, there was a rumor that Schwenckfeld would write to the landgrave about the *Dialogue* (Lenz, II, 73, ff.). No doubt Schwenckfeld heard the rumor of Bucer's authorship, and if he had wanted a good ground for attack, he could hardly have found one more discreditable to the reformer, if it had been true.

[94] Ficker and Winckelmann, I, 19. He was not the only one offended by the *Dialogue* (Lenz, II, 246). The reconciliation was in 1544.

[95] Lenz, II, 72.   [96] *Ibid.*, p. 78.

[97] The Ammeister was Matthias Geiger (Lenz, II, 81, n. 6).

[98] Lenz, II, 81.   [99] Rockwell, p. 124, n. 1.

[100] Not in 1541, as Strobel thinks, for on June 5, 1544, Bucer wrote to A. Blaurer, ''De infaustissimo et pernicoso illo libello valde me conturbasti.

cused him of writing the *Dialogue*.[101] This poem bears
the title, *Wider das unchristlich Gesprechbüchlin von vile
der Eeweiber, So durch eynen geschwinden, aufrürischen
Sophisten (der sich erdichter weisz Huldreych Neobulus
nennen thut) gemachte ist, Eyn kurtz Gedicht, Darinnen
gemelter Neobulus mit seinen eygnen Farben ganz artlich
ausgestrichen wirt. Contra adsertorem Polygamiae.*[102] In
this poem three characters appear: Neobulus, a young
man, and an old man. The old man complains that the
doctrine of bigamy has come too late for his benefit, and
the young man thanks Neobulus for teaching it.[103] Of
Bucer it is said,

> "Von Art ein Jud[104] und falscher Christ,
>   voll geschwinder griff und ein Sophist,
>   der dichter dieses Buchlins ist.
> Ein gleissner und falscher Schrifftgelert,
>   der Gott sein Wort und Werck verkert,
>   zeucht den Mosen fälschlich an
>   auff das er irr mach jederman,
>   will damit sein schalkheyt decken,
>   und ein Türkische sect erwecken."

Hic, qui impresserit, pervestigari non potest; te per Christum rogo, ut
indicia suppedites, quo deprehendi hic miser possit et compesci nocentissima
ista petulantia. Credo te mihi credere; quod editio istius libri et congestio
me invitissimo et summopere dolente facta est" (Schiess, II, 267). *Cf.* G.
Strobel, *Beyträge zur Litteratur besonders des sechzehnten Jahrhunderts*,
II, 423.

[101] Strobel, II, 423-427. Also quoted in Schelhorn, *Ergotzlichkeiten aus
der Kirchenhistorie und Litteratur*, I, 633; and in Janssen, III, 448, n. 1,
where it is translated into verse.

[102] Strobel, II, 423. Rockwell gives the title as follows, "Wider das
Unchristlich Gesprechbüchlein, von vile der Eeweiber, So durch eynen
geschwinden auffrürischen Sophisten (der sich erdichter weisz Huldreych
Neobulus nennen thut) gemacht ist, Ein kurtz Gedicht, Darinnen gemelter
Neobulus, seinen eygnen Farben, gantz artlich aussgestrichen wirt" (Rock-
well, p. 124, n. 1).

[103] Strobel, II, 423.

[104] On the story that Bucer was of Jewish parentage, see above, p. 1.

Neobulus concludes the poem by saying,

"So wil ich die wilden Katzen[105]
umb mich beissen, krummen, kratzen,
mit Teufel und scheltworten hawen drein,
und wütten wie ein wildes Schwein,
Schenden und schmehen jederman,
wer nit mir wil sein daran,
und was ich bösz erdencken kan,
dasz musz on alle scham herausz,
und solt als unglück kommen drausz,
damit will ich mich hawen ausz.
Wie Martin Luther hat gethan,
der nie keyn schelten underlan,
So jemandt wider ihn hat gredt,
und sein leer antast oder gfredt."

In April, 1542, a report reached Bucer's ears that Luther would attack him as the author of the *Dialogue,* and though the report proved to be unfounded, it shows that the rumor of Bucer's authorship was wide-spread.[106] In the Berlin copy of the *Dialogue* there is an inscription by the hand of Abraham Buchholzer, "Bucer may be the author although some say that the book is by Lening."[107] John Forster wrote to Schradi on May 19, 1542, that the author of the *Dialogue* was not only Bucer, but he cooperated with some other servant of the landgrave, so that whatever happened he might be on the safe side. If

[105] This is a reference to Bucer, whose *Explanationes Psalmorum* were published under the name of "Aretii Felini."

[106] Lenz, II, 67.

[107] Rockwell, p. 123, n. 8. Seidemann in his edition of the sixth volume of deWette quotes as proof of Bucer's authorship, a title given in the "Cod. Palat. 435" at the Heidelberg Library, p. 126, "Martini Buceri Buch de bigamia gestellet für den Landgraven zu Hessen, aber nit dermassen gestalt dasz es in deutsch sollte ausgehen." But it seems more probable that this refers to the *Argumenta Buceri.* So also Rockwell understands it (Rockwell, p. 226, n. 6). *Cf.* also *CR.,* III, 850; deWette, VI, 295.

THE *DIALOGUS NEOBULI* 173

the writing was a success, he intended to seek the glory
for himself, so Forster believed, but if not, then he
would have someone else upon whom to throw the guilt.
"If words, if style, if the choice of words, if the names
of the collocutors, if the authorities which he cites, lastly,
if the dialogue method in which he delights above others,
and, indeed, if anyone examines the whole argument and
treatment of the subject very diligently, and collates it
with his other writings, certainly no one will say or decide otherwise than that Bucerism is imitated."[108] Forster's surmise as to Bucer's purpose was incorrect, for
when the book was a failure he did not throw the blame
upon the real author, who must have been known to him.
Besides, there is no authority for thinking that he would
have claimed the glory had the reception of the book been
favorable.[109]

Four years later, in January, 1546, Cochläus, who was
engaged in a controversy with Bucer over celibacy, said,
"A year ago I read a libel brought from Germany,[110] in
which the plurality of wives was defended with seemly
reasons. Some suspect you of being the author of this,
since, indeed, you can hardly disprove that report."[111]
In the same year, Anton Engelbrecht, who had been re-
converted to the Roman Church,[112] repeated this accusa-

---

[108] deWette-Seidemann, VI, 295.

[109] The *Zimmerische Chronik* says in regard to the bigamy of the landgrave, "Er hat ein argen, iedoch gelerten schalk gefunden, war der Martin
Butzer; der liesz ein buch im druck uzgeen, das ain christenmann wol gepure,
zwai eheweiber mit guetem gewissen einsmals zu haben. Aber es ist bei den
Deutschen nit angenommen worden und hat man das buch in seinem wert
bleiben lassen" (*Zimmerische Chronik*, IV, p. 13, 1st edition).

[110] At that time Cochläus was in Breslau.

[111] Rockwell, p. 124, n. 1. Later, in 1546, Bucer wrote to the landgrave
from the Ratisbon Colloquy, "Cochläus ist ein alts arms kind, bullet schwach,
und beisst gar nicht, das sich sein auch seine mitcolloquenten beschemen"
(Lenz, II, 410).

[112] In 1544. *Cf.* Lenz, II, 265. This was not Bucer's first encounter with
Engelbrecht, who had been the official granting him his release from the

tion in a book written against Bucer under the pseudonym
of "Werner von Warresheim."[113] The rumor even followed the reformer to England, and on June 8, 1550, John
Burcher wrote to Bullinger, "Bucer is more than licen-
tious on the subject of marriage. I heard him once disput-
ing at table upon the question, when he asserted that a
divorce should be allowed for any reason, however trifling,
so that he is considered, not without cause, by our bishop
of Winchester,[114] as the author of the book published in
defense of the landgrave."[115]

Dominican Order in 1521 (*Verantwortung*, pp. 5, 9, 33). Later he had
joined the evangelicals and had taken a church at Strasbourg, but his
immoral conduct and other misdemeanors had made it necessary to put
him out of the city (Schiess, I, 442, 450, 459, 466-468, 475, 492, 767). Consequently, he cherished a bitter enmity for Bucer, and was glad of an
opportunity to slander him.

[113] Lenz, II, 429; Röhrich, p. 182; Rockwell, p. 124, n. 1. Bucer wrote
to the landgrave on May 8, 1546, about this attack, "Heisset doctor
Antonius Engelbrecht. Diesem deufel muss ich, weil er sich nit nennet, mit
schriften begegnen, wie ich kan. Aber so der ander sein namen hinbei
gesetzet und sich zu Mentz heltet, wolt ich warlich gern, E. f. g. hetten
sich des gegen dem bischove von Mentz mit ernst beklagt" (Lenz, II,
429, ff.). Bucer replied to Engelbrecht in *Der CXX Psalm*, p. G; *cf*. Schelhorn, I, 633, ff. See below, p. 177.

[114] I.e., Stephen Gardiner. In 1544 he had attacked Bucer when an
English translation of Bucer's account of the Diet of Ratisbon was published (S. Gardiner, *Stephani Wintoni . . . ad M. Bucer de impudenti . . .
conquestio*, 1544). Gardiner himself was accused by Melanchthon of carrying around with him two prostitutes in men's clothing (*CR.*, III, 799), and
Bucer called him "that devilish bishop of Winchester" (Lenz, I, 243)
which was uncustomarily hard language for Bucer to use. He lamented
Gardiner's influence over Henry VIII (Lenz, II, 267).

[115] *Original Letters*, II, 665, ff. Burcher was in Strasbourg at the time
he wrote this letter so it may have been there that he heard Bucer's discourse, but his information about the opinion of the bishop of Winchester
shows that the rumor was abroad in England. His hatred of Bucer is explained by the dread of the Zurichers that Bucer's influence in England
would be used against them because of his disagreement with their interpretation of the Supper (Harvey, p. 54). On Aug. 11, 1549, Bullinger wrote
to Blaurer, "Bucer est in Anglia et plane retinet antiquum; quod ab eo
accepit Germania idem accipiet Anglia. Dominus autem protegat hanc

The belief that Bucer was the author of the *Dialogus Neobuli* lasted down into the twentieth century. When Jacob Baumgarten wrote his *Nachrichten von merkwürdigen Büchern* he judged that the *Dialogus Neobuli* surpassed all other writings in decisiveness and intellectuality. Bucer he thought to be the author, and said, "Among all the suppositions as to the author of this dialogue, the most palpable suspicion falls upon Martin Bucer, who let himself be exploited by the landgrave not only in this affair."[116] Bretschneider, in his edition of Melanchthon's correspondence, assumed that Bucer was the author of the *Dialogue*,[117] and even said explicitly, "the book of Hulderichus Neobulus about bigamy was written by Martin Bucer to please the landgrave."[118] At about the same time the rumor that Bucer wrote the book was accepted by an anonymous historian, who wrote on the history of the bigamy in the *Historisch-politische Blätter* in 1846, and said, "Bucer previously accomplished his purpose with crafty moderation, when, by arranging the arguments and counter-arguments one beside the other, he injected bewilderment into the common mind, whether bigamy might not still be permitted."[119] This writer, who gave a long summary of the *Dialogue,* again showed his belief in Bucer's authorship by saying, "Indisputably Bucer had by the attempt reported above."[120] The last historian to think that Bucer was the author of the *Dialogue* was Tschackert.[121]

a malo et det isti meliorem menten vel meliorem metam. Sed oportet esse in tam ingrato et iniquo seculo instrumenta irae et corruptionis. Dominus Iesus misereatur suorum! Haec tibi plura iam non possum" (Schiess, III, 55, ff.).

[116] Baumgarten, V, 507. Baumgarten's work was published in 1754.

[117] *Cf. CR.,* IV, 761, 768.   [118] *CR.,* V, 75, n. 2.

[119] *Historisch-politische Blätter,* XVIII, 521, ff.

[120] *Ibid.,* p. 522.

[121] P. Tschackert, *Antonius Corvinus Leben und Schriften* (1900), p. 61, n. 4.

In spite of this wide-spread opinion there is sufficient convincing evidence to show incontrovertibly that Bucer was not the author of the *Dialogus Neobuli*. He himself made a number of statements on this point which are trustworthy; and especially those written to the landgrave, because there would have been no advantage in not telling him the truth. Even more convincing than a positive denial of authorship was the indirect statement made by Bucer in a letter to the landgrave on July 19, 1541, "As I have before besought your princely grace, so I beg you again most humbly for God's sake, that you will not let the writing which I prepared for you here, even less the other little book, be issued in such a troubled time: also provide that the style, which is composed in imitation of my own, shall be changed."[122] The "other book" referred to is the *Dialogus Neobuli*.[123] Bucer's acknowledgment of the authorship of the first book, and his statement that the second was written in a style in imitation of his own, are equivalent to an assertion that he was not the author of the second book. The fact that he says that he prepared the first book at Regensburg, shows that it could not have been the *Dialogus Neobuli*, because the landgrave probably brought the latter to the Diet with him.[124] In a letter to Ambrose Blaurer at Constance, written early in March, 1542, Bucer said, "Concerning the *Dialogue* I do not make any false pretences, but I write truly that I am not the author of the writing, however much they insinuate that about me."[125]

When the report that Bucer had written the *Dialogus Neobuli* reached Strasbourg, he was summoned before the council about the middle of March, 1542, and questioned.[126] The magistrates were anxious lest this report,

[122] Lenz, II, 26.   [123] *Ibid.*, p. 26, n. 5.
[124] *Ibid.* Or it may have been brought to him there, *cf.* above, p. 164; see below, p. 181, n. 160.
[125] Schiess, II, 106, 132.   [126] Lenz, II, 65.

if true, would make his service unfruitful, and arouse as much offence against the gospel as the Peasants' Revolt, the sacrament-strife, or the Münster uproar. To the landgrave Bucer reported his answer as follows, "I replied that I had neither instigated such a writing nor had it printed, I was sorry that the people were offended by it; also, neither from your grace nor anyone else, had I ever received any money for composing such or other writings. . . . Now your princely grace knows that I was accused untruthfully in this, and so I humbly ask your princely grace that if there is anyone about your princely grace who would drag me into such suspicion, that he be guarded against."[127] It might be said that Bucer did not tell the truth to the council, but this can hardly be claimed about his statement to the landgrave, who knew all about the matter and could not be deceived. Consequently, there is no good reason to doubt the veracity of his denial that he wrote the *Dialogue* or received any money for doing so. On April 15, 1542, Bucer wrote to the landgrave again, "I beg your princely grace to tell Aitinger not to circulate the report about me, as I am not the author."[128] The truth of Bucer's statement that he was not the author of the *Dialogus Neobuli* is corroborated by the landgrave in a letter written December 17, 1541, in which he said, "which *Dialogue* you did not compose in the beginning, but only somewhat corrected and improved it."[129] To this statement were added the words, later crossed out, "when you learned that it would be published."[130]

It has already been noted[131] that Engelbrecht attacked Bucer as the author of the *Dialogus Neobuli,* and that Bucer replied in his *Der CXX Psalm.* In this book Bucer said, "that I am accused, and it is written that I composed

127 *Ibid.*   128 Lenz, II, 81.
129 *Ibid.*, p. 45.   130 *Ibid.*
131 See above, p. 173.

and published, a book under the name of Huldereichus
Neobulus, on the subject that a man at the same time
may without sin have many wives; that is a spiteful lie
of this shameful libeller, of which God and my conscience
know I am innocent. Therefore he will ever have to prove
the accusation which is worthy the belief of none. And
would God that he would esteem and always hold holy
matrimony as I by God's grace have still held and taught;
then I know well that all pious Christians would give
thanks to God the Lord."[132]

One of the strongest arguments that Bucer did not
write the *Dialogue,* aside from his own statements and
what the landgrave said, is the fact that he did not want
the book published.[133] Yet the very character of the work
shows that it was written for publication, to institute a
public following,[134] and that it would have been useless
had it not been published.[135] The *Dialogue* bears the date
March 27, 1541, making it reasonable to suppose that it
was written mostly during the month of March of that
year. Yet before Bucer even saw the book he was almost
too busy[136] to criticize the short passage on the bigamy
in the landgrave's *Dritte Warhafftige Verantwortung.*[137]
So certain is it that Bucer was not the author of the *Dialogus Neobuli* that the latest compiler of his printed works
has omitted the title.[138]

There is good reason to believe that the real author of
the book was John Lening, pastor at Melsungen. Closely

[132] *Der CXX Psalm,* p. G.   [133] Lenz, II, 26, 65, ff.

[134] *Ibid.,* pp. 65, 78.

[135] *Dialogus Neobuli,* p. A a iii, and ff.

[136] Among other things he was preparing for the Diet.

[137] Lenz, II, 21. In April he was busy at the Diet of Regensburg.

[138] Mentz. Baum lists it among Bucer's printed works (p. 601, no. 56)
and refers to Baumgarten. He does not mention any other author but seems
to doubt Bucer's authorship by observing that "Butzer wird darin gar
nicht als der Verfasser bezeichnet und protestirt selbst gegen die Autor-
schaft."

connected with the bigamy from the first, and a leading spirit in its defense, he had composed the *Rathschlag* of the Hessian theologians in December, 1539,[139] and when Bucer and Melanchthon arrived at Rothenburg, he, with Melander, had prepared them for what was about to happen.[140] It was Lening who wrote "a little book for M" in order to quiet her conscience,[141] and when Melanchthon, in June, 1540, expressed an opinion unfavorable to bigamy, he found three days sufficient time in which to write a confutation.[142] Bucer seems to have recognized that he was a man of some ability, for in March, 1540, he asked Philip to send him to Smalkald, partly in order to discuss the landgrave's "affair."[143] Perhaps Bucer perceived that Lening was not able to hold his tongue very well[144] and wished to caution him against disclosing the secret. In the following December he wrote to Philip, "I wish that Lening had explained to your princely grace what I have written about this[145] in my commentary on Matthew."[146]

It is the universal opinion of contemporary and modern writers that Lening was a bad character. On December 11, 1541, Melanchthon wrote to a friend, "Lening . . . is a monstrosity in body and mind, καὶ ὠμὸς τῇ συζύγῳ. When he gambles with various opinions in religion, it is amazing how much he amuses himself."[147] When he heard of the death of Melander he wrote to Justus Menius, "Dio-

---

139 The "Consilium nostrorum Theologorum" (Rockwell, p. 37, n. 1).

140 Lenz, I, 360.

141 Rockwell, p. 120; Heppe, *op. cit.*, p. 272.

142 Rockwell, p. 69.   143 Lenz, I, 147.

144 deWette, V, 344.   145 I.e., the law of love.

146 Lenz, I, 264. Lening had helped compose the landgrave's reply to the Würtemberg theologians in Nov., 1540 (Lenz, I, 270), and he was among the three Hessian preachers to whom Bucer wished the landgrave to show the results of the secret colloquy at Worms (Lenz, I, 291).

147 *CR.*, IV, 709. Myconius expressed a similarly unfavorable opinion in a letter to Melanchthon on Mar. 26, 1543 (*CR.*, V, 72).

nysius the preacher of Macedon [Hesse] is dead I hear, and I am sorry, for now I fear Lening greatly.''[148] Rockwell, who has examined Lening's life with great care, can find little to his credit,[149] and Grisar has judged Melanchthon's opinion of the man to be a reliable one.[150]

There exists no statement by the landgrave, Lening, or Bucer, to the effect that Lening wrote the *Dialogus Neobuli,* nor has Melanchthon, who was shown the book at Regensburg,[151] and probably told the name of the author, left any definite information. Yet there are still a number of cumulative arguments, which indicate that Lening was the author. First, the printer's manuscript, now kept in the Marburg archives, has the title and corrections in Lening's own hand.[152] This shows without doubt that he was at least connected with the composition of the book. Secondly, Melanchthon has made a statement indicating that he thought Lening was the author. In his letter to Theodore on December 11, 1541, he called Lening a monstrosity, and then continued, ''Wherefore I wish you to spare Bucer. And those insulting libels of Jason[153] will sink into oblivion of themselves. By our writings they would be made more notorious and perchance pursue the career which their authors desire for them. We have expressed our opinion about the subject frequently in other works and still may do so.''[154] Both Ambrose Blaurer and Bullinger suspected Lening of the authorship of the *Dialogue,* as appears from one of Blaurer's letters in which he wrote, ''About the author it is easy to say something. Lening is not in Strasbourg, as you write, but a learned,

148 *CR.,* V, 367.
149 Rockwell, p. 117, n. 1.
150 Grisar, II, 425.
151 *CR.,* IV, 798.
152 Rockwell, p. 121. This manuscript was written by John Pistorius, the pastor at Nidda, who was also instrumental in distributing the *Dialogue* (Rockwell, p. 331; Lenz, II, 65). *Cf.* above, p. 166, n. 76.
153 A reference to Lening (*cf.* deWette, VI, 295).
154 *CR.,* IV, 709.

pious preacher, Lenglin, yet he never published the *Dialogue.*"[155]

Quite significant is the fact that when Bullinger attacked the *Dialogue,* the landgrave sent a copy of the attack to Lening in order that he might write a reply to it.[156] At the same time he sent a copy to Bucer.[157] It was natural for him to ask the author to reply to Bullinger, and so, unconsciously, the landgrave indicated Lening as the man who wrote the book. There is a clear statement by Luther which shows that he thought that Lening was the author, although not entirely certain of the fact. On January 10, 1542, he wrote to Menius that he was strongly inclined to write against the *Dialogue,* "indeed I am wearied by the arguments of that most wicked man, so steeped are they in senseless stupidity and vapid chattering." To this opinion about the book he added, "It has been told me that the author is that Carthusian monster, the pastor at Melsungen. At least I can easily believe it. All those gods have piled their beautiful gifts in that Pandora."[158] The testimony of Corvinus has been noticed.[159] On October 24, 1542, Justus Jonas wrote to John Lang at Erfurt, "I wish Lening were elsewhere. For it is said he composed the *Dialogue* about polygamy."[160]

The circle of men who were on the inside of the secret of the bigamy was a small one. Melanchthon and Luther belonged to this circle, and their statements about the author of the *Dialogue,* although not conclusive, are almost so, because the number of men who might have written the book was also small, and the probability is

---

[155] Schiess, II, 100.

[156] *Cf.* below, p. 215.

[157] Lenz, II, 120.

[158] Enders, XIV, 152.

[159] See above, p. 167.

[160] Kawerau, *Der Briefwechsel des Justus Jonas,* II, 83. There is a manuscript note, signed "Joan Hall," in the back of the copy owned by Professor Rockwell, which states that Lening was the author and that the *Dialogue* was taken to the landgrave at the Diet by Andrew Kolbe.

that Luther and Melanchthon guessed right, if they guessed at all. That so many other reformers also accused Lening shows that there must have been some basis for their suspicion. Every historian of the bigamy who has written since the middle of the nineteenth century has accepted the authorship of Lening as proven; for example, such scholars as Seidemann,[161] Röhrich,[162] Schmidt,[163] Köstlin,[164] Janssen,[165] Rockwell, and others.[166] It may therefore be safely assumed that Lening was the author.

Bucer did not write the *Dialogus Neobuli*. How then did the rumor arise that he was the author? First, although he did not compose the book, yet he had "somewhat corrected and improved it."[167] Bucer himself admitted that some parts of the *Dialogue* were originated by him, but denied that he had inserted them in the book or had it published.[168] Secondly, it is probable that the landgrave told of Bucer's participation in the composition of the book, and though not himself responsible for the report of Bucer's authorship, did not discourage it very actively, to say the least. Bucer wrote to him on November 30, 1541, "But, for the Lord's sake, I still be-

[161] deWette, VI, 294, ff.   [162] Röhrich, p. 181.

[163] G. L. Schmidt, *Justus Menius, der Reformator Thuringens*, I, 256; *Zeitschrift für die historische Theologie*, 1868, I, 445.

[164] Köstlin, II, 519.   [165] Janssen, III, 447.

[166] Rockwell, p. 121, ff. Some of the others are: Varrentrapp in the *Forschungen zur Deutschen Geschichte*, XVI, 16; Lenz, II, 26, n. 5; Rady, p. 100; Dommer, p. 75; Muller in the *Archiv für Reformationsgeschichte*, I, 365; Kawerau in Enders, XIV, 153, n. 1.

[167] Lenz, II, 45.

[168] Schiess, II, 132. The text of this letter is partially unreadable but it seems that he went on to say that he was faithfully promised that the book would not be publicly distributed, and whatever he had written would be for people of sound faith and judgment, and not for the public. Paulus mistakenly says that Bucer admitted his share in the authorship, in a letter in March, 1542. *Cf.* Paulus in the *Historisch-politische Blätter*, CXLVII, 511; Lenz, II, 59, n. 1; Schiess, II, 106.

seech your princely grace not to say that I have composed any part of the work.''[169] This implies, though not necessarily, that Bucer thought the landgrave had told of his part in the writing of it, nor, indeed, could Philip have failed to realize that connecting Bucer's name with the authorship of the *Dialogue* would give it greater prestige. That he did not discourage the report very energetically is shown by Bucer's frequent complaints that men in the landgrave's service, even his old friend Dr. Sailer,[170] had hinted that he was the author, and on March 21, 1542, he besought the landgrave, ''If there is anyone about your princely grace who would drag me into suspicion, take precautions against him. And if Dionysius or Pistorius, or others testify in that manner at Frankfurt, I beg that your princely grace will command them, if they have cause to speak of the matter, to turn aside the unrighteous suspicion from me, and have regard for the service of Christ in which I am.''[171] When Hahn brought the report to Strasbourg that Philip's secretary, Aitinger, had told him that Bucer was the author, Bucer begged the landgrave to impose silence upon Aitinger, yet not to ''feel hard toward either one of them for they are closely related.''[172] To this last complaint the landgrave replied that after he had inquired into the affair, he had ascertained that Aitinger had given a copy of the *Dialogue* to Hahn, but he had said nothing about the author, although he surmised that Bucer was the person ''who revised and modified it.''[173]

Thirdly, as John Forster said, there was a remarkable similarity between Bucer's style and that of the *Dialogus Neobuli*.[174] Even Bucer recognized this and implored the landgrave not to publish the book without changing the

---

[169] Lenz, II, 39.

[171] Lenz, II, 65.

[173] *Ibid.*, p. 82.

[170] *Ibid.*

[172] *Ibid.*, p. 81.

[174] deWette, VI, 295.

style so that it would not resemble his own.[175] It is not at all improbable that the author intentionally imitated him,[176] yet a comparison of the *Argumenta Buceri pro et contra* with the *Dialogus Neobuli* shows some striking differences in form. For example, in the *Argumenta Buceri* the sentences are much shorter and not so involved.

The *Dialogus Neobuli* has been characterized by one Roman Catholic writer as pedantic, involved, and unintelligible,[177] and by another as a cleverly composed book,[178] the "greatest masterpiece of sophistry, perhaps of all the centuries since the Reformation."[179] To a certain extent these criticisms are all true, and yet, in spite of its involved sentences and repetitious mode of argument based on unwarranted assumptions, the *Dialogue* is written with great skill, so as to make bigamy appear not only to be right, but, if that is admitted, also attractive.[180] Throughout the argument for bigamy is negative, and while aiming only to refute its opponents, presents a Utopian view of Christian polygamy which might seem convincing theoretically, if it were not so contrary to the practical and empirical issues involved.

The full title of the book is: *Dialogue, das ist ein*

---

[175] Lenz, II, 26.

[176] *Cf.* the following sentence in Bucer's letter to the landgrave, July 8, 1540, with the title of the *Dialogus Neobuli* (see below, p. 184), "kein Fleisz gespart werden um mit dem göttlichen Wort zu bezeugen, dasz man die von dem Landgraf gebrauchte Dispensation nicht füglich mit kirchlichem oder weltlichem Recht verdammen könne" (Lenz, I, 180).

[177] Grisar, II, 425. Grisar says that the book was of such a style that it was more repulsive than attractive. The subject matter is indeed repulsive, but the way in which it is written makes the book, which is not a small one, interesting and very readable.

[178] *Historisch-politische Blätter*, XVIII, 522.

[179] *Ibid.*, p. 514.

[180] *Cf.* the opinion of Baumgarten, "sondern auch an Fruchtarkeit der Abhandlung die folgenden Arbeiten von ähnlicher Beschaffenheit merklich ubertrifft" (Baumgarten, V, 503).

*freundtlich Gesprech, Zweyer personen, Davon, Ob es
Göttlichem, Naturlichem, Keyserlichem, und Geystlichem
Rechte gemesse oder entgegen sei, mehr dann eyn Eeweib
zugleich zuhaben. Unnd wo yemant zu diser zeit solchs
fürnehme, ob er als eyn unchrist zuuerwerffen und zuuer-
dammen sei, oder nit.* The two disputants are Parzasius
and Eucharius. After they have greeted each other,
Eucharius invites Parzasius into his garden where the
latter asks his friend what troubles him. He replies that
he is perplexed because he has heard a report that the
Lutherans teach bigamy like the Münsterites and the
Turks. Parzasius tells him that this report is a lie, and
asks why people do not hearken to Luther's teachings
against immorality, which is openly permitted among
the priests. Thereupon Eucharius offers to prove that
anyone who takes a second wife like the patriarchs may
be condemned by divine, canonical, imperial, and natural
law; and Parzasius declares that if he will advance his
arguments he himself will refute them. Thus, throughout
the book objections are brought forward against polygamy from these four kinds of law, and are answered.

The line of argument against the condemnation of
bigamy, or polygamy, for the two are not clearly distinguished in the *Dialogue,* may be best presented in outline form. Under the objections from divine law the following arguments are set forth:

1. The singular used in the first divine institution of
   marriage does not forbid bigamy, because:
   a. The word of God as well as the act is necessary: for
      example, the animals have not always gone in pairs
      because they went into the ark two by two.
   b. The singular form in the text, "shall cleave to his
      wife," does not prove monogamy any more than

"love thy neighbor as thyself" means to love only
one neighbor.

  c. "These two shall be one flesh," does not apply, since
     this is not a peculiar quality of marriage, for Paul
     says a man may be one flesh with a prostitute.
  d. The polygamous, patriarchal marriages must have
     been valid ones. If so, then they did not contradict
     the first institution, and so the first institution does
     not preclude polygamy.
2. The polygamy of the patriarchs
  a. Was not a dispensation unless it can be proved that
     the monogamy of the first institution is an essential
     qualification of valid marriage.
  b. Could not have been intrinsically evil for the plural
     wives were given and blessed by God.
  c. Is not condemned by Christ's decision on divorce,
     for by that
     (1) he condemns only the cause and not divorce
         itself,
     (2) and divorce in itself is not evil.
  d. Differs from other Old Testament laws, such as
     those about circumcision, and the dead brother's
     widow, which were for a special time and the Jews
     only, while polygamy was a general ruling.
  e. Was not granted them only for the increase of
     believers, because
     (1) Jacob took Rachel out of love for her.
     (2) David took Abigail for the same reason.
     (3) Deuteronomy XXI shows God also regarded
         the love of man for woman.
  f. Often was followed by domestic troubles (for ex-
     ample, the quarrel between Rachel and Leah) which
     were due to human weakness and not to polygamy
     itself.

3. Lamech cannot be condemned for being a bigamist, for

  a. If the race before Lamech was monogamous, which cannot be proved, yet they were the wicked descendants of Cain.

  b. It is not certain that he was a murderer, and it cannot be argued from this fact that his bigamy was also wicked.

4. What is not condemned in the Old Testament cannot be condemned in the New Testament, because

  a. II Timothy III: 16-17 says, "all Scripture is profitable," etc., and this refers to the Old Testament. "Judge for yourself. All evil can be so fully shown out of the writings of the Old Testament, as also all good taught, that man can be entirely of God and lack in nothing; but no one may prove out of the writings of the Old Testament that having more than one wife in marriage at the same time is condemned in the children of God. Therefore, polygamy cannot be evil and forbidden, for, in addition, the Lord Jesus Christ and his apostles never condemned it. . . . everywhere there is no virtue or good work which such Scriptures [i.e., the Old Testament] do not sufficiently teach, neither any unvirtuous or evil work which cannot also be rejected irrefutably through these Scriptures and condemned."[181]

5. Christians should be more spiritual than people under the old dispensation, but there is nothing about marriage opposed to spirituality, because

  a. God gave the patriarchs their plural wives and blessed them.

  b. No kind of marriage service could be so opposed to spirituality as the immorality now prevalent.

---

[181] *Dialogus Neobuli*, Bl. D iii. Bucer himself fully believed this (*Verantwortung*, p. ciij; *Wie leicht unnd füglich*, etc., 1545, p. 6; Mentz, no. 64).

6. Paul wished that all men were unmarried like himself so as to avoid the cares of marriage; but this does not forbid polygamy on the ground that it would increase the cares of marriage as in the case of Solomon, because

   a. Solomon had too many cares because he took too many wives, and some of them from the heathen.

   b. Paul elsewhere emphasizes the holiness and usefulness of marriage.

   c. Paul would not contradict God's statement that it is not good for man to be alone.

   d. God created woman to be a helpmeet and not a hindrance.

   e. Paul means here that no one shall try to remain unmarried who does not have the gift of celibacy.

   f. It was on account of persecution that Paul advised them not to marry temporarily.

   g. Paul does not mean that all married people care only for worldly things, and *vice versa*.

   h. Nothing in marriage itself is a hindrance to a Godly life, but celibacy is a hindrance to those who are not called to it.

7. That the bishop should be the husband of one wife means, not that bigamy is a hindrance in ordinary life, but only to church service.

8. Matrimonial service is just as holy in bigamy as in monogamy, because

   a. God is one, and he blessed it among the ancients.

   b. Sexual intercourse is not a hindrance to Godly deeds, or to fasts and prayers, because these are not the only Godly deeds, and cannot be observed continually. It is a necessary thing to those who do not have the gift of remaining without it. Every man should abide in his calling, which for some is bigamy. Bigamy is wicked for those not called to it.

9. Polyandry is not right, because it is against nature and God's command.
10. The example of the patriarchal marriages is valid today, because
    a. They took their plural wives to avoid fornication.
    b. Many men today need a wife to avoid fornication.
    c. Neither God, man, nor bigamy, has changed.
    d. There is no divine law against it.
11. The aversion to the thing is due to
    a. A perverted view of marriage as something evil in itself.
    b. A desire to be holier than God himself, for polygamy would help alleviate the present immorality and drive back the Turk.
12. Paul's use of the singular in the texts, "his own wife," and "her own husband," refers to the usual calling, and not to those called to bigamy. The singular is used also in the Old Testament; for example, in the Ten Commandments, at a time when polygamy was common.
13. The husband and wife have a claim on each other's bodies.
    a. But not to their wantonness.
    b. And some wives cannot fulfil all such service to their husbands.
    c. In such a case, if she is a Christian wife, she will tolerate the taking of another wife, rather than force her husband into immorality.
    d. If this is an essential quality of true marriage, and the marriages of the patriarchs were true marriages, then this quality must have been present and fulfilled with each wife, and so this is no objection to bigamy.
14. A Christian should do nothing to offend his neighbor or transgress the commonly accepted law;

    a. But not to the extent of transgressing God's law and calling.

    b. And if he lives among people who would not allow it, he should call upon God for help to contain himself.

    c. And if he does not receive this help, he should keep his bigamy secret until he has won a dispensation from pious people by his good conduct. God himself has deceived the wicked.

15. The marriage vow, according to present common usage, practically includes a vow of monogamy, and a Christian should keep all promises;

    a. But a man should not hold a vow against God's calling. A pious wife would not bind her husband to such a vow, and if she does he should keep his bigamy secret.

16. Eleven theses on bigamy:

    a. There is one God in the Old Testament and New Testament.

    b. He is unchangeable and cannot permit what is wrong.

    c. He permitted polygamy to the patriarchs for their good.

    d. Polygamy in the Lord is good, for it increases good works.

    e. Many people are called today to polygamy.

    f. There is no clear prohibition of it in Scripture.

    g. Christians should not condemn anything without the clear word of God.

    h. A Christian's word that he needs this should be believed.

    i. Obedience of human ordinances should not cause disobedience of God.

    j. The universal horror of bigamy is not due to the Holy Spirit, for men also permit immorality.

k. Avoiding offence to others should not be carried so
far as to cause sin.

II Arguments from Natural Law

1. Natural law is what nature teaches all men.
2. Matrimonial love should be complete, and though such
love can be shown only to one, there are some who are
so called that they can give it to more than one.
3. The law of nature is a light by which God impels men.
God could not direct it against what he has taught in
the Scriptures, and granted his saints. It has already
been shown that bigamy is right according to the
Scriptures.

III Arguments from Canon Law

1. The Fathers were satisfied with the canon of Paul
and did not forbid bigamy to any but church officers.
2. The Neocaesaraean Council imposed penance on polygamists, and forbade priests to be present at such a
marriage.
   a. But though they imposed penance, they did not
   forbid bigamy.
   b. This action was due to a perverted abhorrence of
   matrimonial duties.
   c. The canon law has often made mistakes; for example, on clerical celibacy and fasting.
   d. We should hold only those canons which are according to the Scriptures. They should not declare
   anything sinful which the Holy Spirit does not declare sinful. That Paul warns church officers to be
   monogamists shows that bigamy was prevalent at
   that time. So this council went further than Paul.
3. The general condemnation of bigamy by the church
during the last twelve hundred years is a mistake due
to the fallibility of her leaders.

4. The early church did not consider bigamy a sin deserving penance, because

   a. Ambrose, who was quite ready to reprove the emperors, did not censure Valentinian for his bigamy or his law permitting bigamy.

   b. Pope Leo deposed a bigamous bishop in Africa, but did not punish him further nor make him give up his bigamous wife.

IV Arguments from Imperial Law

1. The law "Codice de incest. et inutilib. nuptia leg. Neminem" punishes bigamy, and the law "Juli, de adulterio leg." makes it dishonorable, but these laws were passed under heathen emperors when divorce was easy and concubines were numerous; and they refer only to two wives with equal rights.

2. Constantine forbade concubines, but only their maintenance within the home. His law was abrogated by the law of Valentinian.

3. Constantine was the son of a *zuweib*. Constantius, his son, had plural wives, and so did Clothair, and Pippin, Charlemagne, Arnold VII, Frederick Barbarossa, and Philip Augustus.

4. The imperial court, if it was composed of understanding people, would not condemn bigamy if a bigamist won its favor by good conduct.

5. Bigamy among us sinful people contains much that is offensive, and gives cause for jealousy and unfaithfulness, but God guides his people as surely now as he ever did, and so there are some to whom bigamy would be as serviceable as to the patriarchs. To those whom he has called God will give the necessary ability.

Such is the argument for bigamy advanced by Parzasius. Eucharius, however, does not acknowledge himself convinced, but merely says in conclusion, "I have examined all this well, and will not undiligently further consider it. . . . I will not condemn anyone who conducts himself discreetly.'"[182]

Due to the loss of the manuscript containing the changes which Bucer made in the *Dialogue,* it is impossible to indicate with any precision the parts of the book for which he was responsible. There are, however, four passages which seem to owe their form, if not their origin, to him, because they resemble so closely what he had already written elsewhere. These are: the passage on divorce,[183] which is similar to what he had written in his commentary on Matthew;[184] the passage dealing with the gift of celibacy,[185] which also agrees with what he had taught in that connection on divorce;[186] and the passage on refraining from giving offence,[187] which might have been molded by Bucer,[188] because the importance of not offending others is first brought forward by Eucharius, who here makes speeches far longer than in any other part of the book, and in this place alone says anything which convinces Parzasius. The passage dealing with the promise of monogamy implied by the marriage vow[189] expresses the same opinion which Bucer had already advanced in the *Argumenta Buceri pro et contra.*[190] Further comparison of Bucer's known writings with the *Dialogus Neobuli* would reveal many other parallel passages, but by such a method nothing certain could be ascertained, for Lening might easily have copied from

---

[182] *Dialogus Neobuli, Bl.* A a iii.
[183] *Ibid., Bl.* D, ff.
[184] See above, p. 20, ff.
[185] *Dialogus Neobuli, Bl.* F ii, ff.
[186] See above, pp. 25, ff., 28, ff.
[187] *Dialogus Neobuli, Bl.* L iii, ff., and *Bl.* A a ii.
[188] *Cf. Argumenta Buceri,* p. 50, ff.
[189] *Dialogus Neobuli, Bl.* O ii, ff.
[190] *Argumenta Buceri,* pp. 12, 48, ff.

Bucer. All that can as yet be definitely asserted is that the Strasbourg reformer revised this book, which was the strongest argument advanced in defense of the land-grave's bigamy, and played such an important rôle in Bucer's own life.

In the summer following the Diet at Regensburg (1541) Bucer was troubled by financial difficulties. Two of his daughters had reached the age when it was necessary to provide for them a dowry, and with his meager salary he was unable to do this.[191] In the effort to secure suffi-cient funds he attempted to gain, through the influence of Elector Louis of the Palatinate, a return of the prop-erty taken into the cloister by his wife in 1511.[192] At Bucer's request the landgrave wrote an intercessory letter to the elector, which was sent to him by the Hessian chancellor, Henry Has, about the middle of July. Chan-cellor Has having suggested that Alexander von der Thann be appointed by the landgrave to negotiate the matter personally, the landgrave, at Bucer's request, commissioned him to do so;[193] but in spite of this assist-ance Bucer was unsuccessful in his efforts. This is shown by the fact that in 1546 he renewed his pleas to Elector Frederick, reminding him of his previous request sup-ported by the landgrave and the elector of Saxony.[194] This second attempt was also a failure, and it was not until November 4, 1559, when his son Nathaniel was able to secure an installment of one hundred gulden, that any of the property was returned.[195]

[191] Lenz, II, 27.

[192] Bucer to the elector of the Palatinate, July 14, 1541, Thesaurus Baumianus, XV, 139-140; cf. Guendalinus to Bucer, May 29, 1532, The-saurus Baumianus, V, 81; Baum, p. 137, ff.; Lenz, II, 27, n. 1. The property consisted of 200 gulden in cash and 100 gulden in inventoried property (ibid.).

[193] Lenz, II, 26, 31.   [194] Ibid., p. 27 and n. 1.

[195] Ibid.

However, the landgrave was interested in the needs of Bucer's daughters, and on August 16, 1541, himself offered to make a fitting contribution for one or two of them, if Bucer would report what was needed.[196] Though sincerely appreciative of this "gracious" offer on behalf of his children, Bucer refused to accept it, preferring to provide for them out of his wife's property in the Palatinate.[197] Thus he hoped to avoid being a burden upon the prince, while promising that if he did not secure enough through the negotiations of Alexander von der Thann, he would let Philip know how much he needed. For two months Bucer did not write to the landgrave again.[198]

During the autumn of 1541 the plague descended upon Strasbourg,[199] and took from Bucer his strong friend and helper, Capito.[200] Hardly had be begun to recover from this blow, when he was borne down under a far greater sorrow by the death of his wife[201] and three of his children.[202] He felt the loss of his wife deeply, for she had been a "gotselige, geschickte" wife, who "now for twenty years has taken off my shoulders all care of the house and children, and overseen everything decorously and advisedly, which for a long time may not be the good-fortune of myself and my three remaining children. But the Lord is only good. Right and good is what he does, to him be eternal praise, Amen! And may he help us to be anxious, so long as he will have us, to serve him truly and usefully

[196] *Ibid.*, p. 29.

[197] *Ibid.*, p. 31.

[198] Lenz, II, 32.

[199] It reached its height in October and November (*cf.* Schiess, II, 88, 92). Bucer was kept busy, in addition to writing and preaching, by the increased duty of attending the sick (Schiess, II, 92).

[200] On Nov. 4, 1541 (Baum, p. 528). Bucer felt his loss keenly (Schiess, II, 92).

[201] On Nov. 18, 1541 (Baum, p. 137, note).

[202] He lost one son and two daughters (Lenz, II, 38). *Cf.* deWette, V, 435; Schiess, II, 92.

until the time comes to find comfort in him and those whom we have sent before.''[203]

It was thus a sad and desolated home to which there came a letter from the landgrave in the latter part of November, 1541,[204] enclosing a present of one hundred florins for Bucer's daughters. Troubled that Bucer had not written to him, and unable to surmise the cause for his silence, Philip assured him that he had overlooked the matter of the one hundred florins, and on behalf of Dr. Ossa, a counselor to Duke Maurice, he requested further information about the religious negotiations at Regensberg.[205] Soon afterwards the landgrave heard the news of Bucer's bereavement, and sent him a consolation which, in spite of its sanctimonious tone, was little short of cruel. ''The departure by death of your beloved wife and little children, in truth makes us very sorry, but we consider that Almighty God took all that away from you in which you have put your temporal comfort here, in order that you might seek your comfort and help only from him, as you doubtless will do. . . . you should not take it too much to heart, for you know that God like a true father chastens his children, and tests them. But we live in the confidence and hope that he will deliver you therefrom with grace.''[206]

Bucer thanked the landgrave for the money he had sent, and said he would use it not for his children's ''schmuck'' as Philip had suggested, but ''zur noturfft.'' This shows how sorely Bucer needed the money, yet he objected to the landgrave's intimation that his failure to write showed a lack of devotion, and a gift of money was necessary to increase his zeal. Not in the least was he angry, but he

203 Lenz, II, 38.

204 To this Bucer replied on Nov. 30, and so it must have come only a few days before (cf. Lenz, II, 32).

205 Lenz, II, 32.

206 Ibid., pp. 44, 46; cf. ibid., p. 52.

resented any mercenary implication that the gift might bring with it,[207] and in order that Philip might understand that he did not serve him for gold, he said in no ambiguous or flattering way, "God knows that I have never served your princely grace, nor any other lords, in divine matters for the sake of material recompense. When I can serve the church and individual consciences to the promotion of their holiness, that itself, irrespective of financial return, sufficiently obligates me to do whatever God will permit me to do. The office is laid upon me. Woe to me if I do not exercise it with all diligence. For he [God] has always more richly rewarded me than my work has been fruitful. Your princely grace has before this given me bountiful gifts. Also I know how your princely grace is burdened with expenses, so that truly I have accepted the present gift, as well as the former ones, not without a twinge of my conscience."[208]

The landgrave's persistent refusal to follow his advice in the matter of the bigamy ever since the Melsungen conference was sufficient reason why Bucer should cease writing to him, and his indiscreet publication of the *Dialogus Neobuli* against Bucer's earnest request, afforded still further reason why the reformer should offer no more advice. The publication of the *Dialogue* had brought just the result that Bucer feared, for in Nürnberg, Swabia, and elsewhere, it was said that he had written the book for gold, and to please the prince. Feeling keenly the gravity of the situation and deeply hurt by the injustice of the charge, which ignored his expectation that the book would be privately printed and distributed, he wrote in self-defence, "My Lord and God knows that I have not sought to avoid my cross for the sake of my person. It is better to suffer insult and persecution in defending the truth, than to have honor and power contrary to it.

207 Lenz, II, 32, 38.   208 *Ibid.*, p. 38, ff.

But my poor service of the Lord will be thereby defeated."[209]

As far as mercenary motives were concerned, the landgrave completely exonerated Bucer, declaring that he had never given him anything on account of the *Dialogus Neobuli,* and he had delayed so long in sending him the one hundred florins, in order to avoid giving occasion for such an accusation against him.[210] There was much in Bucer's relations to the bigamy of Philip of Hesse which merits disapproval and often severe condemnation, but his financial relations to the prince were above reproach. Never did he receive any stipulated remuneration, although from November, 1538, until the close of the year 1542 he was occupied either with journeys and negotiations for the landgrave, or with writing him advice. So long as his salary as pastor in Strasbourg provided his support, Bucer felt that his duty was to do all that he could to advance the kingdom of Christ, without regard for financial return.

Not only did he receive no salary from the landgrave, but Philip rewarded him with very few gifts. Only two presents of one hundred gulden[211] and one hundred florins[212] each are mentioned in their correspondence, and although it is possible that he may have received one or two other such gifts,[213] they were hardly more than enough to pay the expense involved in his service of the landgrave, who acknowledged that he was still indebted to Bucer.[214] When it is considered that Philip gave up his claim to the Saxon inheritance,[215] and promised twenty thousand gulden to Margaret,[216] besides the cost of repair-

209 Lenz, II, 39, ff.
210 *Ibid.,* p. 45.
211 Lenz, I, 168, and n. 5; *cf.* Rockwell, p. 44, n. 5; see above, p. 109.
212 Lenz, II, 32.   213 *Cf. ibid.,* p. 39.
214 *Ibid.,* p. 44.   215 *Ibid.,* I, 331.
216 Rockwell, pp. 35, 318.

ing the monastery at Weissenstein,[217] the gifts he made to Bucer seem very paltry indeed.

With the opening of the new year (1542), Bucer began anew to urge upon the landgrave the suppression of the *Dialogus Neobuli*. There were several reasons why he refused to defend the bigamy openly, and thought it was wrong for the landgrave to do so. Except for Luther, Melanchthon, and the Hessian theologians, he found only two preachers who were willing to uphold the "Wittenberg Rathschlag." These two were Ambrose Blaurer and Dr. Alesius. The rest would go no further than to leave the affair alone, and even Blaurer was strongly opposed to the publication of the *Dialogus Neobuli*. On January 9, 1542,[218] the latter wrote to Bullinger, "It pains me severely, not only that this book has been published in German, but above all that the incontinence of certain princes has moved good men to a treatment of this unnatural subject. God give them a better mind so that they may think upon that which is worthy of Christian warriors in this so evil a time for Germany. . . . I know indeed that many other men of first rank share the opinion of the author, and therefore fear a violent, bloody war, if this evil, or this untimely madness, is imprudently disturbed; on that account I hold it better to keep silent about it, than to arouse the wasps to still greater shame to the church, . . . I will therefore pray that the chiefs of the church direct all their energies to the spreading of the kingdom of God."[219] Bucer reported to the landgrave that he found two miracles in the affair: that all pious Christians tried to hide the landgrave's deed, though they could

217 Tschackert, *Briefwechsel des Corvinus*, p. 80.

218 Lenz, II, 53. Blaurer said he could not condemn the landgrave (Lenz, I, 197). Alesius was at this time a Brandenburg theologian. He remained a good friend to Bucer and afterwards helped him in England.

219 Schiess, II, 99, ff.

not consent to the bigamy itself; and that none would defend the bigamy.[220]

Although his conscience justified him, Bucer refused to testify openly to his support of the bigamy, because thereby he would destroy all the value of any testimony which he might give to the Son of God.[221] "Now God knows that I will gladly support all truth in his name," he asserted, "but that I, by an unnecessary confession with which the Lord would not burden anyone, should ruin my whole reputation and destroy my influence in affairs of vital necessity, your princely grace must consider what result would follow then and how acceptable to God it would be."[222] Not without good authority did Bucer also fear the offence which the *Dialogus Neobuli* would give to the weak, especially if it accomplished its aim of starting a controversy,[223] for he himself had said in his *Argumenta Buceri pro et contra*,[224] offence to the weak should be avoided even in permitted matters.[225] At the Diet of Speier in 1542, and on his way thither, Bucer had been attacked on account of the *Dialogue*,[226] and so for the reasons given above, and his own personal welfare, he besought the landgrave to order the printer to lay aside all copies of the book which he had on hand, and not to issue any more.[227]

---

[220] Lenz, II, 63. As typical of the reception given the *Dialogue* may be taken the opinion of Wolfhart, "Artig ist dasz Du über den Dialog περὶ τῆς διγαμίας mein Urtheil begehrst; doch will ich offen sagen, dasz er nach meiner Ansicht, nicht nur, wie Du schreibst, zur Unzeit, sondern allzu freimütig abgefasst ist, wer auch der Autor sein mag, und dasz er richtiger unterdrückt worden wäre in dieser Zeit, wo ohnedin jedes Laster in Schwang steht. Besser wäre es, dem Türken gegenüber sich als Männer zu zeigen" (Schiess, II, 99). Jacob Otter said, "Neues Unheil weckt der Verfasser des Dialogs De polygamia; ganz andere Erorterungen fordert das grosse Elend der Kirche, Gott erbarme sich und beseitige das Argernis" (Schiess, II, 134).

[221] Lenz, II, 53. [222] *Ibid.*, p. 63.

[223] *Ibid.* [224] *Argumenta Buceri*, p. 50, ff.

[225] Lenz, II, 64. [226] *Ibid.*, p. 63. [227] *Ibid.*, p. 64.

These arguments did not convince the landgrave. Sorry that the reformer had been attacked on account of the *Dialogue,* Philip invited him, in case he found his position at Strasbourg unbearable, to come to Hesse, offering him a salary of five hundred gulden to superintend the church in his lands. His popularity among the nobles, church-officers, and common people would enable him to accomplish much good and correct many lacks, the landgrave declared, ''for there would be found one hundred thousand men in our land who would serve you.''[228]

The prospect of a complete avowal of the bigamy troubled the landgrave even less in March, 1542, than before. Only because the scholars who gave him the ''Wittenberg Rathschlag'' were opposed to it, did he prevent a general following of his example throughout Hesse, but his own personal desire was to allow bigamy ''according to the Mosaic law'' and punish all sexual vice severely. That no pious Christian could be found to defend the thing, disgusted him, especially when he remembered the permission given in the ''Wittenberg Rathschlag,'' and the approval which Bucer had expressed at Rothenburg. He accused the reformer of being faint-hearted, nor could he understand why people were so opposed to the *Dialogue,* when no one had reprimanded Luther for failing to condemn polygamy in his commentary on Genesis.[229] Far from dreading a controversy, Philip declared himself ready to defend the *Dialogue* if it were attacked by any Protestants, and intimated that he was prepared for such an onslaught from Luther. In that event he offered to send a copy of his reply to Bucer for revision.[230]

Regarding himself as a benefactor of the race, the landgrave declared in a spirit of extravagant self-confidence, ''We may at the same time confess it is our opinion and belief, that God Almighty has not permitted this situation

[228] Lenz, II, 69.   [229] *Ibid.,* pp. 68-69.   [230] *Ibid.,* p. 70.

to arise for our sake alone, but we are merely a pioneer
and protagonist of the same, and if we, you, Luther, and
others suffer death, yet there will be found people, who
are more Godly and trusting than we, who will accept this
solution, which is not forbidden by God but is free and
permitted, and at the same time will refrain from adultery
and other evils.''[231] His narrow-minded selfishness hid
from him the truth of Bucer's prophecy that the moment
his bigamy was made an example for a general following
in the manner proposed by the *Dialogue,* then ''the flames
would break forth everywhere'' and the most friendly
hearts would no longer hold their peace.[232]

In response to Bucer's request, Philip sent orders to
his printer in the last part of March, not to issue any more
copies of the *Dialogus Neobuli.*[233] Before Bucer learned
of this action, some Schwenckfelders attacked him again
on account of the *Dialogue* with such severity that he requested the destruction of all remaining copies.[234] The
landgrave was evidently not willing to grant this drastic
demand, for he replied on April 3 that he had merely given
instructions to the printer, also to Dionysius and Pistorius, that he did not wish this affair and Bucer's relation
to it to be revealed.[235]

During March, 1542, probably as Bucer was returning
to Strasbourg through Hesse, he was told that the landgrave had put a new tax upon wood, planning to use this
revenue for the luxurious maintenance of Margaret. How
intimate had grown the relations between the nobleman
and the cobbler's son, may be seen from the fact that
Bucer inquired of the prince himself if the report were
true, and exhorted him to moderation in his expenditures

---

[231] Lenz, II, 70.

[232] *Ibid.,* p. 65. Köstlin says, ''With all the energy and stubbornness
of his nature he fastened on these notions and clung to them'' (Köstlin,
The Life of Luther, p. 507).

[233] Lenz, II, 70-71.   [234] *Ibid.,* p. 65.   [235] *Ibid.,* p. 74.

for Margaret. He then used this incident as the subject for a small discourse on the duties of princes to their subjects; that they should not load them with heavy burdens, but set them a much-needed example in frugality, employing revenues to provide for public needs and uses; not for private extravagance.[236] But the landgrave assured him that he had not levied the tax for such a purpose, nor maintained Margaret expensively, in fact, no better than an ordinary burgher would keep his wife. The wood-tax, he felt sure, was a burden upon no one.[237]

Toward the close of the same month, a disciple of Schwenckfeld once more attacked Bucer on account of the *Dialogue,* even demanding that he should write against it.[238] This the reformer refused to do, but his anxiety about the matter was increased for two reasons. First, he had given the dispensation to the landgrave under the assurance that it would be used secretly, and yet the publication of such writings as the *Dialogus Neobuli* would be regarded by the public as an attempt to make an open introduction of bigamy generally. Secondly, although he was willing to suffer any hardship, yet he felt that for him to testify all that he knew in the affair would only cause offence; and because he was a servant of Christ "to the up-building of the church," he was bound, neither to undermine the trustworthiness of his testimony to the gospel, nor to dishonor himself. To this argument, which Bucer repeated now for the third time, he added the conclusive reason that Christians should be obedient to the common law of the state, unless it caused them to commit sin. So he felt that he could not testify against the general law in public, as the people would interpret such a defense of the *Dialogue.* It was one thing to defend the landgrave's affairs to himself alone, privately, and another to defend a general following of them.

---

[236] Lenz, II, 66, and n. 4. [237] *Ibid.,* p. 74. [238] *Ibid.,* p. 72.

The first Bucer had shown himself quite ready to do, for he had "great testimony of your princely grace's conscience and special needs," but the second he regarded as wrong.[239] For the invitation to come to Hesse[240] "at such a rich compensation," he thanked the landgrave, and declared that for a long time he had desired to serve the Lord under Philip in case he were freed from his "present" service. "But if that should be, we would prefer a salary more in accordance to gospel measure than so high."[241]

In spite of their sharp differences of opinion, they cherished each other's friendship, and Bucer closed his letter on April 2, 1542, with a phrase which is characteristic of this attitude on the part of both. "That your princely grace freely writes me your spirit in that[242] and other things is exactly what I desire. But if your princely grace is offended at my deeds or writings, I beg that you will interpret my language reasonably."[243] While his frankness and sharp treatment of Philip's short-comings exonerate him from any charge of servility or subservience to patronage, it is also to his credit that he still tried to help a man who had trampled upon his advice and ruined the Protestant cause by his alliance with the emperor. Certainly the landgrave must have admired and respected Bucer profoundly, and their faithfulness to each other cannot be sufficiently explained by saying that each was seeking his own advantage.

When Bucer received the news from the landgrave that the distribution of the *Dialogue* would be arrested, he had

239 Lenz, II, 72-73.

240 This invitation was repeated on Apr. 3, 1542 (Lenz, II, 74).

241 Lenz, II, 74.

242 I.e., the invitation to come to Hesse.

243 Lenz, II, 74. It was no doubt due partly to his influence that the city of Strasbourg assumed a favorable attitude toward the landgrave (*ibid.*, p. 77).

spread this information further, and in consequence the excitement against him had quieted down.[244] But in the middle of April, 1542, Michael Hahn brought to Strasbourg more copies of the *Dialogue,* which he had received from Aitinger to distribute. Immediately the complaints against the reformer were revived, and he wrote to the prince, once more begging him to suppress the book completely. Pleadingly he repeated his old arguments that Philip was safe and needed no defense; that he should remember his promises at Regensburg; that it would arouse into open opposition the pious people who tolerated the affair; that it would injure Bucer's service of the Lord; that it would bring disgrace upon the church; and at most the *Dialogue* should be given only to trusted, pious people, after personal argument.[245]

It was over a month before the landgrave replied[246] to this last request, saying, "So much as concerns the further publication of the *Dialogue,* we will comply with your wishes and show it only to trusted people, and have written to the printer to send us all the *Dialogues* which he has on hand."[247] Again he repeated his invitation to Bucer, and offered him two alternatives; one, that he should come to Hesse under the conditions previously stated; the other, that he should spend one half of the year with Philip and the other half with Duke Maurice, "and in both lands help to shape good, Christian discipline and church-ordinances."[248] By this offer the land-

[244] *Ibid.,* p. 78.

[245] Lenz, II, 78-79. A few copies had been sold at the Strasbourg fair (*ibid.,* p. 79).

[246] On May 16, 1542.

[247] Lenz, II, 82. On June 19, 1542, Bucer wrote to A. Blaurer, "As for the *Dialogue* we will conquer the attempts of the devil by patience. I have brought it about that the prince has promised sacredly that he will publish nothing more" (Schiess, II, 128).

[248] Lenz, II, 82.

grave relieved him of any anxiety due to an uncomfort-
able position at Strasbourg, and also removed any ground
for complaint that the publication of the *Dialogue* had
made his condition there intolerable.

The fear that the publication of the *Dialogus Neobuli*
would cause a controversy, not so much with papists as
with evangelicals, was one reason why Bucer had opposed
it.[249] Not only the premonition that such a controversy
might easily lead to new divisions between them troubled
him, but also that the landgrave by his indiscretion would
probably disclose more about the secret, as he had already
done in his polemic with Duke Henry of Brunswick. That
this fear was by no means groundless is shown by the
fact that already before the wedding Justus Menius had
composed, but not published, an opinion against bigamy,[250]
which very nearly led to a postponement of the ceremony.[251] His intention of writing such a polemic became
more definite in September, 1540, for Bruck then investi-
gated the matter, reporting to the elector that Luther
was right in believing that it would not be best to let the
book be issued, for it "would arouse much disputation
and disagreement among theologians," and the landgrave's pastor at Melsungen, Lening, "a very hateful
man although he is learned, will certainly write against
it."[252] For these reasons he advised the elector to forbid
the publication of the manuscript.[253] Along with his own
letter Bruck enclosed a letter from Luther, in which the
reformer, although he was pleased with the little book
of Menius', counseled that it be laid by for a time, because
by arousing suspicion that there might be something in
the affair, it would increase the scandal, and the "Mel-

---

[249] See above, p. 200.

[250] In February, 1540 (Lenz, I, 389, n. 1).

[251] Rockwell, pp. 42, ff., 126, n. 4.

[252] *CR.*, IV, 768, ff.   [253] *Ibid.*, p. 769.

sungen one" might answer it, in which case there was a possibility that he himself would be asked to write.[254] Upon the manuscript of Luther's letter is a note to the effect that the elector did not allow Menius to publish his book because of the controversy it threatened to arouse.[255] At any rate he did not publish it then. Yet before the year was out the landgrave heard of what Menius had intended to do, and wrote to Bucer on January 3, 1541, "But if the holy man, Justus Menius, shall write against us so vigorously then he shall have his answer; and we will not conceal how their highly praised elector committed the sin of sodomy one time in our residence at Cassel, and at the first Diet of Speier."[256]

The publication of the *Dialogus Neobuli* again aroused in Menius a determination to write against bigamy, since von der Thann had given him a copy of the *Dialogue,* and encouraged him to compose a confutation of it secretly.[257] Menius sent the manuscript of this composition to Luther, who replied on January 10, 1542, that he had received it, would give it his consideration, and would see about having it printed after a book which he himself was preparing against Neobulus had been finished.[258] By Febru-

---

[254] Enders, XIII, 182, ff.; *CR.,* IV, 769, ff.; deWette, VI, 296. Both Bretschneider and Seidemann give the date of Bruck's letter, and of Luther's letter enclosed in it, as Jan. 10, 1542. But Lenz has printed a letter from Luther to the landgrave on Sept. 17, 1540 (Lenz, I, 389), whose contents are so similar to those of the letter enclosed by Bruck, as to prove they were written at the same time, and therefore this second report of an attack by Menius must be placed in the late summer or early autumn of 1540 (*cf.* Lenz, I, 389, n. 1; Rockwell, p. 126, n. 5; Enders, XIII, 184, n. 1).

[255] Enders, XIII, 184; *CR.,* IV, 769.   [256] Lenz, I, 302.

[257] Enders, XIV, 154, n. 3; Rockwell, p. 127. On Sept. 27, 1541, Eberhard v. d. Thann wrote to Rudolf Schenck that with the help of Menius he would prepare a confutation of the *Dialogue* though in secret (Enders, XIV, 154, n. 3).

[258] Enders, XIV, 152, ff.; deWette, VI, 426. Luther had not yet read it through (Enders, XIV, 152).

ary 25 Luther had read the pamphlet,[259] and was very much pleased with it. He consulted the elector and with his consent planned to publish it, but because the *Dialogue* had been published anonymously without the author's name or place of publication, he suggested that the pseudonym of "Fidelis Pistobulus" should be used.[260] On May 1, 1542, Luther was still undecided about the publication of Menius' book.[261] Meanwhile it was laid aside and not printed until Menius incorporated it in his book against the Anabaptists.[262] The contents show that Menius was not an unworthy antagonist to Neobulus, for he distinguished between the spiritual and external example of the patriarchs; pointed out that Paul's command to Timothy classifies bigamy as a culpable act; and asserted that there was no clear command of God for polygamy.[263]

Even more threatening than the plan of Justus Menius was Luther's own intention of writing against the *Dialogus Neobuli*. On the first pages of the *Dialogue* Eucharius says to Parzasius, "but what say you to this, that your idol, Luther, has freely written, that he would advise no one, also could forbid no one, to do as the holy patriarchs did with God's favor and blessing: marry a second wife and be the husband of not only one but two wives. . . . also, the taking of two wives is permitted to no one, but your Dr. Luther has permitted it, because he, as a teacher of God, writes that bigamy can still be prac-

---

[259] Myconius praised it highly (*D. Luthers Werke*, Weimar ed. LIII, 187, and n. 12).

[260] Enders, XIV, 196. Enders was the first to publish this letter.

[261] *Ibid.*, p. 257.

[262] Rockwell, p. 127, n. 6.

[263] G. L. Schmidt, "Justus Menius über die Bigamie," *Zeitschrift für die historische Theologie*, 1868, I, 445-460. This is taken from the copy of Menius' opinion in the "Cod. Palat.," p. 435. He also prints an extract from the opinion, in his *Justus Menius der Reformator Thuringens*, I, 257-259.

tised under the new dispensation without sin.''[264] This brazen attempt to secure the protection of Luther's mantle for the ''vile book of Neobulus,''[265] combined with the fact that many people ''rubbed him about the ears'' and urged him to write against the work,[266] appeared to him sufficient reason for taking up his pen to answer ''that evil book with a few words.''[267] Bucer soon heard of Luther's purpose and notified the landgrave that, ''A great many people say that Dr. Luther will write against the *Dialogue,* which your princely grace will ascertain through Philip and others, and also hinder through the elector, because it will cause serious complications. The only remedy for this misfortune is secrecy, completely ignoring all discussion and writing.''[268] Already the storm-cloud of Luther's displeasure had cast its shadow upon Hesse, yet the landgrave, with customary audacity declared that he would reply to Luther by publishing the ''Wittenberg Rathschlag,'' and accusing him of idolatry in retaining pictures and the elevation of the sacrament.[269] Careful consideration, however, showed him that Bucer's plan of procedure was better, and the landgrave, in this case being wise enough to adopt it, wrote a conciliatory letter to Melanchthon on April 1, the day after Bucer's letter arrived.[270] In brief, he said that he had heard that Luther would write against the *Dialogue,* but could not believe the report in view of the approval of bigamy given in the ''Wittenberg Rathschlag.'' By the horrible rumors against himself he had been forced to issue the *Dialogue,* not to institute a general following, but to

---

[264] *Dialogus Neobuli, Bl.* A iii.   [265] Enders, XIV, 241.

[266] *CR.,* IV, 797, V, 75.

[267] *Dr. Martin Luther's sämmtliche Werke* (Erlangen edition), LXV, 206. This undertaking was well under way by Jan. 10, 1542. *Cf.* Enders, XIV, 152.

[268] Lenz, II, 67.   [269] Lenz, II, 70.

[270] *Ibid.,* p. 75, n. 2.

prove that bigamy in itself could not be condemned. He had intended to distribute it only to a few people in secret, but Duke Henry's horrible and vicious slanders forced him to issue it publicly. So he requested Melanchthon to investigate the rumor that Luther would write against the *Dialogue,* and influence him either to give up his plan or modify it.[271] In spite of his calm and pacific tone, however, the landgrave still intended, in case Luther was so inconsistent with his action in 1539 as to attack bigamy and the *Dialogue,* to give Luther his answer, "yet decisively and mildly," and "it would be seen what he previously wrote and granted us and now writes otherwise."[272]

Melanchthon's reply made such a foolish procedure unnecessary, and showed the wisdom of Bucer's advice that the landgrave should exert his efforts to prevent Luther from publishing the book, rather than think of a way in which to fight him. He informed Philip that "when the elector heard of it he requested Luther to refrain, in order to avoid making the affair more notorious, which Luther has done, though he wishes that the *Dialogue* had not been issued."[273] He suggested that Philip himself should write to Luther, and the landgrave carried out this suggestion immediately on April 9 from Grimma.[274] Excusing himself on the ground that many people had tried to influence him against Luther, he assured the reformer of his good-will and requested him not to lose confidence in him. To Melanchthon the landgrave wrote on the same day, "we believe that if we might have only a short conference with Luther himself, we could give him a satisfactory explanation."[275] Luther

[271] *Ibid.*   [272] *Ibid.,* p. 76.   [273] *CR.,* IV, 797, ff.
[274] Lenz, "Nachlese zum Briefwechsel des Landgrafen Philipp mit Luther und Melanchthon," *Zeitschrift für Kirchengeschichte,* IV, 144.
[275] *Ibid.,* p. 145.

hastened to reply to the prince[276] that by stirring up so much filth in such a useless and pernicious way, the "vile book of Neobulus" had frustrated his "loyal" attempts to spare the landgrave. Otherwise he had no ill-feeling towards Philip and remembered him in his prayers.[277]

About the middle of April a report reached Strasbourg that Luther would write against the *Dialogue* and refer to Bucer by name.[278] Since Luther knew that he was implicated in the composition of the book, it is probable that if he had published his writing against it he would have mentioned Bucer, although he has not done so in the fragment that remains. Consequently, the Strasbourg reformer himself wrote to Melanchthon, and at the same time urged the landgrave to make sure that there would be no controversy.[279]

How Philip met Luther on May 5, 1542, for the first time since the bigamy,[280] and how they cleared away many misunderstandings, is described in a letter which he wrote to Bucer eleven days later.[281] "Concerning Luther's writing against the *Dialogue,* we do not wish to conceal from you, that we have just been at Wittenberg and discussed everything with Luther, including our reasons for publishing the *Dialogue*. While so thoroughly satisfied that he agreed to withhold his writing, he criticized several weak arguments in the *Dialogue,* declaring that he did not know it came from us, or he would not have written against it; that with Lamech it was a sin, and that was not a sufficient argument; that only the examples of the patriarchs should have been attested; secondly, he suggested the argument of the necessity which might arise under cer-

[276] Text in Enders, XIV, 240, ff.   [277] *Ibid.,* p. 241.
[278] Lenz, II, 79.   [279] Lenz, II, 79.
[280] Rockwell, p. 198. The landgrave was on a journey to Grimma and Oschatz (Muller in the *Archiv für Reformationsgeschichte,* I, 368). On the landgrave's itinerary see Lenz, II, 76, n. 3.
[281] Lenz, II, 82.

tain circumstances, and, thirdly, the Mosaic command:
if a virgin is won in war, if it pleases him he may take
her, etc., likewise, Moses wrote, if anyone sleeps with a
virgin and the father will give her to him, then he must
take her; likewise, at Tübingen at one time a second wife
was recognized along with the first, etc., this would have
been good reason with which the mouths of people would
have been closed, and so many arguments would not have
been necessary which apart are not strong enough; for it
would be better to have a few good arguments than many
loose ones.''[282]

Thus Luther gave up his plan to write against the
Dialogus Neobuli, and the first part of his writing, which
had been printed, remained a fragment.[283] Resorting
rather to denunciation than argument, Luther declared
that the author was ashamed of his book or he would have
told his name;[284] that the faith of the patriarchs and not
their deeds should be taken for an example;[285] that
Neobulus intentionally interpreted the Scriptures errone-
ously and failed to draw any conclusions;[286] and concluded, ''whoever follows this idiot and book and thereupon takes more than one wedded-wife, and desires that
it should be a righteous thing, the devil will bury him in
the abyss of hell, Amen.''[287]

In March, 1542, there was a real crisis in the history

---

[282] Lenz, II, 82-83. Melanchthon reported of this conference that Luther
gave the landgrave a good answer, ''das der landgraue ausz der Camer zu
mir kham und war seer fro, hatte auch jn sein schreibtefelin verzeichnet die
argument die der herr doctor gesagt, wie von diser sach zu reden, und worumb
ihn das Buch missfallen'' (*Archiv für Reformationsgeschichte,* I, 365-371,
where the letter is printed in full). Sometime during the summer following,
Luther was informed that a book had appeared at Leipzig which justified
bigamy, but he turned the discussion aside to the subject of Solomon's
wives (Kroker, no. 565).

[283] *Dr. Martin Luther's sämmliche Werke* (Erlangen ed.), LXV, 206-212.
[284] *Ibid.,* p. 206.   [285] *Ibid.,* p. 208.
[286] *Ibid.,* p. 209.   [287] *Ibid.*

of the bigamy. Had Luther attacked the *Dialogus Neobuli,* the result would have been a controversy between him and the landgrave, involving not only the complete exposure of the secret, and additional shame to the evangelical cause, but also the possibility of a division with serious results for the Protestants and the liberty of the German states. An open break was prevented when the elector forbade Luther to publish his reply to the *Dialogue,* but it was through the influence and advice of Bucer that the landgrave established more friendly relations with Luther in May, 1542, than had existed for two years previously.

When Henry Bullinger published his commentary on Matthew in the late summer of 1542 he included an attack upon bigamy as defended in the *Dialogus Neobuli.* Bucer had first met Bullinger in 1532, and they had become good friends.[288] In 1537-1538 a coldness arose between Bucer and the Swiss over the doctrine of the Supper, but it was not at that time serious enough to destroy the friendship between the two reformers.[289] But in 1540 it was only by the mediation of Ambrose Blaurer that a complete disagreement was prevented, for he begged Bullinger not to separate from Bucer, though he did appear to concede too much in his desire for unity.[290]

It is probable that the *Dialogus Neobuli* was first called to Bullinger's attention by Ambrose Blaurer, for on November 30, 1541, he offered to send him a copy if he had not already read it.[291] Evidently the copy was sent, for on December 14 Blaurer wrote again, "Accept also the *Dialogue,* concerning which I do not express any

---

[288] C. Pestalozzi, *Heinrich Bullinger,* p. 174.

[289] *Ibid.,* p. 276; *cf. CR.,* XIII, 221-222.

[290] Schiess, II, 48, 50, 51.

[291] *Ibid.,* pp. 94, 95, 97, 99, 100, 112. Bucer had sent a copy to Blaurer (Schiess, II, 93).

opinion, for I have not yet examined the whole question.
As soon as you have read it, send it back, but not without
your judgment because I am deeply concerned about
this thing.''[292] He advised Bullinger not to write against
the *Dialogue*,[293] which the Swiss reformer called ''a
thoroughly foolish book.''[294]

In March, 1542, Bullinger was busily engaged in writing and printing his commentary on Matthew.[295] Each
day a folio page left the press, and meanwhile it was
necessary to revise and write enough to keep the printers
busy, so that the book would be ready for the Frankfurt
fair in August.[296] On August 21, 1542, he recorded in his
diary, ''I have finished the twelfth book of the commentary on the gospel of Christ according to Matthew, which
I began the seventh of August, 1541.''[297] Under the comment on Matthew XIX he said, ''If those had observed
this general orthodox canon, given us by the Saviour
himself, who in these latter days dispute concerning
polygamy, and try to allow one man many wives, they
would not have brought forward with so much confidence
the deeds of the fathers for examples.''[298] Thus clearly
referring to the *Dialogus Neobuli*, which was at that moment the most conspicuous defense of bigamy in Europe,
Bullinger contended that the law of monogamy instituted
by God as the true and only form of marriage, was renewed and revived by Christ; that Paul used the singular

292 Schiess, II, 95.   293 *Ibid.*, p. 100.

294 *Ibid.*, p. 112.

295 On March 17, 1542, Blaurer wrote to him, ''Deine Kommentare zu
Matthaeus gefallen uns wie alles, was von Dir kommt, aussordentlich; sie
zeichnen sich durch angenehme Breite und zugleich klare Kürze aus, und
wir preisen Dich um Diener Gaben willen'' (Schiess, II, 112).

296 Pestalozzi, p. 308.

297 *Heinrich Bullinger's Diarium*, p. 31.

298 H. Bullinger, *In Sacrosanctum Iesu Christi Domini nostri Euangelium
Secundum Matthaeum Commentariorum libri XII per Heinrychum Bullerin-
gerum*, p. 179.

when he said that every man should have his own wife,
etc., and never thought of such a thing as polygamy
among Christians; that the example of the patriarchs
proved nothing in this case, and their just works should
be imitated rather than their polygamy; that a man who
could not cleave to one wife faithfully could hardly be expected to show fidelity to many; that the polygamy of
Abraham was a special concession; and that he and Jacob
did not receive their plural wives from God, but from mistaken human deeds, in the first case that of Sarah, and in
the second that of Laban. With a keener insight than that
shown by any other writer on the subject, Bullinger added,
"And, however these may have gained their wives, it has
been for a long time certain that we should seek the institutions of our life, not from privilege or permission, but
from law, and the law and institution of God is that one
man should be given one wife, until they shall be parted by
death (Romans VII)."[299] Better than perhaps he knew,
he wrote of the defenders of polygamy, "therefore their
fruit tastes anything but sweet to them, so that it is a work
of adding bitterness to bitterness."[300] In conclusion he
begged that the defense of polygamy might not be blamed
upon the gospel, but that all would uphold "holy, simple,
and pure Christian marriage, being content with one dear
wife, who will heal rightly and chastely, easily as steel,
lest we may incur death through fornication."[301]

The landgrave was not pleased when he read this part
of Bullinger's commentary on Matthew, and sent a copy
to Lening, pastor at Melsungen, commanding him to reply
with a personal letter, in which he should "confute his
arguments, and point out what he wrote before and what

[299] H. Bullinger, *In Sacrosanctum . . . Matthaeum Commentariorum*, p.
179.

[300] *Ibid.*

[301] For Melanchthon's comment on this passage, see *Archiv für Reformationsgeschichte*, I, 369, ff.

now, and how the two statements contradict each other."[302] On January 23, 1543, he sent also to Bucer a copy of Bullinger's attack, because "we think, perhaps he may suspect that you composed the *Dialogue,* for he attacks you somewhat."[303] It is quite evident that the landgrave knew that Bucer did not write the *Dialogue* and that Lening did. Philip also offered to send him a copy of Lening's reply when it was ready, so that he could look it over.[304] With Bucer's complaint that he would much have preferred that Bullinger had restrained himself,[305] the landgrave agreed that he too would have been glad if Bullinger had exercised more self-control, and for that reason he had printed nothing against him. He suggested that by means of his friends Bucer should influence Bullinger to refrain from further writings, "for if that is not done, we must come to blows with him."[306]

The landgrave's command to Lening was easier given than carried out in Bullinger's case, but this did not deter the preacher who held his tongue with difficulty, from writing a letter which Bullinger received on February 16, 1543; and to which, two days later,[307] the Zuricher wrote a lengthy reply, expressing his sorrow that Lening was involved "in this affair," and declaring that he only proclaimed his convictions as many had expected him to do.[308] Personally, he would gladly have allowed the dispute to

---

[302] Lenz, II, 121.

[303] *Ibid.,* p. 120.

[304] *Ibid.,* p. 121.

[305] *Ibid.,* p. 122.

[306] *Ibid.,* p. 127. A year after the publication of Bullinger's commentary Bucer had not yet received a copy of it (Thesaurus Baumianus, XIV, 116), and remarked that the Zuricher had no good cause for his attack on polygamy (Schiess, II, 208). There is no evidence that he ever received the copy of the passage referring to bigamy sent him by the landgrave, although it is probable that he did. Bullinger evidently heard a rumor that Lening was the author of the *Dialogue* for he confused the name with that of Lenglin, a preacher at Strasbourg (Schiess, II, 100).

[307] Rockwell, p. 128.

[308] Pestalozzi, p. 277, ff.

sink into silence, but he was not willing to occupy an ambiguous position in the matter.[309]

Bullinger incurred the enmity of the Hessian court by his temerity, and in 1545 Sailer opposed the invitation of the Swiss to the League convention, on the ground that Bullinger could not keep quiet about the bigamy, although when he wrote on Matthew twenty years before, "he did not think about bigamy."[310] Yet Bullinger held to his belief, and there was retained in the third edition of his work on *Christian Matrimony*, published in 1579, a passage found in the second edition of 1548,[311] in which he said, "Firstly, the Lord says in Matthew XIX, as is also prescribed in Genesis II, that marriage is a union of one man with one woman, not of one man with many women, or of one woman with many men. Several of the holy patriarchs had plural wives, but that was by special dispensation, and their deeds cannot be taken as general examples, which may be universally imitated. That several or even many people did so establishes no law. In the passage from Matthew referred to, the Lord reestablished and renewed the primitive rule and therefore whoever at the present time undertakes to introduce polygamy, follows the rule of Mahomet rather than of Christ."[312]

Several times after 1542 there were rumors that an attack would be made on the *Dialogus Neobuli*. The first rumor arose in February, 1543, when Duchess Elizabeth wrote to the elector that she had heard that Luther would attack the *Dialogue*, and, in order to avoid arousing the landgrave from his secrecy, she begged him to forbid the

[309] *Ibid.*, p. 278. Bucer expressed his opinion of Bullinger in a letter to Ambrose Blaurer, Nov. 7, 1543 (Lenz, II, 232).

[310] Lenz, III, 363, n. 1, 518.

[311] The first edition was in 1540 (Pestalozzi, p. 301; *cf. Historisch-politische Blätter*, CXLVII, 567; Rockwell, p. 129, n. 2).

[312] Bullinger, *Der Christlich Eestand, Cap.* III, 7, ff.

218 THE ATTITUDE OF MARTIN BUCER

printing of Luther's reply.[313] Though he had heard nothing of such an intention, the elector ordered Bruck to make
an investigation, which resulted in a report from that
official on March 8, enclosing a letter from Melanchthon
denying the rumor, and asserting that Luther's book had
been laid aside since January, 1542, in the house of the
printer, where someone might have seen it and started
the report.[314] The landgrave too heard this rumor, and
wrote to Melanchthon on March 21 for information, sending a copy of what it was said Luther would publish.[315]
Melanchthon replied on March 28, that "in this year nothing has been printed or written here of the affair of which
your princely grace writes. Luther's writing against the
Dialogue was suppressed and has never been completed."[316]

About the same time Count Christoffel von Gleichen
attacked Bucer, slandering him because of the bigamy
and accusing him among other things of being a Jew. To
gain protection Bucer begged Philip to bring influence to
bear on the count to make him cease from the attack.[317]
Receiving a letter in April from Melanchthon, in which
he was told that "a writing against bigamy and your
princely grace is circulated at Leipzig,"[318] he wrote to the
landgrave on April 15, and advised him to have the circulation of it stopped.[319] It is not known just what this
"writing" was. Melanchthon in his letter to the landgrave
on March 28, 1543, had said, "I have also noticed that the

[313] Rockwell, p. 199; *Archiv für Reformationsgeschichte*, I, 366.

[314] Rockwell, p. 199. Melanchthon thought that the rumor probably began
in Freiburg (*Archiv für Reformationsgeschichte*, I, 370).

[315] Lenz, "Nachlese," *Zeitschrift für Kirchengeschichte*, IV, 148. He
received a copy from Nürnberg.

[316] *CR.*, V, 74. Baumgarten knew of the rumor and of the inquiry of
the duchess (Baumgarten, V, 507).

[317] Lenz, II, 142.

[318] *Ibid.*, p. 145. The letter itself has been lost.

[319] *Ibid.*

elector of Saxony, would be sorry to see anything written by anyone against your princely grace, and his electoral princely grace and many others are greatly annoyed that several in Meissen, and especially at Leipzig, make so many scornful speeches, besides circulating pamphlets which excite, not so much scorn against your princely grace, as hate for the pure Christian doctrine.''[320] From this it seems that the ''writing'' to which Bucer referred was not a printed book such as Luther had planned.[321] The most significant thing in connection with this report was that Bucer added to his letter of April 15, 1543, ''For truly nothing is better than to eliminate all disputes about the subject and suppress them; which I also in the highlands have tried to do, I hope not in vain.''[322] Perhaps if it had not been for such efforts by Bucer, the landgrave would have received more attacks like the one from Bullinger.

When Bucer heard that a certain preacher in Cologne[323] was becoming too zealous in the defense of bigamy, he wrote to the landgrave on March 2, 1544, that the man should be restrained.[324] Being informed that new copies of the *Dialogue* were being circulated, he decided, upon investigation, that they must be copies belonging to the first edition, yet he reminded the landgrave again of his promise to keep as many copies as possible in a safe place.[325] So Bucer's efforts to suppress any argument or controversy over the bigamy[326] and the *Dialogus Neobuli* were gradually successful, and the danger of a conflict between Luther and the landgrave, which would have exposed everything, was overcome.[327]

---

[320] *CR.*, V, 76.   [321] Lenz, II, 145, n. 5.
[322] Lenz, II, 146.
[323] Probably Hardenfeld (Lenz, II, 247, n. 4).
[324] Lenz, II, 247.   [325] Schiess, II, 262.
[326] *Ibid.*, p. 268.
[327] On the subsequent history of the bigamy see Rockwell, p. 130, ff.

The excitement over the bigamy gradually died out. In the autumn of 1543 the landgrave wrote to Bucer that the other princes suspected him of trying to defend his act,[328] but he assured the reformer that he would not oppose a national assembly in order to protect his bigamous marriage.[329] One result upon Bucer's own life is significant of the regret which he felt about the affair. In his commentary on Ephesians, published in 1527, he had said nothing whatever about bigamy,[330] yet when he lectured on the same book at Cambridge ten years after he had signed the "Wittenberg Rathschlag," he explained Ephesians V: 22 as follows, "also it is not to be passed over that monogamy is proved by his *dictum* that wives should be subject to their own husbands." As arguments against polygamy he advanced the following, "Always they[331] were a source of quarrels, and the reason for their permission was the promise of the increase of the posterity of that race, like the stars of heaven and the sands of the sea. But now since the gentiles are made the seed of Abraham by faith there is no longer need for polygamy, and Christ in Matthew restored matrimony to its first institution."[332]

In the beginning of 1543 Bucer was himself accused of bigamy. Though this was only a slander having no connection with his part in the landgrave's case, it is interesting to note the circumstances under which the charge was made. Having been married in June, 1542, to Capito's widow, previously the wife of Oecolampadius,[333] he responded six months later to a call from Hermann von Wied for assistance in the reformation of his diocese of

328 Lenz, II, 200.
329 *Ibid.*, p. 217.
330 *Epistola D. Pauli,* etc. (Mentz, no. 16).
331 I.e., the polygamous marriages of the patriarchs.
332 *Praelectiones Doctiss.*, p. 179 (Mentz, no. 89).
333 Schiess, II, 128.

Cologne.[334] His vigorous activities at Bonn soon aroused the Roman Catholic party into bitter opposition, and among other things they accused him of being a bigamist, because he had married a second wife after the death of the first, thus, so they alleged, transgressing Paul's command that a clergyman should have only one wife.[335] To this attack Bucer replied that the bigamy forbidden by Paul in his command to Timothy was not the marrying of a second wife after the death of the first, but the having of two wives at the same time. This interpretation he supported by the authority of Chrysostom.[336]

As a result of the Smalkald war and the Augsburg Interim, which he refused to accept, Bucer was expelled from Strasbourg by his enemies, and though many positions were offered him in Germany, he chose England as his place of exile.[337] After journeying with Paul Fagius across Europe to Calais, he took ship for England,[338] where he, who had so often provided a refuge in his own home for exiles from all over Europe, was kindly received by Cranmer and Edward VI,[339] and finally given the position of "King's Reader of the Holy Scriptures" at Cambridge University.[340] Though his literary and other activities while in England were prodigious,[341] he still found time for those lectures as Regius professor of Theology, which brought him a great reputation in Eng-

[334] Röhrich, p. 181; Varrentrapp, *Hermann von Wied*, II, 125, ff. The call was first extended to him in February, 1542 (Schiess, II, 104). He arrived in Bonn on Dec. 14, 1542 (Schiess, II, 168).

[335] *Was in Namen . . . zu Bonn*, p. Fiii; *CR.*, V, 122; Lenz, II, 117, 124; Bucer to the Strasbourgers, Feb. 18, 1543 (Thesaurus Baumianus, XIV, 24-25).

[336] *Was in Namen . . . zu Bonn*, p. Fiii; *Scripta duo adv. . . . . Latomi*, p. 77; *Die ander verteydigung*, p. cxlv.

[337] *Scripta Anglicana*, p. 190; *CR.*, *Calvini Opera*, XIII, 56.

[338] *CR.*, *Calvini Opera*, XIII, 235.

[339] *Ibid.*

[340] Harvey, p. 28.

[341] *Cf.* the contents of the *Scripta Anglicana* with Harvey, chapter V.

land.[342] Unfortunately, the climate never agreed with him.
He found it cold, and missed the comforts of his home in
Strasbourg.[343] Under these circumstances it is not strange
that he became seriously ill less than a year after his
arrival,[344] and though managing to continue his labors for
a year longer, he was taken sick for the last time in February, 1551,[345] and on March 1 death came to him,[346] largely
as a liberation from a life made hard by excessive toil,
disease, and undeserved misfortune. He was buried with
great honors, and Calvin, who learned his value during
those years in which Bucer was so heavily burdened by
the negotiations of the religious colloquies and the problem of Philip's bigamy, wrote a eulogy revealing the
depth of his admiration. "I feel my heart almost like to
break when I think of the great loss the church of God has
sustained in the death of Bucer. The Lord grant that I
may leave in life all those whose death I should mourn,
that I may the more joyfully depart from the world."[347]

[342] Harvey, p. 47. He began on Jan. 10, 1550.

[343] *Cf.* his letters home in the Thesaurus Baumianus and in Baum, pp.
553, 555, 558.

[344] Thesaurus Baumianus, XX, 151.

[345] Harvey, p. 90; *cf.* Beza, p. 47.

[346] Harvey, p. 91.

[347] *CR., Calvini Opera*, IX, 60.

CHAPTER VIII

BUCER'S ATTITUDE TOWARD THE BIGAMY

It is by no means easy to understand and state clearly Bucer's attitude toward the bigamy of Philip of Hesse, and it is even more difficult to criticize it. His statements, often intentionally ambiguous and confusing, add to the impenetrability of the veil of secrecy which has not yet been entirely lifted from the affair. Most important of all, he lived in an age very different from our own, when men interpreted the Bible much differently, and, as a rule, more literally than they do today, so that unreserved condemnation of his act would be quite as unjust as to attempt a complete defense of it. Not only his relation to the bigamy, but all the rest of his life, including his own irreproachable conjugal relations, must be taken into account; and when this is done, it becomes clear, that although the reformer permitted Philip to take a bigamous wife, yet he did not do it for immoral purposes. Often misled by the scholastic reasoning which he had learned in the convent, he resorted to distinctions of little ethical validity, yet all this must be allowed its due value, and his intentions given as much consideration as his deeds. It is the purpose of this chapter, not so much to pass judgment upon Bucer's conduct, as to indicate some of his ideas and conceptions which have been ignored by those who were too hasty to condemn or defend.

A general consideration of Bucer's opinion about marriage will help considerably to make his attitude toward the landgrave's bigamy intelligible, because his beliefs about the nature and purpose of matrimony were far different from those of most men today. Adopting an excessively literal interpretation of the seventh chapter of First Corinthians, he followed these two leading lines of thought; marriage is a calling and a medicine. First, the conception of marriage as a calling he based upon Paul's injunction, "Brethren, let every man wherein he is called, therein abide with God,"[1] applying this directly to marriage without any equivocations. In a controversial pamphlet written against Latomus he stated, "First, all men for the most part are so born, and are so made and called by God, that they should serve the Creator in marriage, not in celibacy: only to few is it given to be eunuchs for the sake of the kingdom of God. Secondly, for all those called to marriage, it is not good to live celibate, for that only leads them into a trap: and for that reason God has commanded that all should have, each man his own wife and each woman her own husband, to avoid fornication: for some are not able to avoid this evil, however much they seek the gift of celibacy from God. If they try it they tempt God and cast themselves into danger and misery, unless the Lord delivers them from a situation which does not permit them to take a wife or live with a wife, for in such a necessity the Lord never leaves his people destitute of his spirit and grace, but enables them to live none the less blameless and holy.[2] . . . To contract marriage, Latomus, is neither a strength nor a weakness, but a calling divinely instituted."[3] Such was Bucer's teaching in a nut-shell. He even went so far as to say that in order to be celibate a man must have the gift of chastity,[4] and emphasized the obligation incumbent upon everyone to follow the gift of God.[5] Regarding the ability to remain celibate as a gift from God, he taught that since God alone

[1] I Corinthians VII: 24.
[2] M. Bucer, *Scripta Duo Adversaria D. Barth. Latomi*, p. 93.
[3] *Ibid.*, p. 94.   [4] *Verantwortung*, p. biij.
[5] *Ibid.*, p. c.

knew upon whom the gift of remaining perpetually chaste was bestowed, no man should take a vow of perpetual chastity.[6] This belief he based upon Christ's saying in Matthew XIX that it is not given to all men to be eunuchs for the sake of the kingdom of heaven. Likewise, he held that very few people received this gift, which was specially bestowed upon only a few.[7]

In his second line of thought, Bucer described marriage as a medicine against fornication, because Paul had said, "it is better to marry than to burn."[8] Consequently he attributed the immorality of the clergy largely to the vow of celibacy,[9] and asserted plainly that a man unable to control himself should marry.[10] In January, 1532, he wrote to Ambrose Blaurer congratulating him that the progress of the Reformation in Esslingen had caused the houses of prostitution to be closed, and incidentally remarked that he thought one cause of the evil would be removed if men would marry earlier in life.[11]

Thus Bucer taught that marriage was a calling and a medicine. Such a doctrine adapted itself easily to the landgrave's contention that he needed a bigamous wife in order to avoid an immoral life and consequent damnation, for it was only necessary to admit that the same principles applied to bigamy, and that some men are called to have two wives.

It has already been observed that in 1531 Bucer thought that bigamy was scripturally permissible, and that he used many arguments in his commentaries, such as his interpretation of Matthew XIX which led logically to a

[6] *Ibid.*, p. cij.   [7] *Ibid.*, p. ciij.
[8] I Corinthians VII: 9.
[9] *Verantwortung*, p. ciij.
[10] *Ibid.*, p. cij; *Scripta Duo Adversaria . . . Latomi*, p. 93.
[11] Schiess, I, 317. At Strasbourg it was an article of belief that marriage was necessary to those not otherwise called by God (*Scripta Anglicana*, p. 181).

belief in the righteousness of polygamy.[12] In the *Argumenta Buceri pro et contra* he had reasoned from his teaching on divorce to prove the permissibility of bigamy, and the same arguments were evident in the *Dialogus Neobuli*. Like Luther and Melanchthon he had admitted the possibility of bigamy in the case of Henry VIII, and so, like them, the problem which perplexed him in 1539 was not whether bigamy in itself was right, but whether he should permit it to the landgrave. It was a situation and not a theory which confronted him.

Nothing could show this more clearly than the *Argumenta Buceri pro et contra*, drawn up by Bucer after he was called upon to answer the landgrave's request for approval of his intention to commit bigamy, and yet it was a theory obviously adapted to meet a special occasion, and a special kind of people like the landgrave. Just as he had held previously that certain people should be allowed to re-marry after divorce, because otherwise they could not contain themselves and must become fornicators, so he now said certain men were so constituted that they could not avoid immorality unless they had two wives. For these people bigamy was permissible, if it was committed in a way that would not give offence. Polygamy Bucer regarded not as the rule, but as a valid exception from the rule of monogamy.

Though his theory was thus obviously molded to meet the case of the landgrave, it did not fit perfectly even there, because the landgrave's trouble was not so much the need of two wives, as the need of one wife who would be attractive to him. Had Christina been such a wife, or had he possessed a valid ground for divorce, then he would probably have overcome his vicious habits with only one wife. In his motives for consenting to the landgrave's request, Bucer resembled the Wittenbergers,[13]

[12] See above, p. 27, ff.   [13] See above, p. 71, ff.

believing as he did that there was no better way for the prince to avoid an immoral life, if his conscience assured him that he could not contain himself. Above all, he was reluctant to give his consent, and urged Philip to seek some other way, not so likely to give offence, by which he might control himself.

The arguments in his letter to the Memmingers[14] show that Bucer thought the landgrave's bigamy should be kept secret; that it was a special dispensation not to be imitated by others; that it was allowable as a means of salvation; and that it should be tolerated by Christians, rather than recommended or condemned. As insistent as anyone that the affair should be kept secret, he was not content, as was Luther, with the requirement that a "strong lie" be employed for this purpose, if necessary, for he realized that the landgrave's attitude made an eventual exposure unavoidable, and measures must be adopted to preclude great offence or a possible schism in the evangelical church when the secret was disclosed. Luther and Melanchthon abandoned the landgrave to his own resources; but Bucer tried to help the prince out of his troubles for the sake of the church and the good of his soul. Much too far-sighted to stand idly by while the situation grew daily more ominous, he adopted a method of active endeavor, not to gain an acceptance of a general introduction of bigamy, nor a sanction for the landgrave's deed, but rather the validification of a theory of bigamy under which the landgrave's act might be tolerated and not condemned. This he did chiefly by personal discussion with men whom he thought were open-minded and could be influenced, not only the preachers of Memmingen, but also others, such as Blaurer,[15] Alesius,[16] Schnepf, Brenz, and Osiander.[17] By these methods, however, little was

[14] *CR.*, X, 156-161.
[16] Lenz, II, 53.
[15] Schiess, II, 106.
[17] *Ibid.*, p. 177.

accomplished. He discovered many theologians who were
content not to attack the landgrave so long as he kept
quiet, but only two, outside of those who already knew
the secret, would say that Philip had done right.[18]

Bucer had not undertaken to do anything of this kind
for the landgrave, when he gave his consent in December,
1539. Like Luther, he had understood it to be the intention
of the "Wittenberg Rathschlag" that the bigamy should
appear to the world to be "a common princely deed,"
while his advice could be used to assure the landgrave's
conscience before the judgment of God and the knowledge of a few witnesses.[19] The landgrave's conscience had
troubled him. Bucer, with a few other witnesses, in order
to quiet his conscience, assured him that he did right
before God in taking two wives. As far as Philip's conscience was concerned this was sufficient, and this was all
that Bucer had undertaken to do. That the reformer tried
to influence others to agree with his own attitude was
only the result of his recognition of the landgrave's unwillingness to preserve secrecy after the bigamy was permitted, and of his desire to forestall the opposition which
he perceived must come. In this sense Bucer may be said
to have defended the bigamy more than Luther,[20] but he
never defended it openly or wished to have it made public,
if publicity could be avoided. After 1542 he gave up his
attempts to influence other theologians in favor of such
a bigamy as Philip had committed, and allowed the matter
to sink into silence.

Some account has already been given of the disciplinary
advice Bucer gave to the landgrave after the bigamy began to be exposed,[21] but a fuller discussion is needed here.

---

[18] *Ibid.*, p. 53.
[19] *Ibid.*, I, 195.
[20] Lindsay, "Martin Bucer and the Reformation," *Quarterly Review*,
CCXX, 128.
[21] See above, p. 114, ff.

First, throughout the entire affair Bucer insisted upon complete secrecy, and there is good reason to doubt he gave the prince any definite assurances of open recognition.[22] With great care he concealed the real purpose of his journey to Wittenberg,[23] and at the first sign of a disclosure of the secret he wrote to Philip urging him to take precautions against it.[24]

There were several reasons why the Strasbourg reformer insisted so strongly upon secrecy. By this means he sought to avoid giving offence to those within the church who would object to it, and to those outside who would use it as a basis for slander and attack.[25] After the bigamy began to be exposed, he felt that secrecy was the only way by which the mistake could be rectified, until by discussion the way had been prepared for a favorable attitude.[26] The rumor could be quieted, he believed, if the landgrave observed "only, always, secrecy,"[27] especially since the dispensation by the Wittenbergers and himself had been given for a secret bigamy, and only by keeping the affair secret would the landgrave have any justification for relying upon it.[28] The general Christian law against bigamy was valid, because it did not contradict any divine law, and so no one could break it publicly, he said, although an exception might be allowed secretly.[29] The landgrave had released the reformers from the duty of openly defending the *Rathschlag,* and duty as well as policy demanded that he stand by his agreement,[30] for Bucer was confident that by secrecy Philip could avoid the legal prosecution which he feared, claiming that the law only took cognizance of the overt act of claiming to have two wives.[31]

22 *Cf.* Lenz, I, 330, 354; Rockwell, p. 318, ff.; see above, p. 69.
23 Lenz, I, 118.   24 *Ibid.*, pp. 121, 159.   25 *Ibid.*, pp. 174, 196.
26 Lenz, I, 178.   27 *Ibid.*, pp. 206, 208.
28 *Ibid.*, p. 207.   29 *Ibid.*
30 *Ibid.*, p. 208.   31 *Ibid.*, p. 236.

In his demand for secrecy and the reasons which he
gave Bucer agreed with Luther, but in the wider variety
of methods which he suggested for preserving secrecy,
he was more helpful than the Wittenberg reformer. He
counseled the landgrave to keep closer to Christina,[32] to
punish those who were exposing the secret, and impose
silence upon them,[33] to issue a private writing in which,
without telling the secret, he should defend himself
against the scandalous rumors circulated about him,[34]
and to obtain a promise of secrecy from Duke Henry of
Saxony, who was spreading rumors based upon the information he had secured from Frau von der Sale.[35] Bucer
even proposed that Philip, after nullifying the first marriage-contract with Margaret, should make a new one,
bestowing upon her the status of ''such a concubine as
God had granted to his dear friends,'' while, in reality,
he should give her the treatment and privileges of a
bigamous wife.[36] The imperial law against bigamy would
not be broken by a pseudo-concubinage of this kind, he
urged, but the actual relations with Margaret would remain the same as before. To Bucer, as to the Saxon reformer,[37] it also seemed best that Margaret should be
kept in a secluded place,[38] and as a further means of preserving secrecy he recommended that the landgrave tell
''a holy lie.'' This he distinguished from ''strong lies,''
or ''the breaking of a contract with dishonor,'' and defined as such a lie as Rahab had told, or as the landgrave
told at Melsungen, when he said he had no definite person
in mind, and no definite plans. That is, Bucer recommended the use of ambiguous terms, by which the landgrave would mean one thing and ''the world'' would

[32] *Ibid.*, p. 174.
[33] *Ibid.*, p. 165, ff.
[34] *Ibid.*, pp. 179, 195.
[35] Lenz, I, 175, 178, 179.
[36] *Ibid.*, p. 178.
[37] Lenz, I, 373.
[38] *Ibid.*, p. 180.

understand another. This he justified by the act of Paul; the fact that silence would be taken for an acknowledgment; and the examples of many in the Scriptures, including Christ and even God himself, ''who made false representations to his enemies in order to protect his people.''[39]

Luther advised a strong lie; Bucer, an ambiguous use of terms.[40] Luther justified it by the advantage of the church, the lie of necessity, the secret of the confessional, and examples in the Holy Scriptures.[41] Bucer claimed for his advice only the justification of examples of such conduct in the Scriptures.[42]

Inspired by a democratic interest in the financial, social, and religious welfare of the common people of Hesse, the reformer urged upon the landgrave a better conduct

[39] *Ibid.*, pp. 193, 178.

[40] The landgrave himself recognized this difference (Lenz, I, 202). Bucer would not agree to Luther's demand for a strong lie, but said some sort of lie must be told (*ibid.*, p. 208).

[41] Kolde, *Analecta Lutherana*, p. 362; see above, p. 119.

[42] Rady has said in a contradictory way, ''Bucer . . . weiss in seiner Angst vor dem Reichsgesetze . . . keinen andern Ausweg mehr, als die Lüge. Tag und Nacht sann er auf Mittel sich und den Landgrafen gegen den Kaiser zu schützen und fand nur die drei: 'Verschweigen, Abwenden und falschen Wahn.' Zu diesem Zwecke schlug er (Hagenau, July 8, 1540) folgende vier Wege vor:'' (Rady, p. 85, ff.). Rady then enumerates the four ways proposed by Bucer (*cf.* Lenz, I, 178-180). It is hard to understand how Bucer could find at the same time only one way, and three ways, and four ways, to protect the landgrave from the emperor. Even if the three ways are granted to be all different forms of a lie, yet only two of the four ways mentioned can be so understood on the most charitable estimate, and, as has been shown, Bucer proposed other methods for preserving secrecy which cannot be classified as lies. Denifle (p. 131) has misrepresented Bucer as saying that even Christ and the apostles had recourse to ''lies of necessity,'' but it is hard to see how his reference to Lenz, I, 362, supports this. Köhler discusses Bucer's attitude on the lie in a recent monograph (Köhler, ''Luther und die Lüge,'' *Schriften des Vereins für Reformationsgeschichte*, 1912, pp. 114-118), and repeats Grisar's unfounded statement that Bucer declared he had consented for political reasons (see above, p. 76, n. 117), but gives no authority (Köhler, *op. cit.*, p. 145).

of his government, deeming this equally effective to guard
the secrecy of his act as ambiguous representations. Re-
peatedly after December, 1539, he urged Philip to rule
his lands better and to improve the condition of the common people, for thus he would show penitence for his past
immoral conduct,[43] gain the confidence of his subjects,[44]
and, most important of all, prepare himself to answer for
the way in which he had fulfilled his duties as a ruler.[45]
Not merely did Bucer convey a general admonition, but
he gave definite criticisms and suggestions; for instance,
to spend no more time in amusements, such as the hunt,
than was necessary for recreation,[46] to make use of good
counselors,[47] to supervise the work of subordinate officials to see that it was done correctly,[48] to reduce the
prevalence of drunkenness in his lands and to encourage
the people to save their money.[49] Above all he should put
a high estimation upon the importance of the magistrate's office,[50] read petitions, improve the state of religion and direct the foreign policy.[51] This advice Philip
found it difficult and unpleasant to follow, yet it is evident that Bucer's error in consenting to the bigamy was
productive of some good by establishing such close relations between them that the reformer was privileged to
counsel the landgrave on a matter of so much importance
to his subjects.[52]

The pastoral nature of the relations between the two
men placed Bucer under an obligation not to leave the
prince to his troubles, but to help him all he could. Before the Diet of Regensburg in 1541, he wrote to the land-

---

[43] Lenz, I, 180.
[44] Lenz, I, 121.
[45] *Ibid.*, p. 195.
[46] *Ibid.*, p. 167.
[47] *Ibid.*, p. 121.
[48] *Ibid.*, p. 167.
[49] *Ibid.*
[50] *Ibid.*, p. 180; *cf.* above, p. 26, ff.; Lenz, II, 161-168.
[51] Lenz, I, 167.
[52] *Cf. ibid.*, pp. 182, 203.

grave that when he came to the Diet he should guard his conduct lest any offence be given to the gospel by himself or his people,[53] and in 1544 he did not hesitate to remind the prince that his immoral life had offended both enemies and friends.[54] Free from all mercenary motives,[55] Bucer never conducted himself as a patronized flatterer.[56] Financially Philip never paid him even what his services were worth, and if higher, intellectual, and spiritual values are considered, he patronized the landgrave extensively.

The Reformation was an age of remodeling and initiation, when old standards and beliefs were being extensively overthrown, and new ones established in their places. Of nothing was this more true than of the moral relations of life and the institution of marriage. Clerical celibacy, which had been a universal dogma for centuries, was rejected by all the protesting communions, and an age in which immorality was so common that it was hardly disgraceful, even to clergymen, was beginning to give place to an age of puritanism. In the ardor of his attack upon the prevalent immorality, and the energy of his efforts, it seemed to Bucer that re-marriage after divorce, and bigamy, such as that described, were even advantageous if sexual vice was overcome. Yet at the same time he was influenced by the loose attitude of his time and country toward adulterous relations, and was not so horrified as is the modern mind at the idea that Philip's marriage should appear publicly to be a concubinage. The fact that many other theologians sympathized with his opinions, shows that, judged by his own age, Bucer

---

[53] Lenz, II, 21, n. 4.

[54] *Ibid.*, p. 258.

[55] See above, p. 198.

[56] Thus Varrentrapp incorrectly speaks of Philip as Bucer's "princely patron" (*Forschungen zur Deutschen Geschichte*, XVI, 16).

was not so black as judged by a modern age in which the belief in monogamy is more firmly established.[57]

Always reluctant, Bucer did not push the affair, nor desire that even one person should commit bigamy. The unfortunate marriage at Rothenburg appeared to him to be the only solution for the landgrave's troubles, if his conscience assured him that he could not otherwise avoid an immoral life. In this also, he was influenced by the prejudice of his age against divorce; and it is not just to condemn him by modern standards under which a divorce for incompatibility is possible, and would have solved Philip's connubial difficulties, had it not been for the diplomatic issues involved.[58]

Not the slightest taint of immorality or misconduct is attached to Bucer's private and personal life. Even his cloister-brothers, who never desired to praise him, were obliged to admit that he led a moral life,[59] though there was sufficient opportunity to indulge the lusts of the flesh.[60] In his *Verantwortung* he declared, "And I say, if I had not feared God, and had wished only to seek the lusts of the flesh, then I would in no way have taken her [i.e., his wife]. Women are not so rare. When everything was convenient for me, I might have had two or three instead of one, and changed them every week, and might have been a great lord, like other papists, for a great lordship was offered me by the papal embassy at Worms,

---

[57] There is good reason to believe that Francis v. d. Hulst, who was appointed head of the inquisition in the Netherlands in 1522, was a bigamist (Lindsay, *History of the Reformation*, II, 230).

[58] There is no evidence to support Rady's statement that Bucer departed from the truth when he said the business had been hard upon him, and he would gladly have turned the landgrave aside from it (Rady, p. 84). But all the history of Bucer's relations to the bigamy before he made this statement shows that it was true (*cf.* above, p. 58, ff.). He said at another time, ''Si quisquam est, qui factum et scriptum avertere conatus sit . . . ego certe is; hoc novit Christus, et qui in isto detinentur negotio'' (Schiess, II, 106).

[59] *Der CXX Psalm*, p. Hii.   [60] *Verantwortung*, pp. d-dii.

as many people know.''[61] Bucer's family life was highly
honorable and the best kind of argument in favor of
clerical marriage, when compared with the immoral lives
of the priests of the time. One of the first evangelical
priests to take a wife, he was exiled from Wissembourg
largely on this account, and when he went to Strasbourg
he found it necessary to defend his marriage in his *Verantwortung,* published in 1523.[62] Twenty years later after
his wife's death, Bucer testified to the happiness of their
married relations when he said, ''The dear God has given
me a wife for twenty years, who has been gifted with such
modesty, honor, Godliness, also industry in all cares and
duties of the house, as many pious Christians know, that
through her I have been remarkably helped in my service;
not only in that she has relieved me of all household cares
and temporal business, but also that through her diligence
and her pains, she has so wisely managed the problem of
provision for bodily needs, which sometimes has not been
very bountiful for us, that we have shown much more
hospitality to very many pilgrims and servants of Christ,
than I, if I had been alone could ever have done.''[63] In 1542
Bucer married his second wife, who had been successively
the widow of Keller, Oecolampad, and Capito.[64] His
family cares were already heavy, but he treated his step-
children as well as his own, in affection, interest,[65] and
also in his will.[66]

Though morally irreproachable, Bucer's personal experience enabled him to sympathize with the landgrave.

[61] *Ibid.,* p. dii.
[62] Mentz, no. 3, p. 104; Anrich, p. 19; *Verantwortung,* p. d, ff. See also
Baum, p. 213, ff.; and above, p. 1, n. 3.
[63] *Was in Namen . . . zu Bonn,* p. ciii. *Cf.* Lenz, II, 38.
[64] See above, p. 220.
[65] *Cf.* the letter to his family from England, printed by Baum, p. 556.
[66] Text in Harvey, p. 162; Baum, p. 572; *cf.* Grünberg in the *Realencyclopaedie für protestantische Theologie und Kirche,* III, 612.

He too had bound himself by vows, when almost exactly the same age as that at which Philip was induced to marry his unfortunate wife. Consequently, he thoroughly understood the miserable condition of a man held down by unbreakable vows taken too early in life, and naturally wished to help the prince all he could. Conscientiousness and sincerity marked all of Bucer's relations to the bigamy of Philip of Hesse. There is no evidence in any of his letters that he ever did anything himself, or advised anyone else to do, what he thought morally wrong. He was honestly seeking the best interests of the land-grave and of the church.[67] In many instances his judgment as to what was right may have been at fault, but never did he intentionally do what he could not justify to his own satisfaction from his sole rule of faith, the Scriptures. Even his advice to tell a lie such as Abraham had told was logically right, if once the premise was admitted that the things which the patriarchs did without God's condemnation were worthy examples for Christians to follow. Keenly as he felt the disgrace cast upon him by the rumor that he had written and published the *Dialogus Neobuli,* yet he thanked God for the comfort which came from a clear conscience, and the knowledge that he had honestly tried to do his best for the church.[68] Never should it be forgotten that Bucer had advised Henry VIII in 1531 that he could not condemn the bigamy, and so he cannot be accused of bald opportunism in consenting to

[67] Schmidt has said, ''Lieder kann man kaum annehmen dass das Gutachten, welches er abgab, und die weiteren Bemühungen, denen er sich unterzog, ebenso aus seiner festesten Ueberzeugung hervorgingen wie seine Thätigkeit für eine Vereinigung der Lutheraner und Reformirten'' (Schmidt, *Justus Menius, der Reformator Thuringens,* I, 244, ff.).

[68] *Cf.* this statement by Bucer, ''Ea gratia Domino, me fide gessi in ecclesia, ut multis satis caussae esset, etiamsi scirent mihi aliquid tale accidisse, ut eam stultitiam tegerent et, ne amplius peccarem, monerent'' (Schiess, II, 132).

the bigamy of Philip. Mere desire to keep the landgrave's favor never induced him to permit something he thought was wrong.

These considerations help to explain how Bucer could have made the mistake of allowing Philip to take a bigamous wife, and also diminish the severity of the judgment of modern times upon his error.[69] His error was intellectual and social; not moral. It was due chiefly to two causes: the results of his method of interpreting the Scriptures, and his judgment of the landgrave.

First, Bucer was too literal in his use of the Bible. Because he could find no verbal prohibition of bigamy, he said there was no clear command by which he could condemn it.[70] When such a method of exegesis is used the Bible is indeed far from clear on the matter.[71] In the search for "proof-texts" he failed to see the superiority of the New Testament over the Old Testament,[72] and that the spirit of the New Testament is incompatible with the permission of bigamy. The whole argument which he made for bigamy from the New Testament was an argument from silence.

More important still, he overlooked the fact that many social questions of prime importance upon which the Bible does not lay down any definite legislation, may still be solved by the principles there outlined. Slavery is a most conspicuous example. If Bucer had followed the principles of the New Testament which ordain one moral code for all men, and teach that the only way of overcoming sin is by self-control and not self-indulgence, he would not

---

[69] It is true as Köstlin has said, that in this affair "the reformers let themselves be drawn into guilt" (Köstlin, II, 468).

[70] *CR.*, X, 157.

[71] *Cf.* Faulkner, *op. cit.*, p. 219.

[72] *Cf.* Köstlin, *The Life of Luther*, p. 508; Heppe, *op. cit.*, p. 280. Faulkner fitly speaks of the "sway of the Old Testament which went over into the sixteenth century" (*American Journal of Theology*, XVII, 217).

have made the mistake of establishing one moral code for most men and another lower one for other men, in which their sin should be overcome by yielding to it. Likewise, if he had followed his own teachings on the position of woman as he derived them from the Epistle to the Ephesians,[73] he would not have fallen into the low conception of woman as a medicine against man's immoderate sexual desires. This theory was well established in the age of the Reformation,[74] being due somewhat to the revolt against clerical celibacy, by which it had become clear that marriage did remove a great deal of sexual vice.[75] Bucer's belief in the higher education of women[76] was also far in advance of the extent to which he carried Paul's injunction that every man should have his own wife "to avoid fornication." In arguing the question of bigamy he paid no attention to what modern science calls sociology. Had he done so, he would have realized that the experience of mankind has demonstrated that any kind of polygamy is injurious to the most fundamental of all institutions, the family.

Secondly, excessive clemency was also responsible for Bucer's failure to judge the landgrave correctly. Although he left the extent of Philip's need upon his own conscience to decide,[77] and the landgrave's past life showed his inability to control himself, yet he failed to see that the prince was influenced not only by his own conscience, but also by his love for Margaret. This was not entirely the reformer's fault, because he tried to ascer-

---

[73] See above, p. 220.

[74] *Cf.* Brieger in the *Preussische Jahrbücher,* 1909, CXXXV, Heft, I, 42; Köhler in the *Historische Zeitschrift,* 1905, XCIV, 407.

[75] See above, p. 28, n. 17; *cf.* Faulkner in the *American Journal of Theology,* XVII, 217, 225.

[76] *Cf.* a letter from Bucer to the Marquis of Dorset, Dec. 26, 1550 (Harvey, p. 140). He encouraged Margaret Blaurer to learn Latin (Schiess, II, 805).

[77] Lenz, I, 176.

tain the truth and was misinformed by the landgrave. Again, even granting that bigamy under the conditions stipulated by the "Wittenberg Rathschlag" was right, Bucer misjudged the landgrave in thinking that he would guard the secret of the affair or keep faith with the scholars when confronted by the danger of imperial prosecution. It was chiefly the landgrave's love for Margaret, and his concessions to her relatives, that made him give away the secret through his sister and Frau von der Sale, and forced him to seek his peace with the emperor. Continually ignoring and underestimating these influences upon the landgrave, Bucer vainly appealed to him on the basis of his contract with the reformers and his duty to the church. Likewise, the reformer had not judged Philip of Hesse keenly enough to foresee how he would regard himself, in his egotism, as a prophet and herald of a new blessing to mankind. After the secret was exposed, he still overestimated the landgrave's virtues by believing that the man who had been unable to control himself, even when visited by disease for his immorality, would have the nervous stability to face imperial prosecution calmly and avoid it by silence. Perhaps it is unfair to say that Bucer did not realize this, and it would be more correct to say that though he saw it, yet he tried to stem the tide. In either case, the exposure of the secret and the agreement with the emperor were chiefly the consequences of the landgrave's weakness. Had Bucer understood the man keenly enough to discern these results, he would probably never have given his consent that Philip should take another wife, nor have helped involve Luther and Melanchthon in what became such a serious injury to the cause of the Reformation in Germany; for above all else he demanded that Philip of Hesse should use the "dispensation" in secrecy, and without giving offence or injury to the "church of Christ."

With a better method of exegesis, and a more profound comprehension of the nature of social institutions, Bucer would have regarded bigamy as wrong under any conditions. Failing in this, had he judged the landgrave's character and situation better, he would still never have allowed the bigamous marriage at Rothenburg to take place with his approval. But like all other men he made mistakes, and the greatest of these was when he consented to the bigamy of Philip of Hesse.

Though disagreeing with Bucer's attitude on the Supper, and well acquainted with his share in the scandal, Ambrose Blaurer wrote to Henry Bullinger an estimate of Bucer's character, which, viewed in the light of his relations to the bigamy, cannot be surpassed as an epitome of the reformer's much misunderstood personality, "What you write about Bucer, I fear cannot be entirely conceded; although I also miss many things in him. I love him extraordinarily on account of his rare gifts and especially on account of the entire lack of self-interest which I have continually noticed in him, and his pure striving after the glory of Christ and the extension of his kingdom. At times, however, he may err in the means he employs and accomplish little."[78]

[78] Schiess, II, 121.

BIBLIOGRAPHICAL NOTE

When Martin Bucer died, on March 1, 1551, he left behind him no autobiography, and a searching examination of his printed works reveals only a few, short references to his own life. His *Verantwortung,* published in 1523, contains the largest amount of biographical material, and this is supplemented by a few passages in polemical works, written to defend himself against his enemies in Cologne. While Bucer wrote volumes on exegetical, doctrinal, and political subjects, it never occurred to him that the details of his own life would be of interest to posterity. However, he was an industrious letter-writer, and though much of his correspondence was destroyed, he left behind him a mass of letters, scattered all over Europe, which is the chief source for an understanding of his life and character.

Lamentable as is the non-existence of an autobiography, the failure of any of his contemporaries to write a life of the reformer is equally so. Bucer had many friends, such as John Sturm, John Calvin, and John Sleidan, who were perfectly capable of the task, but who never undertook it. Only his faithful secretary, Conrad Hubert, accomplished anything, for he collected as many of his master's letters as he could, and planned a complete edition of his works. This project was never completed, for only one volume, the *Scripta Anglicana,* ever left the press. This large tome contains chiefly works written during Bucer's exile in England, but with them is mingled a miscellaneous mass of material, comprising letters, extracts from various books, epitaphs, etc. During the centuries that followed, copies of Bucer's works became very rare, until now they are difficult to find even in large libraries. The largest collection is at Strasbourg in the *Bibliothèque universitaire et régionale de Strasbourg*, and the *Collegium Wilhelmitanum*. The Union Theological Seminary Library in New York contains more of Bucer's books than any other library in America. The collection of manuscripts and letters made by Conrad Hubert, is now in the *Archives et Bibliothèque de la Ville* at Strasbourg, to which they were brought from the *Thomasius Archives* at the beginning of the twentieth century. Here they are kept in four different collections and are easily accessible.[1] The "Epistolae Buceri" is the most important collection, and comprises three volumes of manuscript letters, of which the majority were written to Ambrose and Margaret Blaurer. Unfortunately the letters are bound according to a faulty chronological arrangement, and various readers have inscribed hypothetical dates which are often erroneous and misleading. Many other letters are to be found in archives of other cities, chiefly those at Zurich, Basel, and Neuchâtel.

Bucer is one of the forgotten leaders of the Reformation. A recent history of that movement mentions him only incidentally, without giving any connected account of his life and importance. By many people his name is confused with that of Luther, and through ignorance his conduct has often been misjudged. There are many reasons why more is not found about Bucer in the histories of the Reformation. As a result of the Smalkald War he was exiled from Strasbourg and died in a foreign land. He left behind him no sect as did Luther, Calvin, and others, but strove to uphold the unity of the evangelical movement. Later Lutheran influences at Strasbourg

[1] These collections bear the following titles: "Buceriana," "Epistolae ad Hist. Ecclesiam Saec. XVI Pertinentes," "Epistolae Buceri," "Schriften Bucers."

tended to discredit his work and overthrow those things which would have exalted his memory. The chief reason for this silence is the difficulty encountered in collecting and sifting the material bearing on his life. His letters are scattered, his handwriting is almost illegible, and after the death of his contemporaries they were the main source of information.

With the increase of historical activity in Germany, after the Napoleonic Wars, a serious, scholarly investigation of Bucer's life was begun. The work of Jung[2] was a good start and was supplemented by that of Röhrich.[3] In 1860 the first real biography of the reformer was written by Baum as one of the series of biographies of the founders of the reformed churches.[4] Baum's work was based on extensive and original research. He made the most important collection of copies of Bucer's letters, now treasured in the "Thesaurus Baumianus" at the University Library in Strasbourg. In great detail he recounted Bucer's life until 1530, and quoted extensively from the reformer's works and correspondence. But Baum's work was injured by the fact that he combined Bucer's biography with that of Capito, his associate reformer at Strasbourg, and he treated too briefly the most important part of Bucer's life, which came after 1530. Moreover, his work is not always reliable, for he made errors in chronology and often translated his sources too freely. The lack of sufficient references weakens his authority, and his prejudice in favor of Bucer sometimes leads him astray. For example, he says not one word about Bucer's relation to the bigamy of Philip of Hesse.

[2] A. Jung, *Geschichte der Reformation der Kirche in Strassburg und der Ausbreitung derselben in den Gemeinden des Elsasses*. Strasbourg, 1830.

[3] T. W. Röhrich, *Geschichte der Reformation in Elsass und besonders in Strassburg*. Strasbourg, 1830-1832. By the same author, "Martin Butzer," *Evangelisches Jahrbuch von Piper für 1858*, pp. 172-186.

[4] J. W. Baum, *Capito und Butzer*. Elberfeld, 1860.

To his work he added a list of Bucer's publications which is noteworthy for its scholarship but has since been superseded.

Since Baum wrote, four works have appeared dealing with Bucer's life, which are of special importance. In celebration of the four hundredth anniversary of Bucer's birth, Mentz and Erichson published a small volume in which they reprinted one of Bucer's earliest works, listed a number of books containing information about his life, gave a brief guide to the chief libraries containing source-material, and, most important of all, printed a list of Bucer's printed works.[5] This book is indispensable to any student of Bucer's life, and is the product of admirable scholarship. In using it the reader must remember, however, that conditions in the libraries of Strasbourg have been changed since the war and that a few of Bucer's works have been published since 1891. In 1906 Harvey published a dissertation on Bucer's life in England, which throws a great deal of light on that period and might profitably have been used by historians of the English Reformation who have written since then.[6] A very good account of Bucer's theology has been written by Lang, who shows in conclusion the indebtedness of Calvin to the reformer of Strasbourg.[7] Quite recently another biography has been published by Anrich which is scholarly, well-balanced, and written in an excellent style.[8] It is only to be regretted that Anrich did not make his work more comprehensive and give references to his authorities.

There have been written only two works in English on Bucer which are worthy of mention: the article by A. W.

---

[5] *Zur 400 jährigen Geburtsfeier Martin Butzers.* Strasbourg, 1891.

[6] A. E. Harvey, *Martin Bucer in England.* Marburg, 1906.

[7] A. Lang, ''Das Evangelienkommentar Martin Butzer's,'' *Studien zur Geschichte der Theologie und Kirche,* II. Leipzig, 1900.

[8] G. Anrich, *Martin Bucer.* Strasbourg, 1914.

BIBLIOGRAPHICAL NOTE 245

Ward in the *Dictionary of National Biography* and another article by Lindsay in the *Quarterly Review*.[9] Ward's article is little more than a summary of Baum, and although Lindsay appreciates Bucer's importance, his account is too brief to give any idea of the reformer's life. It is unfortunate that no good biography exists in English, for the failure of the historians to give credit to his influence on the Reformation is due more to ignorance than to a lack of such an influence. This ignorance is not so excusable now as it once was, for, since Baum started to work, nearly fifteen hundred of Bucer's letters and those to him, have been printed in the great collections of correspondence such as the *Corpus Reformatorum*. The most important publications containing letters by Bucer have been edited by Lenz[10] and Schiess.[11] The publication of Bucer's correspondence with the landgrave by Lenz, is especially important for a study of the bigamy, and is made extremely valuable by the careful way in which the letters are edited and explained.

Although much had been written about the bigamy, it found its first capable and impartial historian in Rockwell,[12] who was also the first to give anything like adequate consideration to the part played by Bucer. Before Rockwell wrote, accounts of the bigamy had been given in general histories and various biographies of Luther. Rady had faithfully set forth the Catholic condemnation of all that was discreditable in the episode, but it remained for Rockwell to treat the subject in a thoroughly

[9] T. M. Lindsay, ''Martin Bucer and the Reformation,'' *Quarterly Review*, vol. 220, January, 1914, pp. 116-133.

[10] M. Lenz, *Briefwechsel Landgraf Philipps des Grossmüthigen von Hessen mit Bucer*. Leipzig, 1880, 1887, 1891.

[11] T. Schiess, *Briefwechsel der Brüder Ambrosius und Thomas Blaurer 1509-1568*. Freiburg i. Br., 1908, 1910, 1912.

[12] W. W. Rockwell, *Die Doppelehe des Landgrafen Philipp von Hessen*. Marburg, 1904.

historical manner. Some further contributions to an understanding of the affair have been made by Brieger[13] and Köhler,[14] but the extensive discussions by Grisar[15] and Paulus[16] have added little to what was already known. Good, but brief, treatments are to be found in English in the biographies of Luther by McGiffert and Smith, and in a magazine article by Faulkner.[17] None of these say much about Martin Bucer. The best editions of source-material dealing with the bigamy, have been made by Lenz and Enders.[18] These works supersede the older publications by Arcuarius, Neudecker, and Heppe. Much material is also to be found in the *Corpus Reformatorum*. Lenz and Rockwell have both given lists of books touching upon the bigamy. Although the history of the affair is now far better told, there are still many gaps to be filled in, and many questions which find no answer in the documents now known to historians.

The titles of less important works, printed and in manuscript, upon which this study of the attitude of Bucer toward Philip's bigamy is based, will be found in the footnotes, the full title being given the first time a work is cited.

[13] T. Brieger, ''Luther und die Nebenehe des Landgrafen Philipp. I. Die Angebliche Entstehung des Wittenberg Rathschlags in Hessen. Der älteste Entwurf desselben,'' *Zeitschrift für Kirchengeschichte*, XXIX, 174-196.

[14] W. Köhler, ''Die Doppelehe Landgraf Philipps von Hessen,'' *Historische Zeitschrift*, 1905, XCIV, 385-411.

[15] H. Grisar, *Luther*. Freiburg, 1911.

[16] N. Paulus, ''Das Beichtgeheimnis und die Doppelehe des Landgrafen Philipp von Hessen,'' *Historisch-politische Blätter für das katholische Deutschland*, CXXXV, 317-333.

By the same author, ''Die hessische Doppelehe im Urteile der protestantischen Zeitgenossen,'' *Historisch-politische Blätter für das katholische Deutschland*, CXLVII, 503-517, 561-572.

[17] J. A. Faulkner, ''Luther and the Bigamous Marriage of Philip of Hesse,'' *American Journal of Theology*, XVII, 206-231.

[18] E. L. Enders, *Dr. Martin Luther's Briefwechsel*. Kalw. and Stuttgart, 1884, ff.

INDEX

Aitinger, spreads rumor about Bucer, 183.

Alexander von der Thann, appointed to aid Bucer, 194.

Amsdorf, Nicholas, Saxon representative at Eisenach conference, 119 (note 63).

Anabaptists, arise in Strasbourg, 10; opposed by Bucer, 47; attacked by Bucer, 49.

Andrews, Charles M., acknowledgments to, vi.

Anna von der Sale, Philip negotiates with, 62, 73, 102; *Argumenta Buceri* sent to, 85; goes to Rothenburg, 103, 108; exposes secret of the bigamy, 111, 122, 239.

Anrich, Gustav, biographer of Bucer, 244.

Argumenta Buceri, history of, 84; contents of, 87; criticism of, 100, 111, 126, 128, 153, 184, 193, 200, 226.

Augsburg, Bucer conducts reformation in, 8; Diet of, 15; Frau Bucer receives money from, 19, 44; preachers of promise help, 142.

Avranches, Bucer attacks bishop of, 9.

Bastian, Hermann, Anabaptist at Marburg, 50, 52.

Baum, J. W., cited, 178 (note 138); biographer of Bucer, 243.

Baumgarten, Jacob, cited, 175.

Baumgarten, S. J., cited, 164 (note 52).

Bigamy, discussion of in Bucer's writings, 9; papal dispensation for, 36; advised by Bucer to Henry VIII, 42; related to Bucer's teaching on divorce, 27; Philip resorts to, 60; Philip's arguments for, 67; discussed in *Argumenta Buceri*, 87; rumors of the, 107, 109; Bucer's attitude toward, 223.

Bing, Simon, Hessian secretary, 104; cited, 161 (note 36).

Blaurer, Ambrose, recommended by Bucer, 46, 116, 130, 176; suspects Lening, 180; opposes *Dialogus Neobuli*, 199; pacifies Bullinger, 213; sends *Dialogus Neobuli* to Bullinger, 213, 227; defends Bucer, 240; corresponds with Bucer, 242.

Blaurer, Margaret, sends money to Frau Bucer, 19.

Boleyn, Anne, Bucer inquires concerning, 40.

Bonn, Bucer conducts reformation in, 8, 221.

Borries, E. von, cited, 17 (note 102).

Brenz, John, confers with Bucer, 14, 116, 229.

Bretschneider, cited, 175.

Bucer, Martin, importance of, v; birth and boyhood of, 1; enters monastery, 2; meets Luther, 3; leaves monastery, 3; goes to Ebernburg, 4; chaplain in Palatinate, 4; pastor at Landstuhl, 4; marries E. Silbereisen, 4; preaches at Wissembourg, 5; excommunicated, 5; flees to Strasbourg, 6; pastor of St. Aurelia, 7; activities as a preacher, 7; as an educator, 8; as an author, 8; as a polemicist,